Pensions explained

'Pensions are changing every which way. You need to understand what is happening to make the most of the good changes and offset the impact of the bad.'

Jonquil Lowe

About the author

Jonquil Lowe is an economist, and has previously worked in the City as an investment analyst and for Which?, where she was the head of the Money Research Group. Jonquil now splits her time between working as a lecturer in personal finance at The Open University and a freelance researcher/journalist. She holds the Diploma in Personal Finance and writes extensively on all areas of personal finance. She is author of over 25 books, including *Giving and Inheriting* and *Save and Invest*, published by Which? Books.

Pensions explained

Which? Books are commissioned and published by Which? Ltd,
2 Marylebone Road, London NW1 4DF
Email: books@which.co.uk

Distributed by Littlehampton Book Services Ltd,
Faraday Close, Durrington,Worthing, West Sussex BN13 3RB

British Library Cataloguing in Publication Data
A catalogue record for this book is available from the British Library

ISBN 978 1 84490 153 1

Although the author and publishers endeavour to make sure the information in this
book is accurate and up to date, it is only a general guide. Before taking action on
financial, legal, or medical matters you should consult a qualified professional adviser,
who can consider your individual circumstances. The author and publishers can not
accordingly accept liability for any loss or damage suffered as a consequence of relying
on the information contained in this guide.

Publisher's acknowledgements
The publishers would like to thank Gavin McEwan of Turcan Connell for advice on the
law in Scotland and Tony Caher of Campbell & Caher for advice on the law in Northern
Ireland.

Senior Editor: Kerenza Swift
Project Manager: Emma Callery
Designer: Bob Vickers
Proofreader: Kathy Steer
Indexer: Marion Dent
Printed and bound by Charterhouse, Hatfield

Paper: Essential Velvet is an elemental chlorine free paper produced at Condat in
Périgord, France, using timber from sustainably managed forests. The mill is ISO14001
and EMAS certified.

For a full list of Which? Books, please call 01992 822800, visit our website at
www.which.co.uk/books, or write to Littlehampton Book Services.

Contents

Introduction

Saving for retirement has never been more difficult nor more important. The proportion of older people in society is rising as a result of the post-World War II 'baby boom' and medical advances that mean people are generally living longer.

This has conspired with the aftermath of the global financial crisis that started in 2007 to make pensions both expensive and riddled with uncertainty.

Even before 2007, employers – traditionally, important providers of retirement savings schemes – had started cutting back the pension benefits they were willing to offer. Measures to cut the cost of providing State Pensions were also well under way, having started in the 1980s under the leadership of prime minister, Margaret Thatcher. The perverse result is that more of the burden of retirement saving today is falling on the shoulders of you, the individual, who, of all the organisations and agents in society, is probably least able to bear the expense and risks increasingly inherent in saving for a pension. Yet, increasingly, you are responsible for planning ahead so that you will be financially secure when you

reach retirement. It has never been more important to understand how pension schemes work and how to make them work for you.

Risks and costs

Important to an understanding of the risks and cost involved in retirement saving is an appreciation that there are two very different bases on which pensions may be provided: defined benefit and defined contribution.

A defined-benefit pension scheme is one where you are promised a given level of pension at retirement, calculated according to some formula. UK State Pensions are defined-benefit schemes: the current basic pension and the new flat-rate pension, due to start in April 2016, both pay a set amount according to your record of National Insurance contributions and credits. The current additional State Pension depends on your earnings as well.

Salary-related pension schemes offered by employers, such as final-salary schemes (where your pension is a proportion of your pay shortly before retiring), are defined-benefit schemes. You are promised this pension regardless of how the stock market performs, how long

---

Jargon buster

Retirement Used in this book to mean the period of life when you draw a pension. You might not have stopped work altogether.

STATE PENSIONS	EMPLOYER PENSIONS

1980 State Pension increases no longer linked to earnings, only prices.

1988
- Additional State Pension made less generous for people reaching State Pension age from 2000 onwards.
- Tax incentives to encourage contracting-out into personal pensions. First time contracting out on a defined-contribution basis rather than defined-benefit has been allowed.

- Employers no longer allowed to make joining their pension schemes compulsory.
- Everyone has option to have their own personal pension scheme. These are defined-contribution schemes where the individual has their own portable pot of savings not linked to a particular job.

1995 Legislation passed to increase women's State Pension age to 65 (the age for men), phasing in the change over the period 2010 to 2020.

- Large public sector employers negotiate changes with unions to cut cost of some public sector occupational schemes.
- Private sector employers in ongoing trend of cutting pension costs and uncertainty by, for example, switching from final-salary to defined-contribution schemes.

2007 Legislation passed to increase State Pension age in stages to 68 over the period 2020 to 2046.

2008

Legislation passed to introduce a national pension scheme for employees. It will work on a defined-contribution basis with a relatively low employer contribution.

2009 Changes made to accelerate transition of additional State Pension to a flat-rate scheme.

2010 Review announced to look at bringing forward increases in State Pension age and possibly not stopping at age 68.

- Review announced to look at further changes to cut cost of public sector occupational pension schemes.
- Proposed that all public sector and many private sector occupational schemes will be able to cut the cost of inflation-linked increases to preserved pensions and pensions in payment.

2011 Increases to women's and men's State Pension ages accelerated.

2013 Shift to new flat-rate State Pension from 2016 accounced and five-yearly reviews to increase State Pension age.

people are living or other social and economic changes. So these are relatively secure pensions where you are largely sheltered from risks and uncertainties. The main risk is that the pension promise will be renegotiated and the chart on the previous page shows many examples of this affecting both state and employer schemes.

In a defined-contribution (also called a money purchase) pension scheme, you have your own personal pot of savings – your pension fund. The size of the fund depends on how much is paid in by you, your employer and anyone else, how well the invested fund grows and how much is taken away in charges by the providers running the scheme and the investments within your fund. How much pension the fund will buy depends on investment conditions at the time you retire. All personal pension schemes, many occupational schemes and many multi-employer schemes work on the defined-contribution basis. The important point to note is that you are bearing all the risks: if stock markets go down, so does the value of your pension fund; if people live longer

so that the cost of pensions rises, you must save extra, retire later or resign yourself to a smaller pension; if inflation is high, the value of your pension and maybe your pension fund will be eroded. You will need to be constantly vigilant to manage and minimise these risks. But, however well you do this, you are still exposed to the uncertainty of unpredictable shocks – such as the global crisis of 2007 – that can upset even the best-laid plans.

Pensions going forward

At the same time as employers and the State are pulling back from offering secure pensions, the Government is stressing the importance of workplace pension schemes as the main route for avoiding poverty in retirement. To this end, a new policy of auto-enrolment is being phased in over the period 2012–18. Under this policy, your employer has a duty to enrol you in a work-based pension scheme that meets minimum standards. If no other suitable scheme is available, there is a new national pension scheme, the National Employment Savings Trust (NEST). You can opt out if you want to, but the hope is that all employees will, in time, be building up pension savings through their workplace and with the benefit of some contributions from their employer.

In 2012, according to a report by Scottish Widows, fewer than half of

> **'Never before has it been more important to understand how pensions work.'**

 Chapters 7 and 11 look at investment risk and the risk of pension promises being renegotiated and cut back.

UK adults were saving enough for retirement, with over a fifth saving nothing at all. Auto-enrolment aims to address this lack of savings, in particular by overriding or utilising a number of common behavioural traits that we all tend to share. For example, many people acknowledge that saving for retirement is important but fail to get around to doing anything about it. Auto-enrolment exploits this inertia by assuming that once automatically enrolled into a pension scheme, many will not get around to opting out. We also tend to put off making decisions if they seem too complex or make bad decisions if we fail to understand the full implications of the options available (facets of what the experts call our 'bounded rationality'). Auto-enrolment addresses these problems by making the decisions for you: the law decides you will join a scheme; your employer decides which scheme; and the scheme decides how your savings will be invested if you don't.

Auto-enrolment aims in particular to ensure that low- and middle-income earners who have not had pension savings in the past – many of them women wrapping work around family responsibilities – will at last start to build up something for retirement. However, a similar scheme in New Zealand, called KiwiSaver, which started in 2007, has met with only mixed success. Research by the New Zealand Treasury estimates that KiwiSaver has reached only around one-third of its target group and that the vast majority of its members would have been saving around two-thirds of the amount they pay in anyway.

Moreover, the UK auto-enrolment arrangements are a far cry from the final-salary schemes that have been lost. Currently, the average employer contribution to a defined-benefit scheme is around 16 per cent of your pay. The employer contribution required under auto-enrolment will eventually be just 3 per cent (and starts even lower). It is to be hoped that most employers offering pension benefits anyway will continue to make more generous contributions, but there is a risk that they may take the opportunity to level down to the new policy requirement. Moreover, under auto-enrolment, instead of a pension promise, most schemes will build up on a defined-contribution basis with all the inherent risks discussed earlier.

You might feel that with all these costs and risks being heaped upon you, why bother to save at all? But the only certainty is that, if you do not save, you will face a financially tough time in later life. So the onus is on you to manage the risks, keep a check on your retirement planning and save extra. This is a tall order and the reason for this book:

- **Planning your retirement saving** Chapters 1 and 3 provide you with a framework for planning and reviewing your retirement savings.
- **Pensions from the State and employers** Chapter 2 explains what pension you can expect from the State, Chapter 4 explains your rights under auto-enrolment and Chapter 5 shows how the various schemes you may be offered through your job (including NEST) work.

■ **Saving on your own** Much of government pension policy focuses on a partnership between the State and employers to help you build up retirement income. But, of the 29.6 million people in employment, 4.2 million (13 per cent) are self-employed. If this applies to you, you will be all too aware that the full cost of providing your pension already falls on your shoulders, with no employer to help. For you, as well as for employees who are offered a personal pension as their workplace scheme or want to top up their savings, and for some people who are not in work, personal pension schemes are described in Chapter 6. Alternatives to pension schemes are considered in Chapter 12.

■ **Choosing investments and strategies** Increasingly, you are likely to save through a defined-contribution scheme, which includes multi-employer schemes like NEST and all personal pension schemes. With most defined-contribution schemes, you choose how the contributions paid in are to be invested. You need a strategy that gives you the best chance of long-term growth while your pension fund is building up and of reducing the risk of losses as retirement approaches. Chapter 7 looks at a range of strategies and investment funds and Chapter 8 considers the impact of charges.

Chapter 6 looks at your options when you are ready to start drawing your pension.

■ **Coping with change** Very few people these days work for just one employer throughout their whole working life, so Chapter 9 explains what happens to the pension rights and savings you have already built up when you change job, or otherwise leave a scheme, and the choices you have. Chapter 10 includes information about pensions if you are going through a relationship breakdown and what protection and pay-outs pension schemes provide in the event of you or your partner dying.

■ **Your rights** Chapter 11 looks at how safe different pension schemes are, the kind of risks you might run, how you are protected if things go wrong and how to pursue your rights.

■ **Getting advice** Finally, Chapter 13 looks at where you can get help making pension decisions, ranging from informal guidance through to paying for a professional, including how much the latter might cost.

Throughout its pages, this guide signposts you to further sources of information and personalised advice. These sources are summarised in a handy useful contacts section near the back of the book, which also includes a glossary to translate the jargon that is part and parcel of retirement planning.

This guide went to press shortly after the Budget in March 2013 and includes measures proposed in that Budget.

Why pensions are important

Most people can expect some State Pension when they reach older age. While this is valuable and a good foundation on which to build, it is not enough on its own to support a comfortable lifestyle. Thinking about the income you may need in retirement will help you plan ahead and set aside sufficient savings.

Income and lifestyle

The income you have in retirement will be one of the most important influences on the lifestyle you enjoy. Looking at pensioners today, it is clear that a key difference between those on the lowest and highest incomes is whether the person was able to save in a pension scheme while they worked.

A wake-up call

It may seem obvious that you will need an income when you retire, but government data suggests that six out of ten people of working age are not building up any pension apart from whatever the State will provide.

Maybe you are thinking that the State Pension will be enough to live on. Think again! Most people would not choose to live on the £7,500 a year or so that the State is likely to give you. Maybe the future will just somehow take care of itself ? Unlikely. Most of us cannot look forward to an inheritance or a lottery win.

Unfortunately, the only chance of securing a comfortable retirement relies on the hard graft of regular saving over many years. If you're not convinced yet, read on ….

Reasons not to rely on the State Pension

Once basic needs are met, poverty is a relative term. In the UK, it is usually defined as less than 60 per cent of the average income of households generally, adjusted for household size and composition. As a result, in 2013–14, single pensioners are deemed to need £145.40 a week to live on and pensioner couples £222.05 a week. In 2012, the State Pension (see Chapter 2) fell short of this.

However, assuming government proposals for a new flat-rate State Pension go ahead, this is expected in future to provide around £144 a week (in 2012–13 money) for a single person, just about enough to take you out of poverty.

A weekly income of £144 is a little short of £7,500 a year. Most people would find getting by on such a low income possible, but not comfortable. If you want to live on more than £7,500 a year when you retire, you should be thinking about what you can do now to top up the State Pension you expect to get.

> 'Most people would not choose to live on the £7,500 a year or so that the State is likely to give you.'

Income and lifestyle

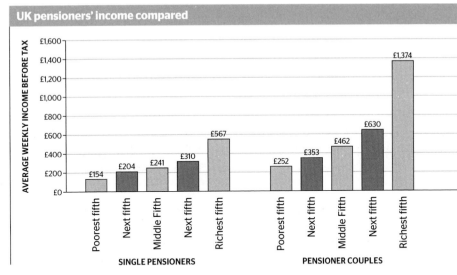

Source: DWP (2012) *The Pensioners' Income Series 2010-11*

Where today's pensioners get their income

The financial experience of pensioners today is very mixed and clearly demonstrates the importance of saving for retirement.

Suppose all pensioners are ranked in order of their income, from the lowest to the highest, and then split into five equal groups as in the chart above. The wealthiest fifth of single pensioners have an average before-tax income of £567 a week (around £29,484 a year), which is enough to support a reasonably comfortable lifestyle. By contrast, the poorest fifth of single pensioners have £154 a week and so are living close to the poverty line. The contrast is even more marked for pensioner couples, with the richest fifth having a before-tax income of £1,374 a week, which is over five times as much as the £252 a week income of the poorest fifth of pensioner couples.

A look at the sources of pensioners' incomes – see overleaf – reveals the main reasons for the big difference in the finances of the poorest and wealthiest pensioners. The poorest couples are heavily reliant on the State Pension and other state benefits. These account for nearly three quarters of their income and they receive only small amounts from other sources, such as occupational pension schemes. What makes the wealthy couples significantly better off is the substantial income they get from occupational pensions, continuing earnings and investments.

> '**The poorest fifth of today's single pensioners are living close to the poverty line.**'

Income sources of the poorest and richest pensioners

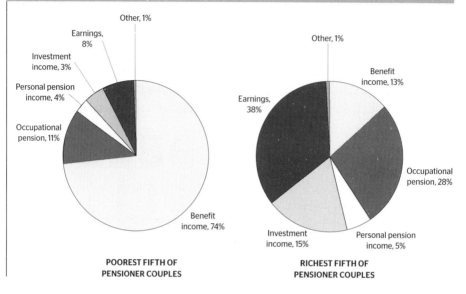

**POOREST FIFTH OF
PENSIONER COUPLES**

**RICHEST FIFTH OF
PENSIONER COUPLES**

Source: DWP (2012) *The Pensioners' Income Series 2010-11.*

With single pensioners, the wealthiest fifth get over a third as much again in State Pensions and benefits as the poorest fifth and, once again, occupational pensions, earnings and investments are the main sources of extra income.

The important messages from this look at today's pensioners are:

■ If you rely purely on the State for retirement income, you are likely to be relatively poor.

■ You can make a big difference to your financial wellbeing in retirement if you plan ahead by saving, for example, through a pension scheme.

■ Carrying on some work can give a big boost to your retirement income.

Planning ahead for retirement

For most people, retirement is a substantial part of life, lasting a couple of decades or more. It follows that ensuring your financial security in retirement requires some forward planning.

Developing a plan calls for a general review of your current finances and careful consideration of how you can build up your savings to generate the retirement income that you will need.

There are five distinct stages to planning your retirement, summarised in the chart on page 17.

Stage 1 involves checking first that other aspects of your basic finances are in good shape. Planning for retirement generally means locking away your money for a long time. Once invested, it is usually impossible to get pension savings back early, even in a crisis. So it is essential that

you have other, more accessible, savings available for emergencies and that you do not have any problem debts that could tip you into a financial crisis – these are crucial considerations if you are being newly affected by the introduction of auto-enrolment (see Chapter 4). You must then weigh up saving for retirement against other goals that are, or may seem more pressing, such as making sure your household would be financially secure if you were unable to work because of illness or the main breadwinner died, saving for a deposit on a house, and so on. However, you need to

How long might retirement last		
If you retired in 2013 at this age	On average you could expect this many years in retirement	
	Men	Women
55	31	34
60	26	29
65	21	24
70	17	20
75	13	15

Source: Office for National Statistics (2011).

bear in mind a couple of important points. First, if you can join a pension scheme through your workplace, this might meet some of your other goals, for example if the scheme provides life cover. Second, failing to save for retirement now could mean you are losing out on financial help from your employer – Chapter 4 has further guidance on this.

At **stage 2**, you need to decide how much income you might need when you retire. You'll find more about this overleaf and on the remaining pages of this chapter.

Stages 3 to 5 are all about checking what pensions you have built up so far, deciding how much extra you need to save and keeping track of your savings as the years go by to check that you are still on target for the retirement you want. Chapters 2 to 9 will guide you through the process.

> **'Planning for your retirement means locking away money for a long time.'**

How much retirement income you want

There is no easy way to predict the amount of income you will need or want when you come to retire. Financial advisers often suggest you should aim for a pension that is two thirds, or perhaps half, your current earnings. That's fine as a rule of thumb, but there are several reasons for taking a closer look at your possible income needs:

- You might spend a lot less once you retire, especially if you currently have a mortgage and/or children to support.
- On the other hand, you might want to allow for higher spending in retirement. This might be planned spending (on, say, foreign travel) or a contingency to cope with, say, age-related health problems.
- Your current earnings might be unusually low because of a career break or family demands.
- You might be earning a great deal now but be happy to settle into a less extravagant lifestyle later on.

You can use the retirement income calculator on pages 18–20 to help you estimate more precisely the retirement income you might need.

If you prefer to use an interactive, computer-based budgeting tool to estimate your retirement needs, see the Tools section of the Money Advice Service website at **www.moneyadviceservice.org.uk/en/tools/budget-planner**.

The five-stage retirement plan

There are five distinct stages to planning your retirement. The flow chart shows how to assess your progress and what action to take at each stage.

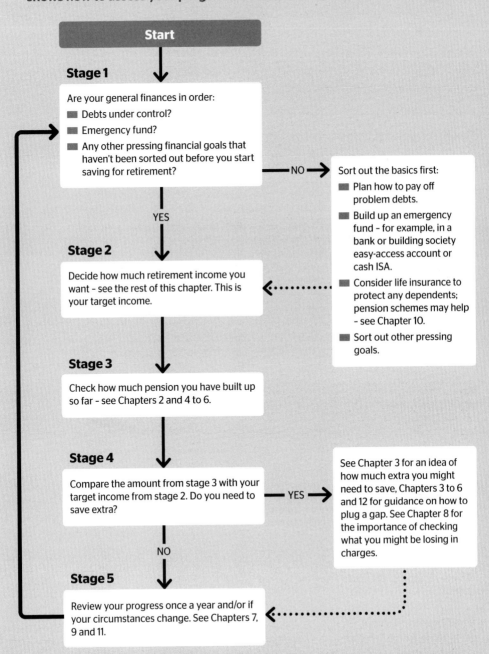

Start

Stage 1

Are your general finances in order:
- Debts under control?
- Emergency fund?
- Any other pressing financial goals that haven't been sorted out before you start saving for retirement?

NO →

YES

Sort out the basics first:
- Plan how to pay off problem debts.
- Build up an emergency fund – for example, in a bank or building society easy-access account or cash ISA.
- Consider life insurance to protect any dependents; pension schemes may help – see Chapter 10.
- Sort out other pressing goals.

Stage 2

Decide how much retirement income you want – see the rest of this chapter. This is your target income.

Stage 3

Check how much pension you have built up so far – see Chapters 2 and 4 to 6.

Stage 4

Compare the amount from stage 3 with your target income from stage 2. Do you need to save extra?

YES →

NO

See Chapter 3 for an idea of how much extra you might need to save, Chapters 3 to 6 and 12 for guidance on how to plug a gap. See Chapter 8 for the importance of checking what you might be losing in charges.

Stage 5

Review your progress once a year and/or if your circumstances change. See Chapters 7, 9 and 11.

Retirement income calculator

This calculator is designed to help you think about the amount of income you might need when you reach retirement. The notes on the following pages will guide you. Fill in the calculator as if you were on the brink of retiring today, using amounts in today's prices. Don't worry about inflation between now and your actual retirement date (see page 21), this will be taken into account later on. If you prefer to use an online calculator, visit the Age UK website at www.ageuk.org.uk/money-matters/pensions/pension-calculator/.

WHAT YOUR HOUSEHOLD MIGHT SPEND		£ PER MONTH
Day-to-day living	A	
Household bills	B	
Transport	C	
Hobbies and luxuries	D	
Health and protection	E	
Saving, borrowing and major expenses	F	
Other expenses	G	
Total monthly expenses *Add amounts A to G*	H	
Total yearly expenses *Multiply amount H by 12*	I	

		Single person or first person		Partner if couple household
Single-person household: copy amount I in the box marked J. Ignore the second column. **Couple household:** decide how amount I would be split between you and continue with separate calculations for each of you, using both columns. *Divide I into two amounts*	J		J*	
Tax factor *Choose the appropriate number from the table on page 20*	K		K*	
Target retirement income *Multiply J by K (and J* by K*)*	L		L*	

Day-to-day living (A)

This covers food, household basics, clothes and so on. Many are things you put in the trolley when you do a main shop. Look at your current supermarket bills: there will probably be just one or two of you in retirement so, if you are currently raising a family, you'd expect these bills to be less.

Household bills (B)

Allow for any rent to continue but, if you are buying your own home, you'll normally have paid off any mortgage by the time you retire. You might spend more time at home, which could mean significantly higher fuel bills. Council Tax and water rates might be about the same, although you might save money by having a water meter installed. What about the phone? Many retired people are low-users. If you decide to 'downsize' to a smaller home, you may find that household bills shrink correspondingly. New appliances might be more efficient too.

Transport (C)

You might save on work-related costs, particularly if you no longer have regular commuting expenses. You might decide not to run a car at all. On the other hand, you might clock up extra miles visiting friends. Bear in mind that people aged 60-odd plus often qualify for reduced, or free, rail, bus, coach and even taxi fares.

Hobbies and luxuries (D)

Would you spend more on hobbies? You may want to enrol in adult education classes to learn a new skill. You might take more holidays, but these could be cheaper if you currently have to take them in the peak season. Would you eat out more often and perhaps go to the theatre and cinema more? You could qualify for pensioners' pub meals and concessionary tickets.

Health and protection (E)

Based on current rules, prescriptions and eye-tests would be free but not usually dental visits or spectacles. Medical insurance becomes expensive as you get older. You might save on life insurance premiums if there would no longer be anyone financially dependent on you. In later old age, you might need to buy in personal care, which, at between £10 and £30 an hour, could soon mount up. You might need eventually to move into a residential or nursing home, which could easily cost around £1,000 a month.

Saving, borrowing and major expenses (F)

You'll save on pension contributions and maybe other savings you make now. You might borrow less, but you'll probably still face occasional big expenses, such as a new washing machine or adaptations to your home. To cover these costs, you could aim to save a set amount each month to achieve them more easily.

Total expenses (I and J)

Add together all the amounts A to F and also G, which is a box for any expenses you expect to have that are not already entered elsewhere in the calculator. Put the total in box H and multiply by 12 to find the year sum. Amount I is the total yearly expenses you expect to have in retirement, so it is also the after-tax retirement income your household will need.

If you are a couple, be aware that pension schemes cannot normally be held in joint names and there are some good reasons why you should be wary of relying on just one of you to make the retirement savings for the whole household (see page 25 onwards). Therefore, at this stage, the calculator asks you to decide how much of the household's after-tax retirement income each of you plans to contribute. Put one amount in box J and the other in J*. From here on, you need to treat the amounts in each column separately.

Tax payable

You can't just set your retirement income target equal to your estimated spending, because most sources of retirement income are taxable. You need to have enough left after paying any tax to finance your spending.

Nobody knows how income will be taxed many years ahead, but it's possible to make a rough adjustment based on the tax system that operates today. In 2013-14, people born before 6 April 1948 still get higher Income Tax allowances than younger people, but these higher allowances are being phased out. However, there is no National Insurance (NI) on pensions, savings income or, if you are over pension age, earnings from a job. This means an older person on the same income as someone younger still typically pays less tax. Based on an Income Tax personal allowance of £10,000 a year and other tax arrangements as they stood in 2013-14, the table overleaf gives a tax factor for use in the retirement income calculator.

Tax factors

If after-tax income is within this band	To find the before-tax income, use a tax factor of
£0 to £10,000	1.0 (in other words no increase)
£10,001 to £24,000	1.1
£24,001 to £42,000	1.2
£42,001 to £54,000	1.3
£54,001 to £77,000	1.4
£78,000 to £89,000	1.5

If you are single, select the appropriate factor and put it in box K. Multiply J by K to find the before-tax retirement income you may need (amount L). This is your target retirement income.

If you are a couple, you need to select the appropriate tax factor for the first of you and put this in box K. Multiply J by K to find your target retirement income (amount L). Now select the appropriate tax factor for your partner and put this in box K*. Multiply J* by K* to find your partner's target retirement income (amount L*). Amounts L and L* together give the total before-tax retirement income your household expects to need.

Case study Craig and Hannah

Craig and Hannah have two children. Currently, they spend around £2,700 a month on food, bills and other expenses. They estimate that, without the costs of raising the children, paying the mortgage and going to work, in retirement they might need only around £1,400 a month. Both of them work, but Craig earns more and has access to a better pension scheme than Hannah, so they reckon Craig is likely to provide around 70 per cent of the household's retirement income and Hannah the remainder. Their calculator entries are shown below. They estimate that Craig's target retirement income needs to be about £13,000 a year and Hannah's around £5,000. However, Hannah, in particular, might want to think about building up a bigger pension than this (see page 25).

			Single person or first person		Partner if couple household
Total monthly expenses *Add amounts A to G*	H	£1,400			
Total yearly expenses *Multiply amount H by 12*	I	£1,400 × 12 = £16,800			
Single-person household: copy amount I in the box marked J. Ignore the second column. **Couple household:** decide how amount I would be split between you and continue with separate calculations for each of you, using both columns. *Divide I into two amounts*	J	70% × £16,800 = £11,760		J*	30% × £16,800 = £5,040
Tax factor *Choose the appropriate number from the table above*	K	1.1		K*	1.0
Target retirement income *Multiply J by K (and J* by K*)*	L	£11,760 × 1.1 = £12,936		L*	£5,040 × 1.0 = £5,040

The impact of inflation

When planning many years ahead, it is essential to take account of the effects of inflation. As prices rise over the years, the same amount of money buys less and less. For example, if prices double, a fixed amount of money will buy only half as much. The higher the rate of inflation, the more you have to save to reach your income target.

Some pension schemes give you automatic protection against inflation (see Chapters 2 and 5), but many don't and it will be up to you to decide what protection to build into your planning (see Chapter 6). The first step is to be aware of the effect that inflation might have.

Fortunately, pension statements and projections these days must all be adjusted for inflation so that the figures you are given are expressed in today's money. This gives you an idea of the standard of living you might expect and helps you assess the amount you need to save. To make the adjustment, the provider has to make an assumption about future inflation. For example, you might assume that over long periods, future inflation might average 2.5 per cent a year. If inflation turns out to be higher, your eventual pension will be worth less than you had expected. If inflation turns out to be lower, your pension will be worth more.

Jargon buster

Inflation A sustained rise in the price level. In the UK, inflation is often measured as the change in the Consumer Price Index (CPI) or Retail Prices Index (RPI). Both are based on the prices of a large basket of goods and services, typical of the items that an average household buys.

Today's money The amount of money today that would be worth the same in terms of what it might buy as a sum of money that you will get at some time in the future. For example £100 in ten years' time would be worth £50 in today's money if prices doubled over the ten-year period.

> ' As prices rise over the years, the same amount of money buys less and less.'

See the table overleaf for help in calculating the long-term impact of inflation on future income and lump sums.

Providers of non-pension investments (such as unit trusts and investment trusts, see Chapter 12) do not have to give you statements and projections adjusted for inflation. If you use these other investments for your retirement savings (or any long-term savings goal) you may need to make your own adjustments. You can do this using the table below.

Key tips

■ Make allowances for inflation when you plan ahead.

■ Plan to save extra if your pension scheme (or schemes) does (do) not offer any automatic protection against inflation.

Case study Graeme

Graeme, aged 40, decides to invest £11,520 in a stocks-and-shares individual saving account (ISA) – see Chapter 12 – and set this aside for retirement age 65. The documents from the provider suggest that the £11,520 might grow to just over £30,000 over the intervening 25 years. That sounds like a tidy sum, but Graeme realises it is likely to be worth less than £30,000 today because of inflation. He uses the table below to get an idea of how much less. He assumes inflation will average 2.5 per cent a year, so looks down the second column until he comes to the row for 25 years. He reads off the figure £539. This tells him that the £30,000 he might get in 25 years' time may be worth only the same as £16,170 today (30 x £539).

Value in today's money of £1,000 you receive in the future				
Number of years until you receive the money	Average rate of inflation			
	2.5% a year	5% a year	7.5% a year	10% a year
5	£884	£784	£697	£621
10	£781	£614	£485	£386
15	£690	£481	£338	£239
20	£610	£377	£235	£149
25	£539	£295	£164	£92
30	£477	£231	£114	£57
35	£421	£181	£80	£36
40	£372	£142	£55	£22
45	£329	£111	£39	£14
50	£291	£87	£27	£9

The Government publishes current inflation rates for the whole economy. But these are averages. You can estimate your own personal inflation rate by going to **www.neighbourhood.statistics.gov.uk/HTMLDocs/dvc14/index.html.**

Retirement saving options

By now, you should be convinced of your need to save for retirement and will have a broad idea as to how much your target retirement income might be.

The question addressed in the remaining chapters of this book is: what are the most suitable ways to save, taking into account any help you can get with the cost, the likely return from investments, and any risks involved?

Basically, there are three ways to tackle retirement saving, as shown in the diagram overleaf. The first way (labelled '1' in the diagram) is the State Pension. Most people will get this (see Chapter 2 for details), but as you have already seen this, on its own, is unlikely to be enough to support the retirement you want. Nonetheless, it is a good foundation on which to build. And do not underestimate the value of the State Pension: as you will see in Chapter 3, if you had to save for it directly (instead of paying for it indirectly through taxes), you would need to build up a fund of at least £170,000.

Help with the cost

The second way (labelled '2' in the diagram) is saving through 'registered pension schemes'. These are occupational pension schemes, personal pension plans and multi-employer schemes, such as the National Employment Savings Trust

(NEST). There are two reasons for choosing these forms of saving. Where the scheme is offered through your workplace, increasingly your employer will contribute towards the cost of building up your retirement income. This help from the employer is explored in Chapters 4 and 5.

The second reason is that the Government provides tax incentives when you use a registered scheme. These take the form of:

- Tax relief on the amount paid in.
- The money in the scheme grows largely tax-free.
- Part of the savings that build up can be taken as a tax-free cash sum when you start to draw your pension. (Although the rest of the savings must be taken as pension, which is taxable.)

Jargon buster

Basic State Pension Part of the State Pension (see Chapter 2), which nearly everyone gets.

Registered pension scheme A scheme designed to provide a pension and often other benefits too (such as life cover and pensions for survivors if you die), which qualifies for advantageous tax treatment.

Taxable Describes income or gains on which you may have to pay tax depending on your personal circumstances.

Using a registered pension scheme can therefore make saving for retirement more affordable because of the help you get from the Government through tax reliefs and, depending on the type of scheme, from your employer as well.

Other ways to save

In general, a registered pension scheme is just a 'tax wrapper' that goes around whatever investments make up the pension fund inside.

The tax wrapper ensures that the investments inside benefit from the tax treatment outlined above, but you can choose to invest in the same sorts of investments without the benefit of the tax wrapper. For example, a pension scheme may invest in shares and bonds, but you can buy shares and bonds directly without belonging to a pension scheme or you could buy them through an investment fund, such as a unit trust.

So you can hold the same investments that would go into a pension scheme without having a pension scheme at all. In that case, you lose the special tax treatment, but typically you gain flexibility. For example, you cannot usually draw any money from a pension scheme before the age of 55, but you can cash in most non-pension investments at any time, regardless of age.

Chapter 3 looks at the factors to consider when putting your retirement savings inside the tax wrapper of a pension scheme. Chapter 12 looks at other investments and strategies and, for a more detailed discussion on this, see the Which? book *Save and Invest*.

Building up retirement income

Although the State Pension is a good foundation, most people need to save more for their retirement.

3. OTHER SAVINGS

For example, individual savings accounts, unit trusts, a second home (see Chapter 12).

2. REGISTERED PENSIONS SCHEMES

Special tax-efficient savings for retirement. Can be via workplace or personal schemes.

1. THE STATE PENSION

A foundation on which to build your pension planning.

Women and pensions

Women pensioners tend to have less income than their male counterparts. In building a retirement plan, women need to consider what steps they and their partners can take to make their financial future more secure.

Special issues for women

These days, the rules of any particular pension scheme – whether the State scheme, an occupational scheme or a personal plan – do not discriminate between men and women. Man or woman, you pay the same to access the same package of benefits. But this does not mean women in general end up with the same pensions as men, because women are more likely to take breaks from work or take part-time or flexible jobs so that they can look after a family. As a result, women are more likely than men to have periods during which they are not paying into a pension scheme. If they work while raising a family, their salaries may be lower, which – since pension contributions or benefits are normally linked to pay – feeds through to a low pension too, or their jobs often come with less generous pension arrangements. If you are a woman living with your partner, you may feel that this does not matter if your partner is making retirement savings for you both, but you should be aware of these facts:

■ Although the State scheme recognises wives, husbands and civil partners for now, this is due to end in 2016 and does not, in any case, apply to unmarried partners. This means if your partner dies before you, you would not necessarily be eligible for financial help from the State.

■ Occupational schemes and personal pensions typically pay survivor benefits to a bereaved partner, whether married or not. However, some schemes have recognised unmarried partners only recently and, as a result, support for an unmarried partner may be low.

■ The legal system recognises that wives, husbands and civil partners may have a claim on retirement savings built up by the other party in the event of divorce, but you may end up with a much lower retirement income than you had been expecting.

> **'Women are more likely than men to have periods during which they are not paying into a pension scheme.'**

■ The legal system does not give similar rights to unmarried partners who split up. If your unmarried partner was building up pension savings for you both, he or she can walk away with all those savings.

You'll find more information about these points in Chapter 10. The key issue to understand is that your planning for retirement will be more robust if you and your partner split the household retirement savings between you so that you each build up some savings in your own name.

Summary

In this chapter, you have seen that saving for retirement is important if you want to avoid living on a very low income. The amount you need to save (the topic of Chapter 3) depends on the amount of retirement income you expect to need. You can estimate this using either a rule of thumb, such as two thirds of your current income, or a calculator like the one on pages 18–20.

Retirement planning needs to fit into your overall financial situation, so you should aim to sort out basics, such as debt problems and building up an emergency fund, before you devote resources to retirement. In choosing how to implement your plan, pension schemes can be a particularly cost- and tax-effective way of saving for retirement. It is important to review your plan regularly to make sure you stay on target for the retirement income you want.

A robust retirement plan will take into account risks that may materialise over the years. A key risk is inflation, which eats into the buying power of your money over time. Women in particular should think about minimising the threat to their retirement security in the event of the death of a partner or relationship breakdown.

Key Tips

For women:

■ Try to build up pension savings in your own name that remain yours regardless of family changes (see Chapters 4 to 6).

■ If you are relying on a partner's pension scheme, check your rights under the scheme and encourage your partner to make decisions that protect or enhance your rights (see Chapter 10).

■ If you are going through a separation or divorce, make sure you claim a share of the family pension rights (see Chapter 10).

For their partners:

■ Consider paying into a pension scheme in your partner's name (see Chapter 6).

■ Be aware of how the decisions about your pension scheme(s) may affect your partner – for example, nominate her to receive any death-in-service lump sum, consider paying extra to increase a survivor's pension (see Chapter 10).

The State Pension

2

Changes since April 2010 mean that most people were on track to get a full basic State Pension when they retire (and might have had some additional State Pension, too). But if you will retire after April 2016, you will probably get a new single flat-rate State Pension instead. If you need extra retirement income, one option could be to delay the date when you start drawing your State Pension.

State Pensions

The State Pension may not seem very generous but it provides a valuable foundation on which to build your retirement income. There are steps you can take to protect your entitlement to State Pension, and to boost the amount you get once you start to receive the payments.

The State and your retirement planning

Chapter 1 suggested three ways to save for retirement: State Pensions, registered pension schemes and other savings and investments. The diagram below splits these up into three tiers of retirement

planning. The State Pension is the only compulsory part of the UK pension system. If you work, you must contribute to it; if you don't work, in many cases, you are credited as if you are paying in. The State Pension currently has two parts: the basic State Pension, which nearly everyone gets; and the additional State Pension, which is mainly for employees.

The basic State Pension is the first tier. In 2013–14, the full basic pension provides just over £5,700 a year for a single person. As discussed in Chapter 1, if that was all the pension income you had, you would be below the poverty line and eligible for means-tested benefits to top up your income. The main means-tested benefit for pensioners is Pension Credit and you will find brief details of how this works starting on page 48.

However, most people reach retirement with some second-tier pension as well. Second-tier pensions are mainly pension schemes you belong to through your workplace or equivalent personal pensions if you don't have access to a work-based scheme – for example, if you are

---

Pension sources

State Pension is the foundation of your retirement income. On top of this you can build additional savings, through pension schemes and other investments.

THIRD TIER PENSION
Other savings and investments –
see Chapters 3 and 12
Extra contributions to second tier
pension schemes - see Chapters 4 to 6

SECOND TIER PENSION
Personal pensions - see Chapter 6
Occupational pensions - see Chapters 4 and 5
Additional State Pension - see this chapter

FIRST TIER PENSION
Basic State Pension - see this chapter

self-employed. But the second tier also includes the additional State Pension. A little bit of history explains why this is so.

Back in the early 1970s, the Government was concerned about pensioner poverty. It observed that the pensioners who were reasonably well off were those who'd had the benefit of occupational pension schemes during their working years. Could the State provide a top-up similar to an occupational pension to lift other pensioners out of poverty? The answer eventually adopted from 1978, was the additional State Pension – at that time, called the State Earnings Related Pension Scheme (SERPS). This scheme covered employees and, through a system called 'contracting out' (see page 38), its cost was shared between the State and employers. The additional State Pension has evolved since (see page 36), but has, to date, remained an important part of the second tier of retirement planning, since the basic and additional State Pensions together, on average, take pensioners above the poverty line. However, from 2016, the basic and additional State Pensions are due to be replaced by a single flat-rate State Pension, worth around £144 in today's money. The State Pension will then become purely a first-tier pension at a level sufficient to abolish, for most people, the risk of having to claim means-tested benefits like Pension Credit. While that is good news for some women, the self-employed and many public sector employees, others may find that they end up with less State

Pension than they had expected under the pre-2016 rules or that cuts in their workplace pension offset a gain in State Pension (see page 39). Moreover, at £144 a week, the State Pension will still not provide a particularly generous income. Occupational pensions and third-tier retirement planning – voluntary extra savings and investments – are therefore important as ways to top up your retirement income even further.

State pensions are not retirement saving in the pure sense, because you do not build up your own fund of savings. Instead you pay National Insurance (NI) contributions – a tax on your earnings – which are recorded and entitle you to claim a specified amount of pension. The State scheme works on a 'pay-as-you-go' basis so that the National Insurance you pay now is actually used to pay the pensions of people who are currently retired. In a similar way, when you come to retire, your State Pension will be paid out of tax on the earnings of people who are working then.

State Pensions and inflation

Since April 2011, the Basic Pension is increased each year by the better of price inflation, earnings inflation or 2.5 per cent a year. Earnings tend to rise at a faster rate than pensions, so this so-called 'triple lock' is a good deal for pensioners. The additional State Pension is increased only in line with price inflation (as measured by changes in the Consumer Price Index, CPI). If prices fall (deflation), there is no increase in those pensions linked to price inflation, but the pensions are not cut.

The basic State Pension

The basic pension is paid to everyone who has been credited with enough National Insurance contributions. It is often called a 'flat-rate' pension, because everyone who qualifies for the full pension gets the same. But people who have a less complete National Insurance record get a reduced amount.

How much?

In 2013–14, the full basic pension for a single person is £110.15 a week (£5,728 a year). A couple where both partners (whether married or not) have built up their own right to claim the basic pension could receive up to twice this amount, in other words, 2 × £110.15 = £220.10 a week (£11,456 a year).

Under current (pre-2016) rules, a wife can claim a basic pension or extra basic pension based on her husband's National Insurance record. Since 6 April 2010, a husband or a civil partner can also claim basic pension based on their partner's record, provided the partner was born on or after 6 April 1950. To be eligible, both spouses or civil partners must have reached State Pension age. The maximum basic pension that can be claimed in this way is £66 a week in 2013–14, or enough to top up the basic pension to that level. Therefore, a couple relying on these rules could receive a maximum of £110.15 + £66.00 = £176.15 a week (£9,160 a year). Unmarried partners cannot benefit from these rules.

First-tier pension
Maximum basic pension (2013–14)
Single person: £5,728
Couple: £11,456 or £9,160

Building up basic pension

The amount of basic pension you get depends on the number of tax years during your working life in which you have paid or been credited with enough National insurance contributions. Each of these years is called a 'qualifying year'. 'Working life' has an official definition and means the tax years from the one in which you reach age 16 to the last complete tax year before you reach State Pension age. For example, if your State Pension age is 65, your working life will be 49 years.

Jargon buster

National Insurance contributions A tax paid by most people who work. There are different types of contribution, called 'classes'. Paying some classes of contribution entitles you to claim state benefits, such as the State Pension.

Tax year A period of a year running from 6 April to the following 5 April. For example, '2013-14' means the year from 6 April 2013 to 5 April 2014. Generally, both taxes and state benefits are set in relation to tax years.

Working Tax Credit (WTC) A state benefit for people who are in work, but on a low income.

Basic State pension entitlement		
When you reach State Pension age	Qualifying years required for full basic pension	Qualifying years required for any basic pension
6 April 2010 to 5 April 2016	30	1
6 April 2016*	35	10

*Assuming government proposals become law.

For people who reach State Pension age between 6 April 2010 and 5 April 2016, to get the full basic pension, you have to have 30 qualifying years and each year gives you at least some pension.

Assuming government proposals go through as expected, from 2016, you will need 35 qualifying years for the full pension and at least 10 years to get any State Pension at all.

Who gets it?

The following people are building up basic pension:

- Most employees, provided they earn at least a minimum amount (£109 a week in 2013–14) or are getting Working Tax Credit.
- Self-employed people, unless they have opted not to pay National Insurance contributions (this is possible where their profits are less than £5,725 for the 2013–14 tax year).
- People who are being credited with National Insurance, for example, while claiming state benefits during a period of illness, unemployment or maternity leave.
- People not in the above categories who volunteer to pay National Insurance contributions.

Jargon buster

Qualifying year A tax year that counts towards your basic State Pension, because you have paid or been credited with enough National Insurance contributions.

State Pension age Age at which you become eligible to claim the State Pension. This is being gradually raised and, depending on when you were born, is between 65 and 68 for men and between 61 and 68 for women (see page 40).

Working life The tax years from the one in which you reach age 16 to the last complete tax year before you reach State Pension age.

Case study David and Gemma

David has a working life of 49 years. But he worked in the Far East for a long time and has built up only 17 qualifying years to count towards his basic State Pension. The 17 years qualify him for only 17/30ths of the full pension. In 2013–14, this would mean a basic pension of 17/30 × £110.15 = £62.42 a week.

Although David and his wife, Gemma, have no children, Gemma stopped work once they married and, in consequence, has only three qualifying years on her own National Insurance record. In 2013–14, this qualifies her for £110.15 × 3/30 = £11.02 a week of basic pension. But she can also claim some basic pension based on David's record. The maximum pension under these rules is normally £66 (see opposite) but David is entitled to only 17/30 of the full basic pension entitlement, so the spouse entitlement is also reduced to 17/30 × £66.00 = £37.40 a week. In total Gemma can claim a basic pension of £11.02 (on her own record) + £26.38 (on David's record) = £37.40 a week.

To check the number of qualifying years you have paid or been credited with National Insurance contributions (NICs) contact the Future Pension Centre for a statement on 0845 3000 168 or via the website **www.gov.uk/future-pension-centre**.

Qualifying years

There are different types of National Insurance contribution and not all count towards building up basic or new flat-rate pension. In general, only Class 1 contributions (paid by employees), Class 2 contributions (paid by the self-employed) and Class 3 contributions (voluntary) count, but there are some complications and these are summarised in the table opposite.

For a year to count as qualifying, you must basically have paid a whole year's worth of contributions: for example, 52 weeks of earnings of at least a minimum amount on which you have paid Class 1 contributions (or are treated as having paid them), 52 Class 2 contributions, or a mixture of Class 1 earnings and Class 2 contributions covering the full 52 weeks.

Key tip

If you are self-employed and your profits are low, think carefully before deciding not to pay Class 2 contributions. At just £2.70 a week in 2013-14, they can be a good value way of building up basic State Pension.

Periods when you are not paying National Insurance usually appear as gaps in your National Insurance record and can reduce the basic pension you'll eventually get. But, in some situations, when you are out of work owing to illness or on maternity leave, for example, you can get National Insurance credits. Before 6 April 2010, for periods spent looking after a young child you were awarded Home Responsibilities Protection (HRP). Since that date, you simply earn credits if you are caring for an eligible child and earlier periods of HRP have now been converted to credits in your National Insurance record.

National Insurance credits

In some situations you may get National Insurance credits, which plug what would otherwise be gaps in your National Insurance record. You might get credits in the situations described below, opposite and overleaf:

- At the start of your working life For the years in which you had your 16th, 17th and 18th birthdays if you were still at school and were born on or after

Jargon buster

Lower earnings limit (LEL) The lowest level of earnings that count towards the record on which certain state benefits, such as your State Pension, are based.

Primary threshold The level of earnings at which employees start to pay National Insurance contributions.

Upper accruals point (UAP) The highest level of earnings that count towards the record on which your State Pension is based.

Upper earnings limit (UEL) Historically, the level of earnings at which employee National Insurance contributions stopped, but nowadays the threshold at which the contribution rate changes.

As well as basic State Pension you may be eligible for additional State Pension (S2P/SERPS). Under the 2016 changes, your rights to any additional pension already built up are to be protected. See page 36 for details.

National Insurance contributions that count towards the basic pension

Type of contribution	Paid by	Details for 2013-14
No contributions but earnings between LEL and PT	Employees	Earning between £109 and £149 a week.
Class 1 full rate on earnings between PT and UAP	Employees	Earnings between £149 and £770. Usually paid at 12% but less if 'contracted out' (see page 38).
Class 2	Self-employed	Flat rate of £2.70 a week. Those with earnings for the year of less than £5,725 can choose to opt out.
Class 3	Out of the labour market and not receiving NI credits	Flat rate of £13.55 for each week.

Key to abbreviations
LEL = lower earnings limit; PT = primary threshold; UAP = upper accruals point; UEL = upper earnings limit. LEL, PT and UEL usually increase each year. UAP is fixed.

National Insurance contributions that do not count towards the basic pension

Type of contribution	Paid by	Details for 2013-14
No contributions but earnings below the LEL	Employees	Earning less than £109.
Class 1 married women's reduced rate	Employees	5.85% of earnings between £149 and £797 a week and 2% above £797.
Class 1, full rate, on earnings above the UAP	Employees	12% of earnings between £770 and £797 a week and 2% on earnings above £797.
No Class 2 contributions	Self-employed	Those with earnings for the year of less than £5,725 who have chosen to opt out.
Class 4	Self-employed	9% of earnings for the year between £7,755 and £41,450 and 2% on earnings above £41,450.

Key to abbreviations
LEL = lower earnings limit; PT = primary threshold; UAP = upper accruals point; UEL = upper earnings limit. LEL, PT and UEL usually increase each year. UAP is fixed.

6 April 1957 and reached these ages before 6 April 2010. You should have been given these credits automatically.

■ While training For the years in which you take part in an approved training course if you were born on or after 6 April 1957. Going to university does not count as an approved course. You should normally get these credits automatically.

■ When you earn less than the lower earnings limit (£109 a week in

2013–14) and you are claiming Working Tax Credit (or previously Working Families Tax Credit or Disabled Person's Tax Credit). You should get these credits automatically.

■ While temporarily working abroad if the UK has a reciprocal agreement with the country in which you are working and you are paying contributions there.

■ If your spouse or civil partner is in HM Forces and you are accompanying them abroad on an assignment.

■ **While out of work because of unemployment or illness** If you're claiming Jobseeker's Allowance or Employment and Support Allowance, you should get these credits automatically. If you are getting Statutory Sick Pay and the year in which you get it would not otherwise be a qualifying year, you need to claim this credit by writing to the NICO Contributor Group by 31 December following the end of the tax year in which you were on sick leave.

■ **While you are on maternity, paternity or adoption leave** and receiving Statutory Maternity, Paternity or Adoption Pay and the year in which you get it would not otherwise be a qualifying year. You need to claim this credit by writing to the NICO Contributor Group by 31 December following the end of the tax year in which you were on leave.

■ **You are a parent** of a child under the age of 12 for whom you are getting Child Benefit. Credits are awarded automatically. You are also eligible if you are a foster carer, but in that case you will need to claim the carer's credit. Since 7 January 2013, if either you or your partner (if you have one) earn £50,000 or more, you will be subject to extra Income Tax to claw back part or all of the family's Child Benefit. You can avoid the tax charge by giving up the Child Benefit. But, if you do this, make

Case study Clare

Clare left school in 1975 at age 18 and went on to university to study English Literature for three years. She gets National Insurance credits for the three years in which she had her 16th, 17th and 18th birthdays and was still at school. But the three years at university do not qualify for credits and appear as a gap in her National Insurance record. However, Clare's State Pension age is 67 (see page 45 for how pension age is increasing). This means she has a working life of 51 years. Only 30 of these years need to be qualifying years for her to get the full basic pension. Therefore, she can have 21 years' worth of gaps in her record without any impact on the basic pension she will get.

Jargon buster

NICO Stands for National Insurance Contributions Office, the part of HM Revenue & Customs that deals with the collection and recording of National Insurance contributions.

To contact NICO by post you should write to: National Insurance Contributions Office, Benton Park View, Newcastle Upon Tyne NE98 1ZZ. You can also call the helpline on 0845 302 1479.

sure you still register your claim to Child Benefit so that you continue to get National Insurance credits towards your State Pension.

- **You are a carer** looking after someone with a disability or frail through old age. You get credits automatically if you are claiming Carer's Allowance. Otherwise, you will need to make a claim for the carer's credit.

- **You are on jury service** and your earnings are below a certain limit (£109 a week in 2013–14). This applies to the years from 1988–9 onwards. You need to claim this credit by writing to the NICO Contributor Group by 31 December following the end of the tax year in which you were on jury service.

- **You are a man under State Pension age but older than the State Pension age for women** You qualify if you are not paying National Insurance contributions or already getting credits for some other reason. You do not have to sign on as unemployed and should get these credits automatically. Women's State Pension age is gradually increasing and when it matches the State Pension age for men from November 2018 onwards, this type of credit will no longer be available.

With many of the above credits, you are not eligible if you are a married woman and you have chosen to pay reduced rate Class 1 contributions during periods when you are an employee, or not to pay Class 2 contributions during periods of self-employment. This is because you are expected to rely on your husband's National Insurance record for your pension.

From October 2013, many of the State benefits for working age people mentioned above will start to be replaced by a new benefit called Universal Credit. At the time of writing, the Government had not announced how National Insurance credits would be linked to Universal Credit, but it is expected that rules similar to those described above will apply.

Key tip

Working life is normally much longer than the 30 qualifying years (35 if the 2016 changes go ahead) that you need for a full basic pension. This means you can have quite a lot of gaps in your National Insurance record without losing any basic pension.

Case study Charvi

Charvi stayed at home, looking after her three children for a total of 18 years. During this time, 16 years fell before 6 April 2010 and Charvi was awarded Home Responsibilities Protection (HRP) to help her qualify for the State Pension. From April 2010 onwards, the HRP years are converted into National Insurance credits. From April 2010, Charvi got carer's credits for the two years that she spent at home looking after the youngest child. The 18 years of credits earn her 18/30 of the full basic pension and count towards the 30 years she needs to qualify for the full amount when she eventually reaches retirement.

To find out more about giving up Child Benefit but continuing to register your claim in order to get National Insurance credits, see **www.hmrc.gov.uk/childbenefitcharge/stopstartpayments.htm#7**.

The additional State Pension

The additional State Pension is a second-tier pension mainly for employees, but also people who cannot work because of disability or caring responsibilities.

When it started in 1978 it was called the State Earnings Related Pension Scheme (SERPS). From 2002, it was modified and the name changed to the State Second Pension (S2P).

The additional pension you get when you retire is based on your combined membership of both SERPS and S2P. Both are currently earnings-related pensions, so the amount of pension you get depends on the average of your earnings over the years you have been in the scheme. The precise calculation is complex, but broadly, your earnings between various limits determine the amount of pension you'll get. Changes were made in 2010 that mean the additional pension would, by about year 2030, have become a flat-rate pension worth around £70 a week in today's money.

However, the Government has proposed that instead of leaving the additional pension to wither in this way, it will be replaced by the new, single flat-rate pension to be introduced from April 2016. Under the proposals, you will have a 'foundation amount' of State Pension based on your National Insurance contributions and credits up to April 2016. This will include any rights to additional pension built up so far. If your foundation amount is higher than the new flat-rate pension, the extra will be protected. So you will not lose any additional pension already built up. However, because S2P is relatively generous to low-income employees (see opposite), many will end up with less State Pension under the new flat-rate scheme than they might have expected under the current rules.

Who gets it?

SERPS was available only to employees with earnings at least equal to the LEL (£109 a week in 2013–14). You could not build up SERPS if you were not working, for example, because you were long-term sick or at home caring for children, or someone who was disabled. S2P addresses some of these drawbacks so, since 6 April 2002, the additional State Pension has been open to:

■ Employees earning at least the LEL.
■ People caring for one or more children under the age of 12 (previously 6) for whom they are claiming child benefit.

People who qualify for carer's allowance through looking after someone who is ill or disabled.

Some people who are unable to work because of illness or disability, provided they are entitled to certain disability-related benefits.

Some people are not covered by the additional State Pension, either SERPS or S2P. These include self-employed people, employees earning less than the LEL and married women who have opted to pay Class 1 National Insurance contributions at the reduced rate and employees who are 'contracted out'.

Over your whole working life, you may have some periods when you belong to the additional State Pension scheme and other periods when you do not. The pension will be based on your average earnings over your whole working life (or since 1978 if you reached age 16 before then) with earnings set at zero for periods when you were not eligible for the scheme.

How much is additional State Pension?

The amount of additional State Pension you get depends on your earnings. The maximum in 2012–13 was just under £162 a week. In practice, however, the high earners who would qualify for this level of pension have usually been contracted out for long periods, so the average additional pension actually paid out today is much lower. The average

Jargon buster

Contracted out Describes the situation where, instead of building up additional State Pension, a person is saving for retirement through an occupational pension scheme or a personal pension. Some of the National Insurance contributions that would normally have gone towards the additional pension are used instead to provide benefits from the occupational scheme or personal pension. Since 6 April 2012, contracting out has been restricted to defined-benefit schemes only and is due to be abolished altogether from 2016. See page 38.

additional pension being received in March 2011 was £26.39 a week (£1,372 a year).

The Government forecasts that the average State Pension (basic and additional combined) being paid out in 2013–14 will be £124 a week (£6,448 a year). If plans to replace the basic and additional pensions with a new flat-rate basic pension of £144 week go ahead, this would be equivalent to £7,488 a year.

S2P, but not SERPS, is designed to give special help to people who are working, but on low incomes, or unable to work because of caring duties or disability. For S2P purposes, they are treated as if they have an income equal to a set amount called the low earnings threshold (LET). In 2012–13, the LET was £14,700.

First-tier pension	
Expected State Pension (Assuming 2016 changes)	From the State: £7,500

To check your basic State Pension and additional State Pension entitlement you can request a State Pension statement from Future Pension Centre on 0845 3000 168 or via the website **www.gov.uk/future-pension-centre**.

The additional State Pension

Graduated State Pensions

Some people who worked between April 1961 and April 1975 might get graduated State Pension. This is an earlier earnings-related additional State Pension scheme. The maximum pension that is paid is small – generally less than £10 a week.

A person with this level of earnings throughout their working life would in theory qualify for an additional pension of around £70 a week (£3,622 a year) at 2012–13 rates.

Contracting out

When SERPS was first introduced, it was intended to be the State equivalent of an occupational pension scheme (see page 29) and, to limit the cost of the scheme to the State, it included arrangements for employers to provide an equivalent pension in place of SERPS. These arrangements were given the name 'contracting out'.

Defined benefits

Under the original arrangement, employers (not individual employees) chose whether or not to offer a contracted-out occupational scheme to their employees. Such a scheme had to provide a pension (called a guaranteed minimum pension) and other benefits broadly at least

as good as the SERPS pension being given up. While employees belonged to a contracted-out scheme, they were not building up SERPS and, in recognition of this, both they and their employer paid a lower-than-normal rate of National Insurance contributions. This type of contracting out is on a 'defined-benefit' basis (because the scheme – like the additional State Pension scheme – pays a pension of a specified or defined amount). For more information about defined-benefit schemes, see Chapter 5. There have been changes to the way defined-benefit contracting out works, but you can still be contracted out of S2P on largely the same basis. Moreover, since 6 April 2012, this is now the only form of contracting out allowed. However, when the State Pension changes to a flat-rate (expected 2016), even this type of contracting out will be abolished.

Defined contributions

From 1988 until 5 April 2012, another type of contracting out became possible: contracting out on a 'defined-contribution' basis. Once again, employers could decide to offer a contracted-out scheme to all their employees. But, alternatively, individuals could decide to contract out independently by having a personal pension scheme to replace the additional State Pension they were giving up. There were some important features of contracting out on a defined-contribution basis:

- You and your employer carried on paying National Insurance at the normal rates, but part of

'S2P is specifically designed to help people on low incomes.'

your contributions were returned (called a 'rebate') and, together with some tax relief, paid into the pension scheme.

■ Defined-contribution schemes do not promise any particular amount of pension or other benefits. Instead, the amount paid in – in this case the rebate plus tax relief – is invested and grows to build up a pension fund. At retirement, you use that fund to buy a pension. So the amount of pension you will eventually get depends on the size of the rebates, how well the fund grows, how much is taken away in charges, and the rate at which the fund can be exchanged for pension. There is more about defined-contribution schemes in Chapters 5 and 6.

While contracting out on a defined-benefit basis is a largely a risk-free exchange for you, the employee – you give up some State Pension but get more or less the same pension instead from an employer's scheme – contracting out on a defined-contribution basis is very different. You gave up a set amount of State Pension but the invested rebate may produce a higher or lower sum. In an era of booming stock markets that may have seemed a gamble worth taking – though in fact it was always very difficult to decide whether contracting out might be a suitable choice. Nowadays, the consensus is that contracting out on a defined-contribution basis is nearly always a poor decision, which is why it has been abolished since

6 April 2012. Contracted-out defined-contribution pensions you already have are now to be treated like any other defined-contribution pension – see Chapters 5 and 6.

Contracting out and the 2016 changes

If, as proposed, the State Pension becomes a single flat-rate pension from 2016, the additional pension will cease to exist. Therefore, contracting out must cease as well. So, if you are currently contracted out (which has to be on a defined-benefit basis), when the changes come in, you will see the following changes:

■ Your National Insurance contributions will increase.

■ Your employer, who will also have to pay higher National Insurance contributions, is likely to make some changes to your pension scheme. You may be asked to pay higher contributions. You may be asked to accept reduced benefits. Your employer may propose closing the defined-benefit scheme altogether. However, if you are in a public sector scheme, current agreements do not permit further changes to your scheme even though your employer will be paying increased National Insurance contributions.

You will still get any contracted-out pensions that you have already built up. There will be a reduction to the flat-rate State Pension you qualify for to reflect the amount you are getting from the contracted-out schemes you belonged to before 2016.

Your State Pension age

You cannot start to draw your pension before you reach State Pension age. Moreover, for most people, that age is rising, making working life longer than you may have expected.

Likely changes in the future

Few people can be unaware of the current crisis in pension provision. As people are living longer and the post-war baby-boom generation enters retirement, the population overall is ageing. The shift in the age profile of the population means there are relatively fewer workers than in the past to pay the pensions of relatively more retired people. As a result, a number of changes have been, and continue to be, made to reduce the future cost of the State scheme. One of the key changes currently in progress is raising the State Pension age. First, women's State Pension age is being increased

Key tip

You can check your State Pension age and the date on which your State Pension is due to start using the calculator on the Gov website: www.gov.uk/calculate-state-pension.

until it matches that of men from 2018 onwards; then the age for both men and women will rise

The increases are being phased in and your own particular pension age depends on when you were born. The table shows the increases as they stood at the end of 2012.

The increase to age 67 had yet to be ratified by Parliament, but in early 2013, the Government announced that it would bring forward legislation as soon as possible to confirm that change. Thereafter, the Government is proposing that it will review the State Pension age every five years. The intention is that the Government will define a standard proportion of adult life that a person can expect to spend in retirement. Then, as average longevity increases, State Pension age will be raised in order to keep that proportion constant. The analysis of life expectancy on which the decisions

Case study Lesley

Lesley was born on 10 August 1953. This means her birthday falls 5 months after 5 April 1953 (counting the part-month as a whole month). Therefore she must add 15 months to age 63 in order to find out her State Pension age. This comes to 64 years and 3 months. She can start to receive her pension from the beginning of the tax month in which she reaches this age - the tax month starting 6 November 2017.

Your State Pension age	
Your date of birth	**Your pension age**
Before 6 April 1950	60 (women); 65 (men)
6 April 1950 to 5 April 1953	Between 60 and 63 (women)*; 65 (men)
6 April 1953 to 5 December 1953	Between 63 and 65 (women)*; 65 (men)**
6 December 1953 to 5 October 1954	Between 65 and 66*
6 October 1954 to 5 April 1960	66
6 April 1960 to 5 April 1961	Between 66 and 67*
6 April 1961 to 5 April 1977	67
6 April 1977 to 5 April 1978	Between 67 and 68*
6 April 1978 onwards	68

* For each month by which your birth date falls after the start of the transition period, add one month to the State Pension age.
** For each month by which your birth date falls after the start of the transition period, add three months to the State Pension age.
For this purpose, a month runs from 6th day of one month to 5th day of the next and a part-month counts as a whole month.

will be based is to be carried out by the Government Actuary's Department, but the decision will also be informed by a report from an 'independent-led body' that will take into account wider factors, such as variations in life expectancy. This raises the prospect that your State Pension age in future might be based not just on your date of birth, but perhaps your health, occupation or even postcode too – in other words, the sort of factors that commercial companies take into account when deciding how much pension to offer in exchange for your pension fund (see Chapter 6).

Life expectancy

In 2011, the Office for National Statistics reported that life expectancy of the UK population was 10 years higher for people living in Kensington and Chelsea than for those living In Glasgow.

'**Your State Pension age in future might be based not just on your date of birth but perhaps your health, occupation or even postcode.**'

Keeping track of your State Pension

You can, at a pinch, work out your own entitlement to the basic State Pension, but it's well nigh impossible to calculate your additional State Pension. Save yourself the effort by getting a State Pension statement from The Pension Service.

You can phone or write to request a pension statement by post. Alternatively, you can register with the Government's online service (the Government Gateway) and then get statements online. Your eventual State Pension will depend on what happens over the whole of your working life, but the statement is based only on what you've built up so far. However, the statement includes some guidance on how much extra pension you may get for each additional qualifying year between now and your State Pension age. You can use this to estimate your likely total State Pension.

If you belong to an occupational pension scheme (see Chapters 4 and 5) or have a personal pension (see Chapter 6), you will get regular statements indicating the pension you may get from the scheme.

In some cases, these may be combined statements, in which case they also include a State Pension estimate based on your own National Insurance record.

Information you need to get a State Pension forecast

- Your National Insurance number.
- The types of contribution you are paying (for example, Class 1 if you are an employee, Class 2 if self-employed – see page 38).
- Your current salary if you are an employee.
- If applicable, details of your current marriage or civil partnership and your husband's, wife's or civil partner's National Insurance number, in case your pension can be increased by using their record. (Your partner will not be contacted.)
- Details of any previous marriages or civil partnerships, in case your former or late partner's record can help to boost your pension. (Former partners will not be contacted.)
- Details of any time spent working abroad.

Example of what a State Pension estimate tells you

Your weekly amount of basic State Pension: £76.02.
Your weekly amount of additional State Pension: £14.91.
Your total weekly amount of State Pension: £90.93.

Increasing your State Pension

If you have received a State Pension statement, it may have alerted you to think about ways in which you can increase your State Pension, for example, by filling gaps in your National Insurance record or deferring the start of your State Pension.

Alternatively, you may have received a letter from HM Revenue & Customs saying you have a gap in your National Insurance record and suggesting that you might want to take action to fill it. At any time, you can ask the Revenue's National Insurance Helpline on 0845 302 1479 to check your record and advise on whether you have any gaps.

Filling gaps in your record

Periods of your working life when you were not paying National Insurance and did not qualify for credits or HRP will appear as gaps in your record. For people reaching State Pension age between 6 April 2010 and 5 April 2016, you need only 30 qualifying years for the full pension. Depending on your pension age (see page 40), your working life may be from 44 to 52 years. Therefore,

under the post-April-2010 rules, you can have substantial gaps in your record without any reduction in your basic pension.

Under the proposed 2016 rules, you will need 35 years for a full pension, which still leaves scope for considerable gaps. However, it is expected that you will need at least 10 years to get any pension at all, so it may be especially worthwhile filling gaps if you will be under that threshold.

You may be able to pay voluntary Class 3 National Insurance contributions to fill gaps in your record. But you need to think carefully whether this is worth doing in your case. Follow the steps in the checklist below.

Normally, you can go back a maximum of six years to fill gaps in your record. But, if you will reach

---

Is it worth paying Class 3 contributions?

Do you have a gap in your National Insurance record?

Check the length of your working life: your State Pension age (see page 40) minus 16.

If you do nothing to plug the gap, do you still expect 30 (or 35 and at least 10) of the years in your working life to be qualifying by the time you reach State Pension age?

If you expect to have fewer qualifying years, are you within the time limits for paying Class 3 contributions to plug the gap?

State Pension age before 5 April 2015, special rules let you fill any gaps up to six years in total going back as far as 6 April 1975. In 2013–14, each weekly Class 3 contribution costs £13.55, so a full year's worth costs $52 \times 13.55 = £704.60$.

Making Class 3 contributions can't increase your additional State Pension. However, Class 3 contributions do currently count towards the State bereavement benefits that your wife, husband or civil partner could claim if you were to die (see Chapter 10). In the case of bereavement benefits, you must have paid or been credited with National Insurance contributions for roughly nine tenths of your working life in order for your spouse or partner to receive the full rate of bereavement benefits. This means Class 3 contributions could increase

entitlement to bereavement benefits, even though they cannot increase your basic pension. However, bereavement benefits based on a partner's National insurance record are due to cease for anyone reaching State Pension age on or after 6 April 2016. Moreover, you should compare the outlay of paying Class 3 contributions for this purpose with the cost of buying life insurance instead. If you are unsure whether paying Class 3 contributions would be worthwhile for you, contact your local Citizens Advice Bureau for help.

Married women: switching contributions

Until 1977, married women could elect to pay Class 1 National Insurance at a reduced rate (or, if applicable, opt out of paying Class 2 contributions). Making this choice meant they stopped building up State Pension in their own right and would, instead, rely on their husband's record for a pension (see page 30).

Although no new arrangements of this kind can be made, a woman who made the choice in the past was originally allowed to continue the arrangement indefinitely. Alternatively, she can end the arrangement at any time (and it automatically ends in some circumstances, such as divorce).

If you are a woman still covered by this, is it worth switching to paying

Key tips

- You get the full basic pension, generally, once 30 of the years in your working life are qualifying years. This means that you can usually have substantial gaps without any loss of pension, so there would be no point paying Class 3 contributions to plug gaps beyond that length.

- If voluntary contributions are worthwhile, in 2013-14, a full year of Class 3 contributions costs £704.60 and buys you £190.93 a year of pension, index-linked and payable from State Pension age for life. You need to survive only 3.7 years after retiring to break even on the deal.

If you decide to switch to full-rate contributions, complete form CA9 available from HM Revenue & Customs and see the guidance on the Revenue website at **www.hmrc.gov.uk/ni/reducedrate/marriedwomen.htm**.

Is it worth a married woman switching to full-rate contributions		
Reason for the switch	Worth doing?	Why/Why not?
To get more basic State Pension	Unlikely	If you'll reach State Pension age before April 2016, you would usually need 18 qualifying years of your own before you could claim more State Pension than you can get based on your husband's National Insurance record.
To get more flat-rate pension	Possibly	If you'll reach State Pension age from April 2016 onwards, under new proposals you will not be able to claim a pension on your husband's National Insurance record and will need a minimum number of qualifying years, expected to be ten, for your own State Pension. If you have time to build up ten years, it would be worth making the switch.
To get more additional State Pension	Maybe	If you are an employee earning at least the LEL (£109 a week in 2013-14) switching to the full rate means that you would also start to build up additional State Pension. S2P offers a particularly good deal for people on low earnings. Any additional pension you build up should be protected under the 2016 changes.

full-rate National Insurance and so starting to build your own State Pension? The table above considers the pros and cons.

Deferring your State Pension

Another strategy for boosting your State Pension is to delay its start, in which case the current rules let you have a bigger pension when you do begin to draw it, or alternatively a cash lump sum. Under the post-2016 rules, you will still be able to earn extra pension, but not a lump sum.

You cannot start your pension before reaching State Pension age (see page 40), but you can choose to

start drawing it later. You can put off drawing your pension for as long as you like – there is no time limit. You must defer your whole pension, including any additional and graduated pensions, as well as your basic pension. You earn an increase or a lump sum on the whole amount deferred.

If you defer your pension and your wife, husband or civil partner claims a pension based on your record, they do not have to defer their pension as well.

If your pension has already started to be paid, you can decide to stop the payments in order to earn extra

How much extra pension you might get for each £100 a week of pension deferred [a]

Length of deferral	Total pension given up	Extra weekly pension earned	Weekly pension when it does start	How long you need to survive to break even (years)	Average life expectancy (years) assuming you were aged 65 when you deferred	
					Men	Women
3 months	£1,300	£2.60	£102.60	9.6	21.4	24.1
6 months	£2,600	£5.20	£105.20	9.6	21.4	24.1
1 year	£5,200	£10.40	£110.40	9.6	20.6	23.1
2 years	£10,400	£20.80	£120.80	9.6	19.7	22.2
5 years	£26,000	£52.00	£152.00	9.6	17.2	19.5
10 years	£52,000	£104.00	£204.00	9.6	13.3	15.2
15 years	£78,000	£156.00	£256.00	9.6	9.8	11.2

a State pensions are increased at least in line with price inflation (see page 29), so all values in this table are automatically expressed in today's money (see page 21).

How much lump sum you might get for each £100 a week of pension deferred

Length of deferral	Total pension given up [a]	Lump sum in cash terms assuming bank of england base rate is 0.5% [b]	Value of the cash sum in today's money [c], assuming inflation averages:	
			1% a year	2.5% a year
1 year	£5,200	£5,266	£5,214	£5,138
2 years	£10,400	£10,664	£10,454	£10,150
5 years	£26,000	£27,680	£26,337	£24,465
10 years	£52,000	£58,997	£53,409	£46,088
15 years	£78,000	£94,429	£81,336	£65,200

a State pensions are increased at least in line with price inflation (see page 33), so the value of pension given up is automatically expressed in today's money (see page 21).

b Lump sum earns base rate + 2% a year. Base rates as at end-2012. Amount shown in this column is the cash sum you would get on a future date before any adjustment for inflation.

c Inflation between now and the date you receive the cash sum would reduce the buying power of the money (see page 21). These columns give a more realistic idea of the value of the cash sum by expressing it in today's money, given various assumptions about inflation.

pension or a lump sum. But you can only defer your pension once.

You do not have to decide at the outset whether to go for extra pension or the lump sum – you can leave that decision until you are ready to start your pension. But, if you want the lump sum, you will have to defer your retirement for at least a year. The minimum deferral period if you choose extra pension is much shorter at five weeks.

You can earn an increase in the pension when it does start of 1 per cent for every 5 weeks you put off the pension. This is equivalent to an increase of 10.4 per cent for each whole year. The extra pension is taxable in the same way as the rest of your State Pension.

Alternatively, provided you put off claiming your pension for at least a year, you can earn a one-off lump sum instead of extra pension. The lump sum is taxable but only at the top rate you were paying before getting the lump sum – in other words, whatever the size of lump sum, it does not result in you moving into a higher tax bracket. The size of the lump sum is calculated as if the amount of pension you deferred had been put into a savings account where it earned interest at a rate of 2 per cent above the Bank of England base rate.

The tables opposite show some examples of how much extra pension or lump sum you might get as a result of deferring your pension. Extra pension offers the more certain deal in terms of investment return unless you die unusually young or defer for a very lengthy period. Looking ahead, the lump sum option offers

Case study Ralph

Ralph is 65 and could start drawing his State Pension of £130 a week. But he is self-employed and plans to carry on running his business for at least another two years, so he does not need his State Pension yet. He decides to defer the pension. Looking ahead, Ralph expects to start his pension at age 67, getting £120.80 a week in today's money, index-linked for life for each £100 of pension deferred. Since he is giving up £130 a week of pension, he can therefore expect an enhanced pension of 130/100 x 120.80 = £157.04. Based on current interest and inflation rates, Ralph thinks that earning extra pension is likely to give him a better deal than taking a lump sum. However, he will make his final choice in two years' time.

an uncertain investment return, but when you come to make the choice at the time your pension starts, you will know exactly what lump sum is on the table and you can then compare it with the extra-pension option.

'If your pension is already being paid, you can stop payments in order to earn extra pension or a lump sum.'

Pension Credit

In 2013, the basic State Pension on its own, even at the full rate, is well below the minimum income that the Government guarantees to pensioners. If this were your only income you could claim Pension Credit to top it up.

It can be very hard to save any money for a distant retirement if your income while you are working is low – other needs may be just too pressing. Even if you do manage to put a bit aside, the amount of pension you accumulate is likely to be small. A question if you find yourself in this position is: will your savings be too small to make any difference to your finances in retirement, given that you may be able to claim means-tested state benefits? If so, then saving anything at all for retirement could be a waste of money.

Jargon buster

Means-tested Describes state benefits that you receive only if your income and, in some cases, your savings are below a specified level.

Pension Credit and couples

'Couple' means a married couple, a same-sex couple who have registered their relationship as a civil partnership and unmarried/unregistered partners living together.

Case study June

In 2013-14, June had a State Pension of £110.15 a week and a personal pension of £20 a week, giving her a total weekly income of £130.15. This is £15.25 less than the Pension Credit guarantee credit for a single person (£145.40), so June qualifies for guarantee credit of £15.25. She is also entitled to savings credit of £8.91. Pension Credit has boosted her income to £130.15 + £15.25 + £8.91 = £154.31 a week.

This is a fundamental argument behind the Government's proposal to shift to a new flat-rate State Pension from 2016 of around £144 a week in today's money. This weekly sum is broadly equal to the minimum income that pensioners are deemed to need to live on. So, if the majority of people retired on incomes of at least that much, there would be no need to claim means-tested benefits and thus no disincentive to make private savings for retirement.

To claim Pension Credit you can telephone a special Pension Credit claims line on 0800 99 1234.

However, the Government has said that the new £144 a week State Pension will not apply to existing pensioners, many of whom will continue to need top-up benefits. In 2013, the main means-tested benefit for pensioners is Pension Credit. The benefit has two parts: a guarantee credit and a savings credit. Depending on your circumstances, you might qualify for either or both of these elements.

Two types of credit

Any person over a qualifying age (equal to women's State Pension age – see page 45) whose income is less than a set amount, called the minimum guarantee, is entitled to claim a top-up to bring their income up to that level. In 2013–14, the standard minimum guarantee is

£145.40 a week for a single person and £222.05 for a couple. The savings credit provides a bit extra to reward people who have made their own modest savings for retirement. In 2013–14, the maximum savings credit is £18.06 a week if you are single and £22.89 if you are a couple.

Examples of Pension Credit for a couple

Your income from all sources	Income above threshold at which savings credit starts	Guarantee credit	Savings credit	Your income including Pension Credit
£50.00	£0.00	£172.05	£0.00	£222.05
£100.00	£0.00	£122.05	£0.00	£222.05
£150.00	£0.00	£72.05	£0.00	£222.05
£222.05 [a]	£38.15	£0.00	£22.89	£244.94
£250.00	£66.10	£0.00	£11.71	£261.71
£260.00	£76.10	£0.00	£7.71	£267.71
£270.00	£86.10	£0.00	£3.71	£273.71
£280.00	£96.10	£0.00	£0.00	£280.00

a Level of the guarantee credit

You can get an estimate of how much Pension Credit you might be entitled to by using the online calculator at **www.gov.uk/pension-credit-calculator**.

Useful resources about State Pensions and National Insurance		
Reference	Title	From
CA5603	To pay voluntary National Insurance contributions	HM Revenue & Customs
None	How to increase your State Pension if you reach State Pension age between 6 April 2010 and 5 April 2015 - Buying voluntary contributions	The Pension Service
BR19	Pension statement application	The Pension Service
CPF5	Your pension statement explained (combined pension forecast)	The Pension Service
SPD1	State Pension deferral - your guide	The Pension Service
NP46	A guide to State Pensions	Department for Work and Pensions

Summary

This chapter has shown how the State Pension provides a useful foundation on which to build your retirement savings. Taking the basic and additional State Pension (or an equivalent 'contracted-out' pension) together, the State scheme is just about sufficient to take you out of poverty in retirement, even though it is unlikely to be enough on its own to meet your retirement income target.

The State scheme is complex. Rather than trying to work out your entitlement for yourself, get a State Pension statement either from The Pension Service or via a combined pension statement from an occupational scheme you belong to or personal pension plan you have.

Consider whether you might be able to boost your State Pension, for example, by starting it later than the date on which you reach State Pension age. Bear in mind, however, that State Pension age is increasing anyway.

The box above draws together some of the most useful paper-based resources about State Pensions if you want to know more. Increasingly, government information is moving to the internet, and you will find a wealth of information on both the Gov (www.gov.uk) and HM Revenue & Customs (www.hmrc.gov.uk) websites.

Pension gap

3

A pension gap is the shortfall between the income you want in retirement and the pensions you are on track to get. Forecasts and benefit statements help you check what you are likely to get. To close a gap, there are various steps you can take to boost your retirement income.

Achieving your retirement goal

Chapter 1 invited you to think about how much income you will need in retirement. Chapter 2 considered how much pension you might get from the State. You might already be building up other pensions too, for example, through a scheme at work. The key question is: do you need to save more?

The national pension gap

Surveys by the pension provider, Scottish Widows, regularly find that barely half the UK population is on track for a comfortable retirement. The other half of the population is saving too little, with a fifth saving nothing at all for retirement.

This lack of retirement saving was behind the recommendations in 2006 of a Pensions Commission, set up by the Government to review and advise on pension provision in the UK, often called the Turner Commission, after Adair (now Lord) Turner, its chairman. The Commissions's recommendations have been translated into a package of legislative measures that are reforming the State

Pension system and introducing a new national system of auto-enrolment into workplace pension schemes (see Chapter 4). At the time of the Commission's review, the Association of British Insurers estimated that Britons were under-saving for retirement to the tune of £27 billion a year and this was dubbed the nation's 'pension gap'.

As the Turner Commission pointed out, when faced with a pension gap, there are four options for society:

- Accept that pensioners will be poorer.
- Increase taxes or cut spending on other things, in order to pay better pensions.
- Save extra.
- Retire later.

Setting aside the first option (poorer pensioners) and accepting that only governments can control the second (increasing taxes or

> ' If you personally face a pension gap, the ways to close it are to save more and/or retire later.'

For an interactive tool that estimates how much pension any extra savings might produce, visit the Tools section of the Money Advice Service website at **www.moneyadviceservice.org.uk/en/tools/pension-calculator** or the Age UK pension calculator at **www.ageuk.org.uk/money-matters/pensions/pension-calculator/**.

cutting other spending), at a personal level you are left with just the last two options. If you personally face a pension gap, the ways to close it are to save more and/or retire later.

Do you have a gap?

It is very easy to underestimate the cost of retirement. Not every individual is saving too little, but the evidence suggests that a very sizeable proportion of people are.

The calculator overleaf will help you check whether you are on track for the retirement you want or whether you need to start saving extra. If you are a couple, each of you needs to fill it in separately. Use the extra column in the calculator for your partner's data, if you want to build up a picture for your household as a whole. The calculator uses annual figures throughout.

■ Start by bringing forward the target retirement income (amount L) that you worked out in the retirement income calculator on page 20.

■ If you do not already have a recent State Pension statement, get one now (see page 42) and enter your expected pension as amount M. If the statement is giving you a weekly sum, you will need to multiply it by 52 before putting the figure into the calculator.

■ You may belong to a pension scheme at work, be contributing to a personal pension plan and/ or have pension rights in an old employer's scheme or previous personal plan that you are no longer contributing to. Gather

'Check whether you are on track for the retirement you want.'

together benefit statements (see pages 103 and 128) for all of these. On each one, find the figure for the amount of pension you can expect from the normal retirement age in today's money. Take care not to include any estimate of your pension from the State, because this is already entered in the calculator at amount M. If you have several employer schemes and personal plans, jot down the pension from each, add them together and enter the total as amount N.

■ Add your State, employer and personal pensions together (amount O) and subtract the total from your target retirement income (amount L) to find your pension gap (amount P).

This calculator is a bit rough and ready, because it assumes that all your pensions will start paying out at the same age. In practice, life can be more complicated, so you may need to adjust some of the figures up (if you will retire later) or down (if you will retire sooner) and pages 60–1 gives you an idea of how you might do this. You may be planning to retire before your State Pension starts (either because you want to retire before State Pension age or you are planning to defer your State Pension). In that case, you will need to plan whether you can manage without that

Pension gap calculator

	SINGLE PERSON OR FIRST PERSON		PARTNER IF COUPLE HOUSEHOLD	
Target retirement income *From the retirement income calculator (Chapter 1, page 20)*	L		L*	
Expected State Pension *From State Pension statement (Chapter 2, page 42)*	M		M*	
Pensions you are already building up *From benefit statements (Chapter 5, page 103, and Chapter 6, page 128)*	N		N*	
Total pension income so far *Add amounts M and N*	O		O*	
Your pension gap *Subtract O from L*	P		P*	

'You have a pension gap if amount P in your calculator is bigger than zero.'

income from the State scheme and this may mean saving extra to bridge that gap. Retirement planning is more of an art than a science, so you will need to think through issues like these, but the pension gap calculator provides a useful starting point.

If amount P in the calculator is bigger than zero, you are currently unlikely to achieve the retirement income you want: you have a pension gap. The next step is to work out how much you may need to save to plug your pension gap, but this depends, in part, on the way you choose to save. This chapter looks just at saving through a pension scheme. For information on other ways to finance your retirement, including non-pension investments, see Chapter 12.

Case study Gina

Gina is 50. After a break bringing up children, she returned to work and is now employed by a logistics firm. She is divorced, so must provide for herself both now and in retirement. Her target retirement income is £16,000 a year and she puts this in box L in the calculator.

For State Pension purposes, her years caring for the children were protected and now count as credits in her National Insurance record (see page 33), so she is on track for a full basic State Pension and some additional pension too. Her State Pension statement, says she can expect a State Pension of £127.74 a week, which she rounds to £6,600 a year. This is Gina's amount M.

Gina worked before she had a family and will get a small pension forecast to be £1,600 a year from her old employer. In the divorce settlement, Gina did not get any share of her husband's pension savings, because she kept the family home instead. Assuming she stays in her current employer's scheme, she is forecast to have a pension of £3,900 a year. She adds these pensions together and enters £5,500 in box N.

Gina follows the instructions in the calculator and works out that she currently has a pension gap of £3,900 a year.

		SINGLE PERSON OR FIRST PERSON
Target retirement income	L	£16,000
Expected State Pension	M	£6,600
Pensions already building up	N	£1,600 £3,900
		£5,500
Total pension income so far *Add amounts M and N*	O	£12,100
Pension gap *Subtract O from L*	P	£3,900

Saving via pension schemes

For many people the best way to plug a pension gap is to start saving (or save extra) through a pension scheme. There are tax advantages and can be other powerful incentives.

Tax advantages

We have already looked briefly at the advantages that saving through a pension scheme has over other types of saving. These include:

- Tax relief on the contributions paid into the scheme.
- The resulting pension fund builds up largely tax-free.
- Part of the savings can be taken at retirement as a tax-free lump sum (though the rest must be drawn as taxable pension).

Using a pension scheme means you get tax relief while you save, but, apart from taking a tax-free lump sum on retirement, you are eventually taxed on the money you receive as pension income. You defer tax rather than save it altogether. Whether you save tax in the long run depends on two factors:

- The rate at which you get tax relief while you save, relative to the rate at which you pay tax when you retire. You get tax relief on pension savings up to your top rate of tax, but there is a cap on the amount you can save each year that qualifies for tax relief (see page 64). Most people get tax relief on contributions while they are working at the basic rate. If you pay tax on your pension in retirement at a lower rate than the rate of tax relief you had, you gain from the tax deferral. If you pay tax at a higher rate in retirement, you may lose.
- The tax-free lump sum. The tax rules broadly allow you to take a quarter of your pension savings as a tax-free cash sum rather than as taxable pension. This part of your savings benefits from tax relief on the way into the pension scheme and freedom from tax on the way out, regardless of the rates of tax you pay while working and in retirement.

The table opposite demonstrates how you win or lose from the tax treatment if you opt to save through

---

Jargon buster

Contribution Money paid into a pension scheme by you or someone else, for example, your employer.

Pension fund A pool of investments into which contributions are paid and that is used to provide pensions and other pension scheme benefits as they fall due for payment.

Tax deferral Putting off a tax bill until a later time. This could save tax if your tax rate in future is lower than now.

a pension scheme. The table assumes that your invested pension fund grows at a rate of 4 per cent a year, after charges, over a 20 year term and that you take the maximum possible tax-free lump sum at retirement. An effective rate of return in the table greater than 4 per cent means you gain from the tax treatment. An effective rate of less than 4 per cent means you lose.

You might think that pension schemes would offer a poor deal if you're a non-taxpayer while working, since the tax incentives appear irrelevant. But with some types of pension scheme, including NEST (see Chapter 5), personal pensions and stakeholder pension schemes (see Chapter 6), everyone is given tax relief at the basic rate (20 per cent in 2013–14) on the contributions they pay into pension schemes, regardless of their actual rate of tax. If you are a non-taxpayer you still get tax relief at 20 per cent, which is effectively a bonus.

Key tips

The table shows that:

- ■ Most people are winners from saving through pension schemes.
- ■ The only non-winners are non-taxpayers and basic-rate taxpayers who (unusually) end up paying tax at the higher or additional rate when they retire.
- ■ The higher your tax rate while working, the bigger the win (but see page 64 for limits on the amount you can pay into pension schemes).
- ■ The greater the fall in your tax rate after retirement, the better the pension scheme deal.
- ■ To be a winner from pension schemes, non-taxpayers need to choose schemes that give tax relief on their contributions (see Chapters 4 to 6).

Winners and losers from pension schemes [a]

Your top rate of tax when you pay into the scheme	The top rate of tax on your pension when you retire			
	0%	20%	40%	50%
0% [b] non-taxpayer	W 7.5%	W 5%	1.8%	0.9%
20% [b] basic-rate taxpayer	W 7.5%	W 5%	1.8%	0.9%
40% [c] higher-rate taxpayer	W 12%	W 9.4%	W 6.4%	W 5.6%
50% [d] additional-rate taxpayer	W 13.3%	W 10.8%	W 7.8%	W 6.9%

Key: W = winner. Percentages are effective annual return after tax treatment.
a Based on tax rates in 2013-14, investment return 4% a year after deduction of charges and a 20-year investment term. Assumes contributions qualify for basic rate tax relief at source (see page 111) and that rate of tax when you pay into the scheme applies to the whole of your contributions, but this might not in practice be the case (see page 111).
b Non-taxpayers paying into an occupational scheme (see Chapter 5) would not get tax relief. Figures here assume they pay into a scheme such as NEST or a personal pension, where they do get the benefit of 20% tax relief (see Chapters 4 to 6).

To understand the pros and cons of different types of scheme see Chapters 4 to 6. Tax rates are an important consideration but there are other benefits and drawbacks you need to consider.

Other features of pension schemes

Tax incentives are a strong reason to save for retirement through pension schemes. With occupational pension schemes and increasingly most workplace schemes (see Chapters 4 and 5), another powerful incentive is that your employer pays contributions into the scheme on your behalf – these are effectively an extra part of your pay package. Running a pension scheme is a complex business requiring input from a variety of professionals, including actuaries, lawyers and fund managers. They all need to be paid and there are costs too in buying, selling and safely keeping the investments in the pension fund. The higher the charges, the less money left to provide pensions and other benefits. Occupational pension schemes and multi-employer schemes usually have relatively low charges. But, with personal pensions and similar schemes that you take out on an individual basis, charges are often high. See Chapter 8 for more information.

The main drawback of saving through pension schemes is that they are inflexible. They are designed specifically to provide an income in later life. Usually you cannot get your money back early and when you can get at your money most of it must be drawn in the form of a pension. If you want greater flexibility, you may want to consider alternatives to pension savings as discussed in Chapter 12.

Trivial pensions

If the value of your pension scheme savings from all the schemes you have (occupational and personal) comes to no more than a specified amount, the pension you get will be very small and is called a trivial pension. In the tax year 2013–14, the specified amount is set at £18,000. In this case, you may be able to draw the whole of your savings as a lump sum instead of as a pension – called 'trivial commutation' – though not all schemes allow this. You must be aged at least 60 and savings in all the schemes must be converted to lump sums within a 12-month period.

In addition to the overall limit above, if the value of the savings you have built up in any particular scheme is £2,000 or less, this counts as a 'stranded pot' or 'small pot' and can also be converted to a lump sum. This applies to any number of occupational schemes in which you have savings, but a maximum of two personal pensions.

Only a quarter of any lump sum will be tax-free – the remainder will be taxed as income for the year in which you receive the sum.

If you are interested in taking trivial commutation or turning stranded and small pots into a lump sum, contact your normal tax office for advice (you can find the address on tax notices and documents you've been sent or through the Revenue website www.hmrc.gov.uk).

How much should you save?

The amount you might need to save to fill a pension gap depends not just on the income you want, but also on when you intend to start drawing it. Retiring later reduces the amount you need to save, while retiring earlier makes the amount soar.

If you have a pension gap, the key question is: how much (or how much extra) do you need to save to plug the gap? The tables on page 60 give some idea, assuming you save through a pension scheme and get tax relief at the basic rate that is added to your savings.

The tables show the amount you would need to save each month, after deducting tax relief at the basic rate, in order to produce £1,000 a year of pension (pre-tax) in today's money. You'll need to save less if your employer is willing to contribute or you get tax relief at more than the basic rate.

The following assumptions have been made:

- Your monthly contributions increase in line with earnings assumed to increase by 3 a year.
- Your contributions are net of tax relief at the basic rate (20 per cent).
- The pension fund investments grow by 4 per cent a year after charges have been deducted.
- At the chosen retirement age, the pension fund is converted into a pension that increases during retirement in line with

price inflation. This is typically achieved by buying an annuity. Since 21 December 2012, as a result of European legislation, the same annuity rates apply to both men and women. (Previously, women faced lower rates reflecting the fact that they tend to live longer than men of the same age.)

- The table for couples assumes the pension is taken out by one partner and carries on paying out at two thirds of its previous rate if that person dies first.
- All amounts are in today's money assuming inflation averages 2 per cent a year between now and retirement.

Note that the tables also assume that all your savings are used to provide pension income. You will need to allow extra if you intend to draw off some of your pension savings as a cash lump sum.

> **'Starting your pension planning earlier in life lowers the proportion of your income that you need to save.'**

Savings per month to produce each £1,000 a year of pension

SINGLE PERSON

Your age now	Your planned retirement age				
	55	60	65	70	75
20	62	42	28	19	12
25	78	52	34	22	14
30	101	65	42	27	17
35	136	84	52	33	21
40	195	113	68	41	25
45	314	162	91	53	32
50	676	261	130	72	41
55		561	210	103	56
60			451	166	80
65				357	128
70					276

COUPLE

Your age now	Your planned retirement age				
	55	60	65	70	75
20	68	50	38	25	17
25	85	62	46	30	20
30	110	78	56	37	24
35	148	100	70	45	29
40	212	135	91	57	36
45	341	194	122	73	45
50	734	312	175	98	59
55		671	282	141	79
60			607	227	113
65				488	182
70					392

Starting early, saving more

Looking down the columns of the tables above, you can see that the monthly cost of saving for retirement rises the later in life you start. For example, the column for a single person retiring at age 65 (top table) shows that you need to save £42 a month to produce a £1,000 a year of pension if you start at aged 30. The cost rises sharply to £68 a month if you wait until age 40 and £130 if you wait until 50. Conversely, the cost is only £28 a month if you start saving from age 20.

Starting to save early in life not only spreads the cost over a greater number of years, but also gives you a bigger boost from 'compounding'. Compounding means you earn a return not just on the money you pay in, but also previous returns that have been reinvested.

Bear in mind that the tables show the monthly cost of each £1,000 a year of pension. You need to scale

Key tips

■ To keep the cost manageable, start saving for retirement as early in life as you can.

■ There is no lower age limit for having a pension plan - it could be a novel and valuable gift for a child.

■ If you can't save enough for the retirement income you want, consider whether you could retire later.

up the relevant figure from the table by the number of thousands of pounds of income you want. In the example above, paying £68 a month from age 40 may seem affordable, but that is designed to produce just £1,000 a year of pension. If you want £10,000 a year, you will have to invest 10 × £68 = £680 a month (£8,160 a year).

You can see that leaving your pension planning until late in life may mean saving a large proportion of your income. Leave it too late and you simply may not be able to afford to save enough for the retirement income you want.

Case study Geoff

Geoff, aged 40, hopes to retire at age 65 with an income of £20,000 a year. Currently he's on target for only £15,000 so he has a £5,000 pension gap. The table opposite shows that he needs to start saving £68 a month for each extra £1,000 of income, so he needs to save 5 × £68 = £340 a month to plug the gap. If he puts off starting to save for just five years, the cost rises steeply to 5 × £91 = £455 a month.

Working longer

The tables opposite also illustrate why planning to work longer makes your pension more affordable. You can see that, as you move across any row, each column corresponds to a later retirement age and the cost of each £1,000 of pension falls.

For example, suppose a single person (top table) aged 35 starts saving for retirement and wants to retire at age 60. The table shows that you need to save £84 a month for each £1,000 a year of pension. If you aim instead to retire at age 65, the cost falls to £52 a month. The cost falls for two reasons: firstly, you will be saving over a longer period (equivalent to starting to save earlier); but, secondly, you will also benefit from a better rate when you come to convert your pension fund into pension, because retiring later means the pension will not be paid out for as long. See Chapter 6 for more information about converting a pension fund into pension.

These days, employers cannot normally insist that you retire at any particular age, so the way is open for you to work longer if you want to. Occupational pension schemes can set a normal pension age from which your pension usually becomes payable. But you may be able to defer the start and earn extra pension, and, provided the scheme rules and your employer allow it, you do not have to retire in order to start drawing a pension from your present employer's scheme. This opens the way for partial rather than full retirement. For example, you might – provided your employer and the pension scheme rules allow it – cut back your working hours and make up the consequent drop in pay by starting to draw a small pension. Deferring the rest of your pension means it will be larger once it does start. Planning ahead to adopt this strategy means you can reduce the amount you need to save.

If you are self-employed, you make your own decisions about when to cut back or stop working. You are more likely to have personal than occupational pensions and you may be able to arrange these to progressively increase your pension income in step with cutting back on your work and earnings. This is called 'phasing' your retirement – see Chapter 6 for details.

Ambitions like Natalie's (see case study below) to retire very early are looking increasingly unrealistic. As people live longer, retiring at 55 could mean spending as long or longer in retirement than working. Most

Case study Natalie

Natalie, aged 30, thinks it would be great to retire at 55 with a private pension of, say, £15,000 a year. But, if she starts to save now, she needs to contribute 15 × £101 = £1,515 a month – that's over £18,000 a year and far more than Natalie can afford. By planning on a later retirement age of 65, she reduces the outlay to 15 × £42 = £630 a month (just under £7,600 a year) which is still a lot but more manageable.

people simply could not save enough while working to fund so many years of leisure.

Reviewing the situation

The figures in the tables on page 60 are based on assumptions. There is no escape from using assumptions when you are making financial plans for the future, because nobody knows in advance what will happen. The assumptions are reasonable guesses but they are very unlikely to be exactly right and – as the 2007 global financial crisis and subsequent recession showed – unexpected events can throw everyone's calculations into disarray. Therefore, it is essential that you check your retirement planning on a regular basis – say once a year. This will enable you to make, hopefully, minor and affordable adjustments as you go along to keep your planning on track.

Age discrimination

Age discrimination has been illegal since 2006. Your employer cannot make you retire at a specified age unless there are objective reasons for doing so. For example, it has been argued that some jobs with the emergency services, requiring high levels of physical fitness, and work as an air traffic controller, which requires exceptional mental fitness, justify setting a specific retirement age.

To check out how much pension a set level of monthly savings might produce at retirement, try the online calculators at **www.moneyadviceservice.org.uk/en/ tools/pension-calculator** or **www.ageuk.org.uk/money-matters/pensions/ pension-calculator/**.

After calculating your pensions gap at the start of this chapter, here is a quick overview of your options.

```
┌─────────────────────────┐
│          Start          │
└─────────────────────────┘
             │
             ▼
┌─────────────────────────┐            ┌──────────────────────────────┐
│ Are you prepared to tie  │    NO →    │ Consider alternatives to     │
│ up your savings until at │ ─────────→ │ pension schemes (see         │
│ least age 55?            │            │ Chapter 12), for example:    │
└─────────────────────────┘            │  ■ Individual savings        │
             │                         │    accounts (ISAs).          │
            YES                        │  ■ Unit trusts and similar   │
             │                         │    investments.              │
             ▼                         │  ■ Property.                 │
                                       └──────────────────────────────┘
```

Are you prepared to tie up your savings until at least age 55? — **NO** → Consider alternatives to pension schemes (see Chapter 12), for example:
- ■ Individual savings accounts (ISAs).
- ■ Unit trusts and similar investments.
- ■ Property.

YES

Are you currently building up a pension in an occupational pension scheme (see Chapter 5)? — **NO** → Consider joining an occupational scheme if there is one open to you (see Chapter 5) or, other workplace scheme (see Chapters 4 and 5).

Otherwise consider saving through a personal pension (see Chapter 6) or alternatives to pension schemes (follow the arrow above).

YES

Do you need to save extra to meet your target retirement income? — **YES** → Check whether you can pay additional voluntary contributions to the occupational scheme (see Chapter 5).

Alternatively, consider saving through a personal pension (see Chapter 6) or alternatives to pension schemes (follow the arrow to the right).

NO

Review the situation at least yearly to make sure you are still on track.

Limits to saving through pension schemes

Since 2006, most people have been able easily to pay as much as they want into a pension scheme, making it feasible to plug even a large pension gap.

Annual contributions

There is no limit as such on how much you pay into pension schemes each year, but you will want to stay within your annual allowance (see below) and you will get tax relief only on contributions up to this amount:

- A basic amount of £3,600, or
- If higher, an amount equal to your 'relevant earnings' for the tax year. This means your UK earnings on which you have paid Income Tax. They include wages, salaries and so on from a job plus the taxable value of any fringe benefits (such as a company car, medical insurance or cheap loans), profits from your business and/or income from property you let out on a commercial basis as furnished holiday accommodation.

Relevant earnings do not include income from other property, savings, investments, pensions, state benefits and so on.

This is called your 'annual limit for relief'. It applies to the sum of your contributions to all the pension schemes you might have.

Some types of contribution do not count towards the limit, for example, contributions paid by your employer and transfers you receive as part of a pension sharing arrangement on divorce (see Chapter 10). Otherwise contributions paid in for you by someone else – for example, if your husband or wife makes payments into your scheme – do use up part of the limit.

If you go over your annual limit for relief, any tax relief on the excess contributions must be paid back. The pension scheme will normally organise repaying any tax relief that was paid directly into the scheme. You have to arrange repayment through your tax return of any relief that was given direct to you. The excess contributions can be left in the scheme or repaid to you.

Your Annual Allowance

You have an Annual Allowance each year that sets the amount by which your total pension savings can

---

Jargon buster

Annual limit for relief The maximum contributions you can make to pension schemes each year that qualify for tax relief. The limit is £3,600 or, if higher, your total UK earnings for the year.

increase. In any tax year when your savings increase by more, you have to pay tax on the excess at a rate of 40 per cent.

For the tax year 2013–14, the Annual Allowance is £50,000 and is due to fall to £40,000 a year from 2014–15. However, you can also carry forward any unused Annual Allowance from the previous three years and in the years 2010–11, 2011–12 and 2012–13, the allowance was £50,000. See the case study (Arif) on page 66 for how these carry forward rules can help you make a large contribution.

The Annual Allowance applies to the increase in value of all your savings through pension schemes. How you measure the increase in value depends on the type of scheme:

- **Defined-benefit scheme** (see Chapter 5). Each year you usually see an increase in the amount of pension you are promised at retirement. To convert this into a value that can be compared with the annual limit, the pension is multiplied by a factor of 16 but you ignore any increase in line with inflation. For example, if your promised pension goes up by £1,000 a year more than inflation, this is treated as an increase in your pension savings of $16 \times £1,000 = £16,000$. You also take into account any increase in a tax-free lump sum payable automatically at retirement.
- **Defined-contribution scheme** (see Chapters 5 and 6). The increase in value is the sum of contributions paid into the scheme by you, by someone else on your behalf and, if applicable, by your employer.

- **Cash-balance scheme** (see Chapter 5). The increase in value is the change in the amount of pension fund you are promised at retirement, but you ignore any increase in line with inflation.

The Annual Allowance applies each tax year. But for each scheme you need to look at the increase over its 'pension input period' (PIP). This is usually the 12 months up to the scheme anniversary date – your pension provider can tell you what the PIP is. To find the total increase in savings for the tax year to compare against your Annual Allowance, you add up the increases over all the PIPs ending in that tax year. For example, if you had one scheme where your savings increased by £6,000 over the 12 months to 31 June 2013 and another where your savings increased by £8,000 over the 12 months to 31 December 2013, the total for the tax year 2013–14 would be £14,000.

The yearly growth in most people's pension savings will be much less than their Annual Allowance. Only a small proportion of the population is likely to have to worry about exceeding this allowance. This may apply to you if, for example:

- You run your own business and have left starting to save for retirement until late in life and now need to make large contributions to catch up;
- You've been in a defined-benefit scheme for many years and now you are given a large pay rise (say, on promotion) that feeds through into a big increase in your promised pension;

Case study Arif

Arif has inherited £70,000 on the death of his mother. He would like to pay as much as possible of this into a pension scheme. His relevant earnings in 2013-14 are £80,000 so he can get tax relief on the whole of a contribution of £70,000 (see Chapter 6 for how this tax relief is given and how much it comes to).

However, at first sight, it looks as if a £70,000 contribution would exceed Arif's Annual Allowance. But he only paid £5,000 into his pension scheme last year, so he has £50,000 – £5,000 = £45,000 of unused Annual Allowance from last year that he can add to his 2013-14 £50,000 allowance and so comfortably cover the whole £70,000 contribution.

Jargon buster

Defined-benefit scheme Type of pension scheme that promises you a set level of pension that is typically based on your pay and length of time in the scheme.
Defined-contribution scheme Type of pension scheme where the pension you get depends on the amount paid in, how well the invested contributions grow and the amount of pension you can buy at retirement with the resulting fund.
Cash-balance scheme Type of pension scheme that promises you a set amount of pension fund at retirement for each year you have been in the scheme. The pension you get then depends on how much pension you can buy with fund.

■ Or you are a high earner who would normally make large contributions each year.

If any of these apply to you, consult a financial adviser (see Chapter 13).

Your Lifetime Allowance

Your Lifetime Allowance is an upper limit on the value of benefits (pensions, tax-free lump sums and payments to your survivors if you die) that can be drawn from all of your pension schemes over your lifetime. If you go over the limit, however, a special tax charge is payable.

However, the standard Lifetime Allowance for the tax year 2013–14 is £1.5 million, which is due to fall to £1.25 million from 2014–15. The value of most people's pensions and other benefits is well below this. If you think you could be affected, get help from a financial adviser.

Summary

This chapter has shown how you can translate your retirement goal into a concrete amount that you need to save each month. It has also suggested ways to adapt your goal if it will cost more than you can afford. Because you are planning for the future, which cannot be known with certainty, it is essential that you review your retirement plan regularly and adjust it as necessary to stay on track.

To work out how much you can put into your pension scheme(s) without breaching your Annual Allowance, use the calculator on the HM Revenue & Customs website at **www.hmrc.gov.uk/tools/pension-allowance/index.htm**.

Auto-enrolment

4

Over the next few years, nearly all employees will automatically be put into a pension scheme at work. Employers must contribute, so, for most people, this is good news. However, the amount of pension that you build up may not be enough to plug your pension gap.

Pensions for all

Official estimates suggest that at least seven million people in the UK are not saving enough for retirement, particularly those on low to middle incomes. The Government aims to change this by phasing in a new policy under which nearly everyone will automatically join a pension scheme at work.

Why auto-enrolment?

In the past, employers could – and often did – make membership of the pension scheme a compulsory condition of employment. The Thatcher government reforms of the 1980s, with their focus on individual choice and responsibility, swept away compulsory membership and so, for many years now, it has been up to you to choose whether or not to join any work-based pension scheme.

You have seen in Chapter 3 that the State Pension alone is unlikely to provide you with enough retirement income. Moreover, if your employer will contribute towards the cost of saving for a pension, a work-based scheme can be a valuable part of your total pay package as an employee. The Government reports that when they talk to workers, there is usually agreement that saving for retirement is a good idea and a work-based scheme an attractive way of doing so. Frequently, workers go away from such discussions full of good intentions but inertia takes hold and it remains a fact that around half of the people who could join a pension scheme at work fail to sign up.

To tackle this problem and, following the teachings of behavioural economists like Richard Thaler and Cass Sunstein (authors of the influential best-seller Nudge), the Government decided to stand choice on its head. Since October 2012, it has been implementing a policy that places a legal duty on employers automatically to enrol most employees in a work-based pension scheme within one month of starting work. You can opt out if you want to but, if the behavioural economists are right, inertia will persuade the majority to stay in.

Who is affected by auto-enrolment?

Auto-enrolment started on 1 October 2012 with the largest employers and is being gradually extended to the whole workforce by February 2018. Most employees, down to those working for the smallest employers, will have been automatically enrolled by the start of April 2017. Between then and February 2018, relatively new employers (who have started to take on employees from 2012 onwards) will be brought into the scheme. If they want to, employers can choose to come into the auto-enrolment scheme earlier than their legal deadline – called their 'staging date'.

Once the relevant staging date arrives, your employer must write to you telling you about your rights to save for a pension through a work-based scheme. What your rights are depends on whether you already belong to a work-based pension scheme that at least meets certain minimum requirements, how old you are and how much you earn.

If you already belong to a scheme through work to which your employer contributes, you are unlikely to see any change as a result of auto-enrolment. Your employer should write to you within two months of the staging date to confirm that you are already in a suitable pension scheme. If this applies to you, you might prefer to skip reading the rest of this chapter.

If you are not already in a pension scheme at work or you are in a scheme, but your employer doesn't pay into it for you, the chart summarises how you will be affected by auto-enrolment.

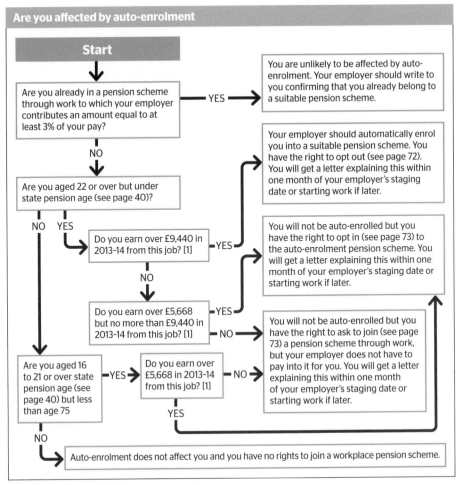

Are you affected by auto-enrolment

Start

Are you already in a pension scheme through work to which your employer contributes an amount equal to at least 3% of your pay? — **YES** → You are unlikely to be affected by auto-enrolment. Your employer should write to you confirming that you already belong to a suitable pension scheme.

NO

Are you aged 22 or over but under state pension age (see page 40)?

Your employer should automatically enrol you into a suitable pension scheme. You have the right to opt out (see page 72). You will get a letter explaining this within one month of your employer's staging date or starting work if later.

NO   **YES**

Do you earn over £9,440 in 2013-14 from this job? [1] — **YES** → You will not be auto-enrolled but you have the right to opt in (see page 73) to the auto-enrolment pension scheme. You will get a letter explaining this within one month of your employer's staging date or starting work if later.

NO

Do you earn over £5,668 but no more than £9,440 in 2013-14 from this job? [1] — **YES** —

— **NO** → You will not be auto-enrolled but you have the right to ask to join (see page 73) a pension scheme through work, but your employer does not have to pay into it for you. You will get a letter explaining this within one month of your employer's staging date or starting work if later.

Are you aged 16 to 21 or over state pension age (see page 40) but less than age 75 — **YES** → Do you earn over £5,668 in 2013-14 from this job? [1] — **NO** →

YES

NO

Auto-enrolment does not affect you and you have no rights to join a workplace pension scheme.

[1] Auto-enrolment applies separately to each job you have.

How auto-enrolment works

For employers to meet their legal obligations, they must enrol you in a pension scheme that meets minimum standards – in most cases, this means they must pay at least a minimum sum into the scheme for you.

A defined-benefit scheme – in other words, a scheme set up by your employer that promises you a given level of pension in retirement, typically calculated as a proportion of your pay while working (see Chapter 5) – almost certainly meets those standards. Broadly, it must offer a pension at least as good as that available from the current additional State Pension scheme (whether or not this employer's scheme is contracted out).

However, most employees these days will be offered membership of some sort of defined-contribution scheme (see Chapters 5 and 6) – in other words, a scheme where you build up your own pot of savings that you use at retirement to buy a pension. The amount of pension you get from a defined-contribution scheme depends on the amount paid in, the amount lost in charges, how well the invested contributions grow and the rate at which the pension fund that builds up can be converted to pension when you reach retirement. The minimum standards that a defined-contribution scheme must meet are that at least a certain amount must be paid into it in contributions.

The table opposite shows the minimum contributions that must be made to an auto-enrolment scheme. The amounts shown in the table apply to your 'qualifying earnings', meaning your pay between certain limits, which in 2013–14 are £5,668 and £41,450. (These limits are the same as those that apply to the standard rate of National Insurance – see page 33 – but the Government reviews the limits each year and will not necessarily retain this alignment with National Insurance.)

Once auto-enrolment is fully operating, the minimum contribution to the workplace pension scheme must be 8 per cent of your earnings between the limits. Your employer must pay in at least 3 per cent of your qualifying earnings and, if your employer pays in at that level, you must pay in at least 4 per cent of your earnings from your pay packet. A further 1 per cent of earnings would then come from tax relief at the basic rate (20 per cent in 2013–14) on the amount you pay in. However, your employer can pay in more, in which case you may be able to pay in less. For example, if your employer paid in a full 8 per cent

Minimum contributions to auto-enrolment pension schemes				
	Contributions as % of qualifying earnings [1]			
Date contributions made	Total contribution	Minimum from employer	Usual minimum from employee	Tax relief on employee contribution
1 October 2012 to 30 September 2017	2%	1%	0.80%	0.20%
1 October 2017 to 30 September 2018	5%	2%	2.40%	0.60%
1 October 2018 onwards	8%	3%	4%	1%

[1] £5,668 to £41,450 in 2013-14.

of your qualifying earnings, there would be no need for you to pay in anything at all.

During a transitional period from October 2012 to September 2017, the minimum contributions are reduced to help both you and your employer gradually adjust to the costs of saving for a pension.

How much pension you might build up

How much pension you build up through auto-enrolment will depend on the type of pension scheme you belong to and a range of other factors, such as how generous your employer's contribution is. Chapters 5 and 6 explain how you can get an idea of the amount of pension you might end up with from different types of scheme.

Case study Chloe

Chloe, aged 30, works for a large coffee shop chain and was automatically enrolled into a workplace pension in October 2012. Chloe earns nearly £217 a week before tax and National Insurance. In 2013-14, 86p a week is taken from her pay packet to pay into the workplace pension scheme. This is topped up by 22p tax relief and £1.08 from her employer, so that her total pension contributions are £2.15 a week.

Key point

Whatever you save towards your pension under auto-enrolment is at least doubled by the addition of your employer's contribution and tax relief.

To check how much you might have to pay into a pension scheme under auto-enrolment, use the calculator on the Money Advice Service website at **www.moneyadviceservice.org.uk/en/tools/workplace-pension-contribution-calculator**.

However, a key point to note about automatic enrolment is that, if your employer provides only the minimal scheme, the amount of pension you build up will be modest. You can see, in the example of Chloe, that on relatively low earnings of £217 a week (£11,266 a year), the total paid into her pension scheme in 2013 is just £2.15 a week (£112 a year). Even when the total contribution rises to 8 per cent of qualifying earnings, the total paid in would still only be £448 a year. Looking back to the table on page 60, and adjusting for tax relief, this is equivalent to saving around £30 a month and might produce an inflation-proofed pension for Chloe of only around £700 a year from age 65. Certainly this is better than no pension, but probably would not have a substantial impact on Chloe's living standards in retirement.

Of course, some people covered by auto-enrolment will be on higher earnings. With pay at the top of the 2013–14 earnings limits but assuming the full 8 per cent contribution, the amount saved would be over £2,800 a year, which, if saved from age 30 to 65, might generate an inflation-proofed pension of over £4,500 a year.

Moreover, a key point to note about auto-enrolment is that whatever you pay in, this is at least matched by the contribution from your employer plus tax relief. This means that, even before any considerations about what investment return you might get from your savings, the money you personally pay in is doubled, which gives a valuable boost to your savings.

Your rights under auto-enrolment

Under the auto-enrolment rules, employees fall into four groups, each of which has different rights. The first three groups have the names given below, which are set out in the legislation and you may see these names on letters you get from your employer. Each group is described in this section.

Eligible jobholders

You are in this group if you are aged 22 to State Pension age (see page 40) earning over £9,440 in 2013–14. Your employer must automatically enroll you in a workplace pension scheme and write to you telling you this is what is happening.

Your employer must pay contributions into the scheme for you. Typically you will have to contribute too (see page 71 for how much) and these contributions will start to be automatically deducted from your pay before you get it.

You have the right to opt out of the pension scheme if you want. To opt out, you must write to your employer. Provided you do this within the first month of being enrolled, any contributions that have already been taken from your pay will be refunded. If you opt out after this, no new contributions will be paid in, but those you have already paid are not normally refundable and will stay in the pension scheme until you start your pension (or may be transferable to another scheme – see Chapter 9).

If you opt out, your employer must periodically (usually every three years) automatically enroll you again if you are still an eligible jobholder. If you don't want to be in the pension scheme, you will then have to opt out again.

Non-eligible jobholders

Although misleadingly called 'non-eligible', this group does have important rights under auto-enrolment. You are in this group if you are:

- Aged 22 to State Pension age and earning more than £5,668 up to £9,440 in 2013–14, or
- Aged 16 to 21 or State Pension age to 74 and you earn more than £5,668 in 2013–14.

Your employer does not have to automatically enroll you into a workplace pension scheme. However, if you ask, your employer must then put you into the same scheme that applies to eligible jobholders. This is called 'opting in'.

Your employer must pay contributions to the scheme for you as set out on page 71 and usually you will have to pay in too.

So basically you have the same rights as eligible jobholders, except that you have to request to join the pension scheme.

Entitled workers

This group includes you if you are aged 16–24 and earn £5,668 or less in 2013–14.

You will not be automatically enrolled into a pension scheme, but, if you ask, your employer must arrange for you to join a scheme through work. However, this scheme does not have to meet any particular requirement and your employer does

Key point

If you are an eligible jobholder or non-eligible jobholder, your employer will pay a substantial part of the cost of saving for your pension. So, opting out of, or not joining, the workplace scheme will be like turning down a pay rise.

not have to pay anything into the scheme for you.

It might be convenient to join a pension scheme in this way because your contributions can be taken direct from your pay packet and handed over to the scheme provider. You will still get tax relief on your contributions in the normal way (see page 56), but you will not get the benefit of any help from your employer.

Everyone else

If you are not in one of the groups above – in other words, you are under age 16 or aged 75 and over – auto-enrolment does not cover you and you have no rights to join a workplace scheme.

'Under the auto-enrolment rules, employees fall into four groups, each of which has different rights.'

Who might want to opt out?

Employers are not allowed to discriminate between workers who join the workplace pension scheme and those who don't – for example, by paying them different salaries. So opting out or not opting in would not seem to make sense. It would be like turning down a pay rise.

However, there are a few situations in which you might not want to be in the workplace scheme. For example:

■ You have more than one job and prefer to put all your pension savings into a scheme offered by just one of your employers.

■ Your priority at the moment is paying off debts that have become a problem and you really can't afford to save for a pension as well.

■ You are very close to retiring (say, within a year or two) and these savings are going to make little or no difference to your retirement income.

■ You are already drawing a pension under a 'flexible drawdown arrangement' (see page 121). This is because to meet the conditions for flexible drawdown, you must not be building up new pension savings.

In other situations, you should think twice about opting out or failing to opt in. Be particularly thoughtful about doing this if you reckon that your partner is setting aside enough retirement savings for you both. Your retirement plans will always be more robust if you have at least some savings in your own name that would be unaffected in the event of relationship breakdown or bereavement (see page 25).

Summary

By early 2018, if you are an employee, you will almost certainly have access to a work-based pension scheme, if you don't already. In most cases, you will be automatically enrolled, so that the decision you have to make is whether to opt out rather than whether you should start to save. Your employer will decide what sort of pension scheme this is and Chapters 5 and 6 describe the types of scheme you could belong to.

In most cases, you are likely to be enrolled into a defined-contribution scheme, where you build up your own personal pot of savings with which to buy a pension. As with any defined-contribution scheme, it is impossible to know in advance whether the contributions will grow well enough to deliver the pension you want. However, your employer must contribute to the scheme on your behalf and this contribution plus tax relief will at least double the amount you personally contribute, giving an important boost to your savings.

Work-based pension schemes

5

By 2018, being a member of a workplace pension scheme will be the norm for virtually all employees. But many of the best schemes – those that promise you a pension linked to your pay – are being replaced. Make sure you know what your employer offers and how this will affect your retirement.

Making the most of work-based pension schemes

Unfortunately, a clear message from Chapter 3 is that pensions are expensive. But one of the major perks of being an employee is that your employer may currently help towards the cost of your retirement savings and under auto-enrolment (see previous chapter), will have to do this.

A myriad of schemes

If you are an employee, you will normally be able to join a pension scheme through your workplace. There are three main types of scheme that might be on offer:

■ **Occupational scheme** This is organised by your employer, who pays into the scheme on your behalf, though you are usually required to contribute too. Membership is offered as part of your overall pay package. When you leave your employer, you stop being an active member of the scheme. The two main types are defined-benefit schemes (see page 82) and defined-contribution schemes (see page 89). Final-salary schemes are normally the most generous and government figures for 2010 show that, on average, employers contributed around 15.8 per cent of pay to such schemes. On average, employers paid 6.2 per cent of pay into defined-contribution schemes.

■ **Multi-employer scheme** Occupational schemes that cover employees working for a range of different employers have long been common in the public sector (for example, the Teachers' Pension scheme and Local Government Pension Scheme) and have also existed in the private sector (for example, in the construction industry). However, they have become more important with the start of auto-enrolment (see Chapter 4). This has been due to the establishment of the National Employment Savings Trust (NEST) and rivals to it – see page 95.

■ **Group personal pension scheme (GPP)** This is a personal pension (see Chapter 6) run by an insurance company. Unless the scheme has been set up under the auto-enrolment rules (see Chapter 4), your employer does not necessarily have to pay anything towards the scheme, but might agree to do so. (A

'Final salary schemes are normally the most generous.'

contribution of 3 per cent of your pay is common.) Your employer might have negotiated with the insurance company for some favourable terms for members, for example, low charges. The scheme is personal to you so, when you leave your employer, you can carry on paying into the scheme if you want to.

◼ **Stakeholder pension scheme**
This is also a personal pension but has some special features, such as a cap on charges and flexible contributions (see Chapter 6). Until auto-enrolment kicks in for smaller employers (see page 68), if your employer has five or more employees and does

Jargon buster

Private sector The part of the economy that is independent of the State.

Public sector The part of the economy to do with the State. For example, public sector workers are people employed by central or local government or state services. They include, for example, NHS staff, teachers, firemen and police.

> ' A salary-related scheme promises a pension based on your pay.'

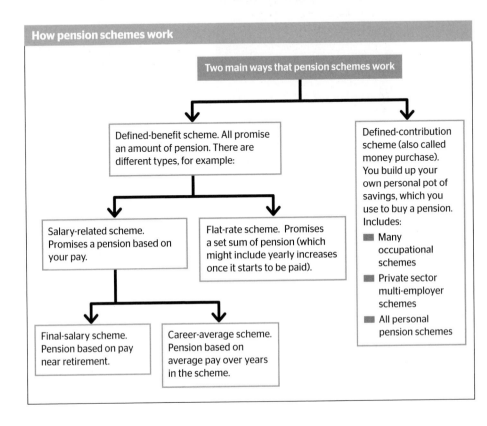

How pension schemes work

Two main ways that pension schemes work

Defined-benefit scheme. All promise an amount of pension. There are different types, for example:

Defined-contribution scheme (also called money purchase). You build up your own personal pot of savings, which you use to buy a pension. Includes:

◼ Many occupational schemes

◼ Private sector multi-employer schemes

◼ All personal pension schemes

Salary-related scheme. Promises a pension based on your pay.

Flat-rate scheme. Promises a set sum of pension (which might include yearly increases once it starts to be paid).

Final-salary scheme. Pension based on pay near retirement.

Career-average scheme. Pension based on average pay over years in the scheme.

not offer either an occupational scheme or a GPP to which the employer contributes at least 3 per cent of your pay, there must be a workplace stakeholder scheme. Your employer does not have to pay anything into your stakeholder scheme, but might agree to do so. When you leave your employer, you can carry on paying into the scheme if you want to.

With all these workplace schemes, there is usually an arrangement for your own contributions to be deducted direct from your pay and passed automatically to the scheme provider.

Once covered by the auto-enrolment rules, your employer must offer a workplace pension scheme, which could take the form of any of the schemes on pages 76–8 provided they meet the minimum requirements. In the case of all types of defined-contribution schemes (whether occupational, group personal pension or stakeholder scheme), the main requirement is that your employer must pay contributions to the scheme on your behalf equal to at least 3 per cent of your pay between limits. See Chapter 4 for details.

There is no essential difference between a GPP or workplace stakeholder scheme and the types of personal pension and stakeholder scheme that you arrange for yourself, so turn to Chapter 6 to find out more about how these schemes work. This chapter looks at occupational pension schemes and multi-employer schemes.

Key tip

■ Occupational pension schemes – in particular, defined-benefit schemes – are an especially valuable part of the pay package. It's usually worth joining, if you have the chance.

Occupational schemes

These offer a pension organised by your employer, who pays into the scheme on your behalf, though, you are nearly always required to contribute too. They are usually hard to beat as a way of saving for retirement.

Employers are not obliged to offer occupational pension schemes. Many do, however, as a way of attracting and retaining staff. You do not have to join, but membership of a good scheme is a valuable part of your pay package.

The basics

Like all pension schemes, occupational ones have tax advantages (see Chapter 3). However, you do not get any tax relief on contributions you pay into an occupational scheme unless you are a taxpayer, since whatever you pay into the scheme is deducted directly from your pay before Income Tax is worked out. Unlike the schemes described in Chapter 6, there is no mechanism for giving a bonus to non-taxpayers (see page 57).

Benefits

The table on page 80 summarises what a good occupational scheme typically offers. Your employer usually pays a substantial part of

Case study Hank

Hank earns £30,000 a year and is a basic rate taxpayer. In 2010-11, his tax bill would normally be £4,112. But Hank pays 5 per cent of his salary into the pension scheme (5% × £30,000 = £1,500 for the year). This reduces his tax bill to £3,812. This means Hank has had tax relief of £4,112 – £3,812 = £300. The tax relief comes to 20 per cent of £1,500, in other words.

the cost of these benefits and often separately meets the bill for running the scheme. These advantages make an occupational scheme hard to beat as a way of saving for retirement. Around half of all full-time employees belong to occupational schemes.

> 'A good scheme is a valuable part of your pay.'

 For information about specific details of your occupational pension scheme, contact the pension scheme administrator, who is usually located in the HR department in a company or workplace.

Restrictions/discrimination

An occupational scheme may be open to all employees or restricted to a particular group – for example, one scheme for works staff, another for management. A scheme is not allowed to discriminate on the basis of sex, sexual orientation, disability or religion.

Chapter 3 looked briefly at the age discrimination laws that came into effect in 2006. (Your employer may not normally set an age by which you must retire.) The legislation also applies in theory to occupational pension schemes but has little practical effect, since most of the age-related rules that are part of occupational schemes' design are exempted. For example, occupational schemes are able to set a normal pension age from which your full pension is payable and to specify

minimum and maximum ages at which you are eligible to join a scheme.

In general, pension schemes may not treat part-time workers less favourably than their full-time counterparts. This includes giving equal access to the scheme.

Jargon buster

Civil partner Since 5 December 2005, same-sex couples have been able to register their relationship as a civil partnership and, for most purposes, are then treated in the same way as husbands and wives. If new laws being discussed by Parliament in early 2013 are passed, same-sex couples in England and Wales will also be able to marry (and convert a civil partnership into marriage) and be treated the same as husbands and wives.

Benefits from a typical scheme	
Type of benefit	**Description**
Retirement benefits	From normal pension age: ▪ Pension ▪ Tax-free lump sum
Early retirement benefits	Reduced pension if you choose to retire early
Ill-health benefits	Pension if you have to retire early owing to illness or disability.
Death benefits	▪ Pension for your spouse/civil partner or unmarried partner if you die before or after retirement. ▪ Pension for children/other dependants if you die. ▪ Lump sum payable to anyone you nominate if you die before the age of 75 (scheme rules may specify earlier age).

For information about all types of discrimination and how to exercise your rights, see the Equality and Human Rights Commission website at **www.equalityhumanrights.com**.

Different types of scheme

There are two fundamental types of occupational pension scheme and some important variations – see the table below.

Main types of occupational pension scheme [a]	
SCHEME	**DESCRIPTION**
Defined-benefit schemes	
Salary-related	The pension you get is worked out according to a formula based on your pay and length of time in the scheme. For more information, see pages 82-8.
Final-salary	This is the most common type of salary-related scheme. For more information, see page 84.
Career-average	Another type of salary-related scheme (usually less generous than final-salary). For more information see page 88.
Defined-contribution schemes (also called money purchase)	
All defined-contribution schemes	Your pension depends on how much is paid into the scheme, how well the invested contributions grow, charges deducted and how much pension you can get for your fund at retirement. Pages 89-94 give a brief introduction. For further information, see Chapter 6.
Hybrid schemes	
All hybrid schemes	Combine elements of both salary-related and money purchase schemes (see below).
Cash-balance	Promises a set amount of pension fund (defined benefit) but amount of pension it will buy is unknown (defined contribution) (see below).

a Table describes most common types. There are others.

Hybrid schemes

Hybrid schemes combine salary-related and defined-contribution elements to reduce the risks you bear by giving you a limited pension promise. They work in a variety of ways. For example, in a final-salary underpin scheme, you are promised a pension at least equal to an amount worked out on a final-salary basis. But the contributions are invested and, if the pension fund would buy a bigger pension than the salary-related one, you get the defined-contribution pension instead.

Cash-balance schemes are a type of hybrid scheme that spreads the risks more evenly between you and your employer. In a pure defined-contribution scheme, your employer pays a set contribution to the scheme on your behalf and leaves you to run the risk of how well or poorly the invested contributions grow. In a cash-balance scheme, your employer promises you a set amount of pension fund at retirement for each year you are in the scheme and pays in however much is needed to keep that promise. So your employer – not you – bears the investment risk while your pension fund is building up. You still bear the risk of a low pension if the cost of pensions rises as people live longer.

Defined-benefit schemes

Defined-benefit schemes are considered the best type of pension scheme, because the employer bears the bulk of the costs and the schemes offer you, the member, a large degree of certainty about the pension you will get.

The pension promise

Defined-benefit schemes are unlike most other types of saving and investment. You are promised (but not guaranteed) a certain level of pension, regardless of the amount you pay in. Commonly the promise is related to your salary – for example, 1/80 of your salary for each year in the scheme. This means you can plan ahead with some certainty because you know roughly how much pension to expect as a proportion of your current earnings.

In a contributory scheme, you'll be required to pay something towards the cost of meeting the pension promise and your employer pays the balance. In a non-contributory scheme, you pay nothing and your employer meets the full cost.

> '**Defined-benefit schemes offer some certainty about the pension you will get when you retire.**'

Who bears the risks?

Most private sector schemes are funded, which means the contributions paid in are invested to build up a fund from which the promised pensions are paid. Whatever you contribute is usually a fixed percentage of your pay – say 5 or 6 per cent. The amount your employer has to pay varies depending in particular on:

■ How well the invested contributions grow. If investment performance is good, the cost to your employer is less. If investment performance is poor, your employer has to pay more.

■ The cost of the pensions once they start to be paid. The major factor here is how long the pensioners live on average. The total cost of a pension for someone who lives many years will be greater than the cost for someone who dies soon after retirement. If – as currently – average life expectancy is rising, the cost of the pension scheme to the employer rises.

To find out more about different types of occupational scheme, consult The Pensions Advisory Service (TPAS) website on **www.pensionsadvisoryservice. org.uk** or call their national helpline on 0845 601 2923.

Jargon buster

Pay-as-you-go scheme Type of pension scheme where the cost of the pensions being paid out today is met from the contributions being collected today from the workers who are members of the scheme.

In this way, with a defined-benefit scheme, your employer rather than you bears most of the risk involved in saving for retirement. However, in recent years, the risks and uncertain future cost of offering a defined-benefit scheme have become too much for many employers because of volatile investment returns, changes in accounting rules and increasing longevity. As a result, many employers in the private sector have closed their defined-benefit schemes to new employees and, in some cases, to existing employees as well. So, indirectly, you do bear some risk – the risk your scheme will be closed and that you will not, after all, be able to build up the pension you had been expecting. You can find more about this risk in Chapter 11.

The situation is a bit different in the public sector where, although pension scheme benefits have been cut back in recent years, most public sector workers – teachers, NHS staff, police, local authority workers, and so on – are still able to join a defined-benefit scheme. Some public sector schemes are funded and others work

Salary-related occupational pension schemes

If your workplace offers this type of scheme, you are almost certain to benefit from joining it. The pros and cons listed below show why this is the case.

Salary-related occupational pension schemes normally offer considerable benefits to their members. Traditional-style 'final-salary' schemes (based on your pay shortly before retirement) are particularly advantageous, with a promised pension that is partly protected against inflation. 'Career-average' schemes (based on average pay over your whole career) offer similar benefits but are less expensive for employers and pay out less to those whose earnings peak in later life.

PROS

- Tax advantages (as for all private pension schemes).
- Predictable pension benefits.
- Some protection against inflation.
- Employer pays some, or all, of the costs of providing pensions and other benefits.
- Employer might separately pay running costs.
- Employer, not you, bears the direct risks of poor investment performance and rising life expectancy.

CONS

- Can be difficult to understand.
- You might lose out when changing jobs (see Chapter 9).
- Scheme might close if your employer finds it too costly or risky (see Chapter 11).
- In worst-case scenario, scheme might close without being able to pay the promised pensions (see Chapter 11).

on a pay-as-you-go basis (as does the State Pension scheme that you looked at in Chapter 2), but either way if the cost of meeting the pension promise increases, the State can, in the last resort, raise taxes or borrow in order to pay pensions as they fall due. At least that was the thinking until recently.

As private sector defined-benefit schemes have been closing, critics have suggested it is unfair that public sector workers should continue to have this perk. Traditionally, the argument has been that public sector workers often receive lower pay than they would working in the private sector and a good pension scheme goes some way to offset this. Whatever the relative merits of these arguments, the Government's drive to rein in huge public sector debts following the global financial crisis that started in 2007 and subsequent recession added to pressure for public-sector pension scheme benefits to be cut.

Final-salary schemes

Final-salary schemes are the most common type of defined-benefit scheme. They are widespread in the public sector, but have been closing down in the private sector where, in any case, they were generally offered only by larger employers.

Final-salary schemes are occupational schemes that offer a pension worked out as a proportion of your pay at or near retirement (or when you leave the scheme if earlier – see Chapter 9).

A big advantage of a final-salary scheme is that your promised pension is automatically protected against inflation while it is building up, because the promised pension rises as your earnings increase.

How much pension?

Different schemes work out the promised pension in different ways, but typically you might get 1/60, 1/80 or 1/100 of your final salary for each year you have been in the scheme. The fraction you get is called the 'accrual rate'. For example, if your final salary is £24,000 and you have been in a 1/60 scheme for 30 years your pension would be $30 \times 1/60 \times £24,000 = £12,000$ a year. The general formula for working out your pension is:

Years in scheme × Accrual rate × Final salary = Pension

The table to the left shows how, for each £1,000 of final salary, your pension would build up in a final-salary scheme. Usually the maximum pension you are allowed is 40 years' worth – for example 40/60 (a pension equal to two thirds of your final

Pension build-up in a final-salary scheme			
Number of years in the scheme	Pension built up for each £1,000 of your final salary £1,000 of your final salary		
	1/60	1/80	1/100
1	£16.67	£12.50	£10
5	£83.33	£62.50	£50
10	£166.67	£125.00	£100
15	£250.00	£187.50	£150
20	£333.33	£250.00	£200
25	£416.67	£312.50	£250
30	£500.00	£375.00	£300
35	£583.33	£437.50	£350
40	£666.67	£500.00	£400

salary) or 40/80 (half your final salary).

At the time of writing, salary-related schemes were required by law to increase pensions in line with price inflation up to a maximum of 2.5 per cent a year. However, the Government was reviewing whether to abolish this requirement. Schemes can choose to make bigger increases.

What is your final salary?

Final salary is defined in the rules of your scheme. It can have a variety of meanings: for example, average pay over the last three years, the average over a three-year period ending within the last ten, or your annual earnings on a specified date. Check what definition your scheme uses.

Only your 'pensionable earnings' are included in the calculation. This might be just your basic salary. A more generous definition would also include overtime pay, bonuses, commission and/or other payments. Some schemes reduce pensionable earnings to take account of the basic pension you will get from the State. One way in which some employers have been trying to contain the costs and uncertainties of running a defined-benefit scheme is to put a cap on pensionable pay, for example, excluding recent pay rises from the definition.

Pensionable earnings are also normally used as the basis for setting the contributions you pay if you are in a contributory scheme.

> **Jargon buster**
> **Accrual rate** In a salary-related pension scheme, the proportion of your pay that you get as pension for each year you have been in the scheme.
> **Pensionable earnings** The definition of pay used by a salary-related scheme when working out the pension it will pay and for setting contributions.

Tax-free lump sum

Most final-salary schemes let you take a tax-free lump sum when you start your pension. You can use this money in any way you like – buy a new car, take a holiday, home improvements, boost your savings, and so on. It can be tempting to take as much tax-free cash as possible but this may be a poor deal.

The tax rules limit the maximum tax-free lump sum you can have. Your scheme's own rules might limit you to a smaller lump sum but, under the tax rules, the maximum lump sum you can take at retirement is broadly the lower of either:
■ A quarter of the value of the benefits you are drawing, calculated by adding together

> **Case study** Dziko
>
> Geoff, aged 40, hopes to retire at age 65 with an income of £20,000 a year. Currently he's on target for only £15,000 so he has a £5,000 pension gap. The table on page 71 shows that he needs to start saving £68 a month for each extra £1,000 of income, so he needs to save 5 × £68 = £340 a month to plug the gap. If he puts off starting to save for just five years, the cost rises steeply to 5 × £91 = £455 a month.

 For advice on what to look out for – and what to do – if your scheme appears to be at risk, see Chapter 11.

the lump sum and the value of the pension. To work out the value of the pension, multiply the annual amount by a factor of 20. For example, if the remaining pension is £12,000, its value is 20 × £12,000 = £240,000 and the maximum lump sum would be £80,000 since this is a quarter of £240,000 + £80,000 = £320,000 or

■ A quarter of your Lifetime Allowance (see page 66) remaining after deducting the value of any pension and other benefits you have taken so far.

The tax rules require that you take any lump sum within three months of becoming entitled to your pension.

Case study Colin

Colin has been a member of a 1/60 scheme for 20 years. He is about to start his pension and his final salary is £27,000. He has the option of taking a pension of 20 × 1/60 × £27,000 = £9,000 a year or taking a tax-free lump sum plus a lower pension.

The scheme rules let him swap £1 of pension for each £12 of lump sum. He reckons he could manage with £7,500 pension, which would let him take a lump sum of 1,500 × £12 = £18,000. This is well within the limits allowed by the tax rules.

If Colin had to use the £18,000 to buy, on the open market, a pension that increased in line with inflation, in late 2012 he would have got only about £633 a year pension - much less than the £1,500 pension he has given up to get the lump sum. This means the commutation factor offered by the scheme is a poor deal.

In a 1/80 or 1/100 scheme, typically the lump sum will be in addition to your pension worked out as above. In a 1/60 scheme, the scheme rules normally require you to give up part of your pension if you want to have a tax-free lump sum – this is called 'commutation'.

The scheme sets a 'commutation factor', which says how much lump sum you get for each £1 of pension you give up. A common factor is 12 so, for example, if you gave up £1,000 a year of pension, you would get a tax-free lump sum of £12,000. Many schemes offer a higher commutation factor to women than men, reflecting the higher cost of pensions for women since they tend to live longer.

It can be tempting to take the largest lump sum possible at retirement since it is tax-free and you can use it in any way that you like. In the past, you were often advised to take a lump sum, even if you needed the pension because you could invest the cash tax efficiently to produce income. But, over the last 15 years, it has become clear that people generally are living longer, which is making pensions more expensive. Commutation factors have not kept up with the increase and are now often poor value. For example, to get good value, someone aged 65 should expect to be offered a lump sum of well over £20 for each £1 of pension given up.

Starting your pension

As with all pension schemes, the tax rules say that you cannot start your pension before age 55. Provided your employer and the schemes rules allow it, you do not have to retire to

Case study Rick

So far Rick has been a member of his 1/80 pension scheme for 26 years. Based on his current salary of £38,000, Rick (now aged 56) can expect a pension at the normal pension age of 65 equal to 35 × 1/80 × £ 38,000 = £16,625 a year. But he would like to retire early at age 60. This means his pension would be based on 30 years' membership. His scheme also makes an actuarial reduction of 6 per cent for each year of early retirement. So his pension from age 60 would be 70% × (30 × 1/80 × £38,000) = £9,975 a year. Retiring just five years early would reduce his pension by 40 per cent.

Jargon buster

Actuarial reduction A cut in your pension if you retire early to reflect the extra cost of paying your pension for longer. Often 6 per cent for each year of early retirement.

start a pension from your employer's scheme. And there is nothing to stop you taking work elsewhere after starting to draw a pension.

Most schemes set their own normal pension age from which your full pension is payable and typically this is 65 at present. Although schemes are allowed to set a lower normal pension age, it is illegal for employers to set a normal *retirement* age unless there are objective reasons for doing so, which is unlikely (see page 80).

Retiring early

If you choose to retire earlier than the normal pension age for your scheme, your pension will usually be a lot lower because:

- It will be based on fewer years of membership.
- Once it starts, the pension will, at best, generally increase only in line with prices whereas while

it is still building up it is increasing in line with your earnings (which tend to increase by more than prices).

- The scheme will usually impose an 'actuarial reduction' to reflect the extra cost of paying your pension over a longer period. A common reduction is 6 per cent for each year below normal pension age.

If your employer is looking for voluntary redundancies, you might be offered a better-than-normal early retirement package – for example, the actuarial reduction might be waived.

Salary-related schemes often pay higher pensions if you have to retire early owing to ill health. For example, there might be no actuarial reduction and the pension might be based on the number of years' membership you would have had if you had been able to work on until the normal pension age. Under the tax rules, your pension can start earlier than 55 if you have to retire early owing to ill health.

Retiring later

If you put off drawing your pension beyond the normal pension age for your scheme, you may be entitled to a larger pension once it does start. For example, in a 1/60 scheme, you might be allowed to carry on building up pension at a rate of 1/60 of final salary for each extra year of membership perhaps up to a maximum of, say 45/60. Alternatively, the pension you had built up by normal pension age might be increased, say, in line with price inflation up to the point at which it starts. Check the rules for your particular scheme.

Case study Holly

The normal pension age for Holly's scheme is 65 but her employer agrees to her carrying on working for another five years. At age 65, she would have qualified for a pension of 31/60 of her final salary. But the scheme lets her continue building up pension at the normal rate, so by age 70 she gets 36/60 of her final salary. As her final salary is then £42,000, she retires on a pension of 36 × 1/60 × £42,000 = £25,200 a year.

Case study Jacinda

Jacinda has been in a career-average scheme for the last ten years. The table below shows her pensionable earnings over those years and how her career-average salary is worked out from them. It is a 1/80 scheme, so based on her membership so far, she has built up a promised pension of 10 × 1/80 × £26,561 = £3,320 a year.

How Jacinda's salary is worked out

Year	Pensionable earnings A	Increase in national average earnings up to 2009 B	Pension earnings revalued to 2009 A × (1 + B)
2003	£16,000	33.0%	£21,286
2004	£17,300	26.6%	£21,898
2005	£19,000	20.7%	£22,927
2006	£21,000	16.4%	£24,436
2007	£23,800	10.7%	£26,350
2008	£25,000	7.4%	£26,847
2009	£27,400	6.7%	£29,248
2010	£28,600	4.6%	£29,901
2011	£31,000	2.3%	£31,713
2012	£31,000	0.0%	£31,000
Average			£26,561

Career-average schemes

A career-average scheme is very similar to a final-salary scheme but, instead of your pension being based on your pay at, or near, retirement, it is based on the average of your pensionable earnings over all the years you have been a member of the scheme.

To contain the cost and uncertainties of providing a defined-benefit scheme (see page 6), some employers – including in the public sector – have been replacing final-salary schemes with career-average schemes. Where employees' pay tends to peak late in their working life, career-average schemes are cheaper for employers, offering less generous pensions. But career-average schemes can work out better for employees whose pay peaks in mid-working-life.

How much pension?

As with a final-salary scheme, your pension is worked out according to a formula:

Years in scheme × Accrual rate × Average salary = Pension

The accrual rate will typically be 1/60 or 1/80. Because salaries tend to rise over time as a result of inflation, usually earnings from earlier years are revalued to put them into today's money before your average salary figure is worked out.

You have already met an example of a career-average pension scheme in this book: the additional State Pension, which you looked at in Chapter 2.

Defined-contribution schemes

Defined-contribution schemes are the main alternative to the salary-related schemes considered in the previous sections. Defined-contribution schemes can seem appealing, because they are easy to understand. But they do not offer any pension promise, making planning for retirement unpredictable and risky.

Defined contribution (also called money purchase) describes any pension scheme where the amount of pension you get at retirement depends on:

- The amount paid into the scheme.
- How well the invested contributions grow.
- The charges deducted.
- 'Annuity rates', which determine how much pension you get from the fund that has built up.

Many occupational schemes are defined-contribution schemes. In fact, increasingly so, since defined-contribution schemes do not expose employers to the costs and uncertainties that are inherent in defined-benefit schemes.

As a result, many private sector employers have been closing their final-salary schemes and switching new – and sometimes existing – employees to defined-contribution schemes instead.

Most other types of pension scheme, including personal pensions and stakeholder schemes also work on the defined-contribution basis. This section looks at features specific to occupational defined-contribution schemes.

Unlike salary-related schemes, with a defined-contribution scheme, your employer simply pays in a set amount in contributions. This means the employer knows just how much it will cost to provide the scheme and bears no risk of costs running out of control.

If investment returns are poor, or pensions become more expensive because people are living longer, you get less pension rather than your employer having to pay more. This explains why employers are keen to switch to defined-contribution schemes. But, for you, the switch is a poor deal exposing you to greater uncertainty and an increased risk that your retirement income will fall short.

Jargon buster

Annuity An investment where you swap a lump sum (such as a pension fund) for an income either for life or a specified number of years. You cannot get your money back as a lump sum.
Annuity rate The amount of pension you get in return for your lump sum.

Pros and cons of occupational defined-contribution schemes

If your workplace offers this type of scheme, you are almost certain to benefit from joining it. The pros and cons listed below show why this is the case.

Salary-related occupational pension schemes normally offer considerable benefits to their members. Traditional-style 'final-salary' schemes (based on your pay shortly before retirement) are particularly advantageous, with a promised pension that is partly protected against inflation. 'Career-average' schemes (based on average pay over your whole career) offer similar benefits but are less expensive for employers and pay out less to those whose earnings peak in later life.

PROS	CONS
Tax advantages (as for all private pension schemes).	Unpredictable amount of pension and other benefits – in other words, you bear all the risks.
Employer pays some or all of the cost.	
Employer sometimes pays running costs separately.	Employer tends to pay less of the cost than with a salary-related scheme.
Simple to understand.	No automatic protection against inflation.
Easy to transfer if you change jobs (see Chapter 9).	

The table above summarises the main advantages and drawbacks of occupational defined-contribution schemes.

How much pension?

You can't know in advance how much pension you'll get from a defined-contribution scheme. But, with an occupational scheme, there are some features that help towards a good pension:

■ **Amount paid in** Your employer contributes on your behalf. Generally employer contributions are nowhere near as high as the amounts employers pay into defined-benefit schemes – see below – and, under auto-enrolment, need be no more than 3 per cent of your pay between limits (see page 70), but they still provide a significant boost to your pension savings.

Private sector occupational schemes

Generally, employer contributions to money purchase schemes are not as high as those paid into salary-related schemes, although they still provide a significant boost to employees' pension savings.

Type of scheme	Average employer contribution	Average employee contributions
Defined-benefit scheme	15.8%	5.1%
Defined-contribution scheme	6.2%	2.7%

Source: Office for National Statistics (2012).

Charges Occupational schemes are often large and can negotiate lower charges than you would pay if arranging your own defined-contribution scheme.

Annuity rates Again, because of their size, occupational schemes can often negotiate better annuity rates than you can get yourself. However, when you come to draw the pension you do not have to take the annuity offered by the scheme – you have the option instead to shop around for your own (see Chapter 6).

There is no requirement for the pension from a defined-contribution occupational scheme to be increased each year in line with inflation. It is left to you to decide whether you want an inflation-linked pension – see Chapter 6 for guidance on making this choice.

Tax-free lump sum

When you become entitled to start your pension, the tax rules let you take up a tax-free lump sum up to the lower of:

- A quarter of the fund that has built up, and
- A quarter of your Lifetime Allowance (see page 66) less the value of any benefits you have already taken.

The scheme might set its own lower limits.

Unlike a salary-related scheme, there are no commutation factors determining how much pension you

> **'With a defined-contribution scheme, you can't know in advance how much pension you will get.'**

give up in order to take a tax-free lump sum. The amount of pension you give up depends directly on the annuity rate at which the pension would have been bought. This is considered in detail in Chapter 6 but, generally, even if you need as much income as possible, it is worth taking the maximum tax-free lump sum. If need be, you can then invest the lump sum tax-efficiently to produce an income.

Starting your pension

The rules are the same as for final-salary schemes. Your pension must not start before age 55. You do not necessarily have to retire to start drawing pension from your employer's scheme and there is nothing to stop you from taking work elsewhere after starting to draw a pension.

Case study Geoff

Geoff has built up a pension fund of £28,000 and the scheme rules let him take up to a quarter of this as a tax-free lump sum. If he starts his pension now, he could have 25% × £28,000 = £7,000.

 To check how much tax-free lump sum you can have and other rules for your scheme, contact your pension scheme administrator or HR department.

Retiring early

If you retire earlier than the normal pension age, your pension will be lower because:

- You will miss out on the contributions that would have been paid in if you had put off drawing your pension until later.
- You reduce the time the pension fund is invested so miss out on some of the growth you might have had.
- The pension fund will buy less pension per year reflecting the fact that it has to be paid out for longer.

Some employers separately offer 'group income protection insurance' to pay out an income up to normal pension age if you have to retire early because of ill health.

> '**Defined-contribution schemes expose employers to fewer costs and uncertainties than defined-benefit schemes.**'

Retiring later

If you retire later than the normal pension age for your scheme, you may get a larger pension when it does start because:

- The pension fund continues to be invested and so hopefully will carry on growing – see Chapter 7 for guidance on how to invest in this situation.
- Extra contributions may be paid in. Check to see if your employer will carry on making contributions beyond normal pension age.

Case study Palab

Palab, 60, has been in a defined-contribution scheme for 30 years. He pays in 5 per cent of his earnings (currently £30,000 a year) and his employer adds a further 6 per cent. He had intended to work on until age 65 but is considering retiring now instead. By 65, his pension fund might buy an inflation-linked pension of £8,400 a year. If he retires now, he will lose five years' pension fund growth, miss out on $5 \times (5\% + 6\%) \times £30,000 = £16,500$ of contributions and get a lower annuity rate because the pension has to be paid for longer. These factors reduce his pension by 40 per cent to £5,000 a year.

Contracting out: choices and changes

A work-based pension scheme may replace part of your State Pension. In some situations, you have been able to choose whether this happens. However, the rules changed from 2012 onwards, so that now only your employer can decide if you will be contracted out and then only through a particular type of scheme.

Chapter 2 described how it is possible to be contracted out of the additional State Pension (see page 36). There are two main ways in which it works:

■ **Defined-benefit basis** This is possible if you belong to a salary-related occupational pension scheme. You can be contracted out on this basis even on or after 6 April 2012.

■ **Defined-contribution basis** This was possible in the past if you belonged to an occupational defined-contribution scheme or a personal pension scheme (which could have been a group personal pension scheme or stakeholder scheme, available through your workplace, or a personal pension scheme you took out for yourself). This form of contracting out has been abolished from April 2012 onwards and a contracted-out pension fund you have built up is now treated in the same way as any other defined-contribution pension fund.

This section answers some common questions about contracting out.

Q Can I choose whether or not to contract out?

A Not since 6 April 2012. The only form of contracting out now permitted is through a defined-benefit scheme. Only some occupational pension schemes are run on this basis and your employer decides whether or not the occupational scheme is contracted out. By joining, you are automatically contracted out of the additional State Pension.

Q Why was defined-contribution contracting out abolished from 2012?

A When you contract out through a defined-benefit scheme, you are promised a pension broadly equivalent to the State Pension you give up. This is not the case when you contract out on a defined-

Jargon buster

Contracting out Giving up some additional State Pension and building up a pension, instead, through either an occupational scheme or, before 6 April 2012, a personal pension scheme. Part of the National Insurance you and your employer pay - which would have gone towards the State scheme - is used to build up the alternative pension.

contribution basis. All defined-contribution pensions are uncertain and depend on how much is paid in, investment growth, charges, and how much pension you can get for your fund at retirement.

This means that defined-contribution contracting out is risky: you may end up with a bigger or smaller pension than you would have had if you had stayed in the additional State Pension scheme. The Government decided it had become too difficult to estimate who might win or lose by contracting out this way.

Q Why did my National Insurance contributions rise when defined-contribution contracting out was abolished?

A Whether or not this happened to you depends on how you were contracted out. If you were contracted out through a defined-contribution occupational pension scheme, both you and your employer paid lower National Insurance contributions to reflect the State Pension given up. When you ceased to be contracted out, your National Insurance contributions reverted to the normal (higher) rate. (Similarly, when contracting out on a defined-benefit basis stops from 2016, you see a rise in your National Insurance contributions if you are currently contracted out.)

There was no reduction in National Insurance while you were contracted out through a personal pension scheme – you paid the full rate contributions, but part was paid as a rebate direct to your pension scheme. When contracting out on this basis ceased from 2012, the rebates stopped. But the amount of National Insurance deducted from your pay was unchanged.

Q What happens to contracted-out pensions I've already built up?

A These carry on. However, special rules that used to apply to pensions from contracted-out defined-contribution schemes have been abolished. So these pensions are now treated just like those from any other defined-contribution scheme. This means you are, for example, free to invest this type of scheme as you like and start drawing the benefits at any age from 55 onwards.

> '**If yours is an occupational pension scheme, your employer decides whether or not to contract out.**'

For more information about contracting out and how the rules have changed, visit The Pensions Advisory Service (TPAS) website at **www.thepensionsadvisoryservice.org.uk**.

Multi-employer pension schemes

Multi-employer schemes are not new – they have existed for many decades in the public sector with, for example, a single scheme covering local government employees whichever local council they work for, a single scheme for teachers working for a multitude of different schools, and so on.

Multi-employer schemes have been less common in the private sector, but have occurred in, for example, the construction industry where workers often move from one employer to another according to the projects being developed.

The advantage of a multi-employer scheme is that, as you move from one job to another, there is no disruption to your pension scheme membership provided the old and new employers both offer membership of the same scheme. By contrast with most occupational schemes, leaving your job would mean leaving your pension rights behind or transferring them, usually with some loss of eventual pension (see Chapter 9).

With the start of auto-enrolment (see Chapter 4), multi-employer schemes have come to the fore. This is because, to ensure that all employers would have access to a suitable pension scheme, the Government set up a new multi-employer scheme called the National Employment Savings Trust (NEST). This scheme and its broad shape are enshrined in law, but NEST is not in any way a state-guaranteed scheme. It operates independently of government and the protection you get as a member should anything go wrong is the same as the protection that applies to any occupational scheme (see Chapter 11).

NEST and its rivals

The introduction of auto-enrolment has also triggered other multi-employer schemes to set up in the UK, which rival NEST. In late 2012, the two main rivals were NOW and The People's Pension. NOW is run by an organisation, called ATP, which has operated a similar pension scheme in Denmark for over 45 years. The People's Pension is run by B&CE, which has 30 years experience offering multi-employer schemes to the construction industry in particular. Both NOW and The People's Pension are open to any employees in any industry.

In general, it is your employer, not you, who decides whether you will belong to one of these multi-

> **'The advantage of a multi-employer scheme is that, as you move from one job to another, there is no disruption to your pension.'**

employer schemes and which one. However, there are some additional rules that apply to NEST that permit self-employed people to join. They also allow employees who are no longer with an employer that offers NEST membership the opportunity to carry on contributing to NEST. Balanced against that, there are some restrictions in the NEST rules that do not apply to NOW and The People's Pension, so deciding which scheme might be best for you means weighing up the various features of each one – see the table opposite.

All three schemes work on a defined-contribution basis and aim to offer a low-cost, straightforward pension choice. Chapter 8 looks at pension scheme charges and puts the costs of these multi-employer schemes into context. Chapter 7 describes the various ways you might choose to invest a defined-contribution pension fund. These three multi-employer schemes acknowledge that when there is too much choice, most people are likely to either put off making any decision at all or make bad decisions. So all three schemes limit the choice available and, if you don't want to make a choice, have default options that are likely to be broadly suitable. The aim is to strip away the complexity that often surrounds pensions, to make saving for retirement straightforward and un-daunting.

NOW and The People's Pension do not limit the amount you can save or your ability to transfer past savings to this scheme or to shift savings you have built up in the scheme to a different scheme later on. The same is not true of NEST. When the legislation describing what NEST would and would not be able to do was passed, the aim was to create a scheme that would work well for low- and medium-income workers who had traditionally been shunned by the mainstream pensions industry as too small to be profitable as customers. To avoid siphoning off larger, more profitable customers, there are restrictions on what can be saved through NEST:

- There is an annual limit on contributions paid in each tax year. This applies to the total from all sources, including, for example, your own contributions and those from your employer. The maximum is £4,400 in 2012–13 and is reviewed each year.
- NEST cannot normally accept transfers of pension savings that have been built up in other schemes (called 'transfers in'). The exceptions are where you have built up savings in an occupational scheme of which you have been a member for between three months and two years (see Chapter 9), or where these are a share of your

To find out more about the National Employment Savings Trust (NEST), visit **www.nestpensions.org.uk**. For information about NOW, go to **www.nowpensions.com**. See **www.thepeoplespension.co.uk** for information about The People's Pension.

Multi-employer schemes compared

	National Employment Savings Trust (NEST)	NOW	The People's Pension
Type of scheme	Defined- contribution	Defined-contribution	Defined- contribution
Charges	Designed to be low (see Chapter 8)	Designed to be low (see Chapter 8)	Designed to be low (see Chapter 8)
Investment choice	Target date fund recommended (see Chapter 7) or choice of 5 other funds if you prefer	No choice. Single investment strategy (see Chapter 7).	Three risk-based profiles (see Chapter 7), or alternatively choice of 7 other funds
Lifestyle fund? (See Chapter 7)	Yes	Yes	Yes
Sharia-compliant fund? (See Chapter 7)	Yes	No	Yes
Cap on amount of contributions that can be paid in?	Yes [1]	No (subject to HM Revenue & Customs limits – see Chapter 3)	No (subject to HM Revenue & Customs limits – see Chapter 3)
Allowed to transfer in savings from other pensions? (See Chapter 9)	No [1]	Yes	Yes
Allowed to transfer savings out to another scheme? (See Chapter 9)	No [1]	Yes	Yes
Can you carry on contributing after leaving your job?	Yes	No	No
Can self-employed people join?	Yes, provided aged 16–74	No	No

[1] Between November 2012 and January 2013, the Government was consulting on whether this rule should be abolished.

former partner's savings that you have been awarded on divorce (see Chapter 10).

■ NEST cannot normally make 'transfers out' – in other words, you may not transfer the savings you have built up in NEST to another scheme. The exception to this rule is where a share of the savings has been awarded to your former partner on divorce (see Chapter 10).

However, at the time of writing, the Government had launched a consultation to see whether these constraints on saving through NEST should be abolished. This was because it feared that the annual contribution cap in particular might be causing complications for employers who would prefer to enrol all employees, including high earners, into the same pension scheme but were prevented from doing so by the NEST constraints.

Increasing your pension

If you are on track for a low pension from your occupational scheme or multi-employer scheme, you have several options to improve the situation. These may include making Additional Voluntary Contributions (AVCs), and possibly joining an employer's salary-sacrifice scheme.

The three main ways of boosting your occupational pension are to:

- Pay extra contributions (see below).
- Start your pension later (see pages 87 and 92).
- Consider salary sacrifice if available (see page 101).

Extra contributions

Many employers run in-house 'Additional Voluntary Contributions (AVC)' schemes, which let you pay in extra to build up extra benefits. They work in various ways:

- **Added pension scheme** This type of scheme is found mainly in the public sector. You pay either a lump sum or extra contributions over a number of years and in return get an extra chunk of pension. Buying added pension in this way is very similar to paying voluntary Class 3 contributions to buy extra State Pension that you looked at in Chapter 2. Both that arrangement and the added pension scheme considered here are examples of defined-benefit schemes because they promise a set amount of pension.
- **Added years scheme** This is available only with salary-related

schemes and found mainly in the public sector (for example, in schemes covering teachers and NHS workers) – though, even there, added years schemes are being phased out and replaced with added pension schemes instead. Your AVCs buy extra years, so that when the formula is used to work out your pension (and other benefits) the amount is higher.

- **Defined-contribution AVCs** This is available with any type of occupational scheme. Your AVCs are invested and build up a fund. This can be used to provide extra pension, buy other benefits such as life cover (see Chapter 10) or increase your tax-free lump sum.

You do not have to use any of the pension arrangements above from your employer. You could instead just pay into your own personal pension plan (see Chapter 6) but arrangements from your employer often have lower charges or may have other features that make them a deal worth considering.

Added pension schemes

You pay additional contributions to buy extra chunks of pension. Typically, the extra chunks might be in units of, say, £250 a year. If the normal pension from the scheme is usually increased once it starts to be paid, the extra chunk is also treated in the same way. There may be maximum extra pension you can buy, say, £5,000.

Generally, you can choose whether to pay monthly contributions either over a set period or between now and your normal pension age. Alternatively, you may be able to pay in one go with a lump sum.

Whether buying added pension is a good deal depends on how much you have to pay for them. This depends on your age at the time you buy the pension and your sex. (Since women tend to live longer than men, as a group, their pensions cost more, and the legislation requiring gender-neutral annuities from 21 December 2012 onwards – see page 114 – does not impose similar requirements on occupational pension schemes.) For details of you own scheme, contact the scheme administrators (usually located in your HR department). Increasingly, pension schemes have a website that may include an online calculator so you can check how much the extra pension will cost in your own case.

Added years schemes

As discussed above, in a final-salary scheme or career-average scheme, your pension is worked out according to a formula:

Years in scheme × Accrual rate × Your pay = Pension

An added years scheme lets you buy extra years so that the 'years in scheme' part of the formula is higher than the actual number of years

Case study Beryl

Beryl, aged 59, is a member of the NHS Pension Scheme. So far, she has built up a pension of around £5,000 a year from the scheme and would like to buy an extra £500 a year (£42 a month) of pension payable from age 65. Under current rules, the pension will be increased each year in line with inflation once it starts to be paid.

The online calculator on the NHS Pension Scheme website tells her that the extra £500 pension would cost her £146 a month if she spread the payments over a period of five years (a total outlay of £8,760). Alternatively, she could pay a one-off lump sum of £7,540 Beryl recently inherited some money when her mother died and decides to pay the lump sum.

for which you have been a scheme member. In most schemes, there is a maximum number of years that you can have in total – say, 40 or 45 – so there is a cap on the overall pension you can build up this way.

Whether buying added years is good value depends crucially on how much you are charged for each year. Generally, the closer you are to normal pension age and/ or the higher your salary, the more expensive the added years will be.

Often you will have a choice of either paying for the added years through an increase in your regular contributions to the scheme over a selected time period or in a single lump sum. You may even be able to use the tax-free lump sum you get at the point at which you start your pension to buy added years at the last minute.

Many public sector schemes that used to offer added years schemes have now replaced them with added pension schemes instead. But if you had already started to buy added years, you can carry on making the payments to complete the deal.

In-house definted-contribution scheme

In-house defined-contribution AVC schemes are essentially no different from any other defined-contribution scheme and Chapter 6 describes in detail how these work. But there are some special features of an in-house AVC scheme that you should consider:

■ **Charges and investment choice** Typically the scheme will be run for your employer by an insurance company or, sometimes, a building society. Your employer may have been able to negotiate a good deal so that the charges are lower than for a scheme that you arrange for yourself. On the other hand, the choice of ways to invest your AVCs may be more limited than you would like. See Chapter 7 for information about investments.

■ **Matched contributions** Some employers are willing to pay extra towards your pension if you do and so may agree to match your contributions up to a set level – for example, 3 per cent of your pay. This would mean that if you paid extra contributions equal to, say, 2 per cent of your salary, your employer would also pay in 2 per cent on your behalf meaning that you benefited from extra contributions of 4 per cent.

■ **Taking the benefits** You could just use the AVC fund that has built up to buy a pension at retirement – and you could first take up to a quarter of the fund as a tax-free lump sum provided the AVC scheme rules allow this. But the AVC fund might be fairly small, in which case you might not get a very good deal on charges when you converted it into a pension. However, the tax rules let you combine the fund from the AVC scheme with the fund or value of your rights from your occupational pension scheme. That means, provided the rules of the occupational and AVC

Case study Sam

Sam, aged 48, is a teacher. She spent over ten years away from paid work while her children were young and then returned to full-time teaching. A few years ago she was on track to complete 27 years membership of the pension scheme by age 60. Based on her current salary of £34,000 a year, she would get a pension of $27 \times 1/80 \times £34,000 = £11,475$ a year. But she decided to buy five added years, and these will boost her pension to $32 \times 1/80 \times £34,000 = £13,600$ a year. She is paying for the added years through an increase to her regular monthly contributions. She is paying over 10 years at an extra cost of £3,350 a year.

Defined-contribution schemes work like conventional savings and investments, where you pay money in, with the hope that it will grow in the future. See Chapter 6.

Key tip

Where your employer offers matched contributions when you pay into the in-house AVC scheme, the scheme is likely to be a better way to make extra savings than other types of defined-contribution pension scheme.

schemes allow it, your tax-free lump sum can be worked out as 25 per cent of the total and paid in all or part from either of the schemes. So you might be able to arrange to take the whole of the AVC proceeds as a tax-free lump sum and draw all the pension from the occupational scheme.

Salary sacrifice

There can be advantages for both you and your employer if you receive part of your pay in the form of employer's pension contributions instead of normal pay.

You get Income Tax relief on contributions you make to your occupational pension scheme, multi-employer scheme or other workplace pension but you do not get any relief from National Insurance contributions. By contrast, whatever your employer pays into the scheme on your behalf is a perk of the job on which you pay no Income Tax and no National Insurance. So it's far more tax efficient if your employer pays into the scheme rather than you.

It is also tax-efficient for employers because they pay no National Insurance on money they pay into a pension scheme for their employees but do on money paid out in the form of salaries, bonuses, and so on.

As a result, many employers offer salary-sacrifice schemes. These let you choose to have varying amounts of your pay package in the form of employer's pension contributions instead of normal pay. Even if your employer does not operate such a scheme, they might be willing to set up such an arrangement if you ask. (Salary sacrifice works just as well for employer payments to a personal pension that you have arranged yourself – see Chapter 6 – instead of a workplace scheme.)

Think carefully before opting for salary sacrifice. It may affect, for example, the State Pension you are building up under current rules (see Chapter 2) and your entitlement to other state benefits linked to income or earnings. For example, assuming you are not contracted out, giving up part of your pay could reduce your additional State Pension (since the amount you get is currently linked to the average of your pay over your years in the scheme). On the other hand, lower pay could mean, say, you qualify for extra state benefits, such as Tax Credits or, from October 2013, Universal Credit.

So far, the Government has indicated that it is happy for salary-

---

For more information from HM Revenue & Customs on taxation and salary-sacrifice schemes, see **www.hmrc.gov.uk/specialist/salary_sacrifice.htm**.

Key tip

Salary-sacrifice schemes save you National Insurance, which may mean you can afford to save more for retirement. In addition, your employer might be willing to pass on to you in the form of extra pension contributions some of the National Insurance they save. Check with your employers to see if they run, or would consider, a salary-sacrifice scheme.

Case study Hank

At present, Hank earns £30,000 a year and pays 5 per cent of these earnings (£1,500) into his employer's occupational pension scheme. His employer offers a salary-sacrifice scheme under which the employer will pay the £1,500 into the pension scheme if Hank accepts a pay cut of £1,400 a year.

The table below compares the position for Hank and his employer if Hank joins the sacrifice scheme. Both gain from the salary sacrifice. Hank still has £1,500 going into the pension scheme for him and also sees his take-home pay rise by £248 despite the £1,400 pay cut. Hank's employer takes over the pension contribution but saves £93 overall through the lower salary and National Insurance bills.

sacrifice schemes to exist and has specifically excluded them from tax avoidance legislation but this could change in future.

Salary sacrifice schemes can be used in conjunction with auto-enrolment. In that case, being automatically enrolled into the workplace scheme would typically be accompanied by a fall in your cash pay. However, your employer cannot force you to auto-enrol through a salary sacrifice arrangement, so, even if you want to stay in the workplace pension scheme, you can instead keep a higher salary and pay your own contributions from that. However, bear in mind that salary sacrifice normally works in your favour. If you have been auto-enrolled on a salary-sacrifice basis and decide to opt out of the workplace scheme altogether, your pay should then revert to its original level.

How Hank and his employer benefit from the salary-sacrifice scheme			
	Before the sacrifice	After the sacrifice	Gain/(loss)
How Hank gains			
Hanks's income	£30,000	£28,600	(£1,400)
How much Hank pays into the pension scheme	£1,500	£0	£1,500
Hank's Income Tax bill	£3,812	£3,832 [a]	(£20) [a]
Hank's NI bill	£2,670.24	£2,502.24	£168
Hank's take-home pay	**£22,017.76**	**£22,265.76**	**£248**
How much goes into the pension scheme for Hank	£1,500	£1,500	£0
How the employer gains			
Cost of salary	£30,000	£28,600	£1,400
Cost of pension [b]	0	£1,500	(£1,500)
Cost of NI contributions	£3,077.95	£2,884.75	£193
Total cost to employer	**£34,578**	**£34,485**	**£93**

a The Income Tax bill rises, because although Hank's pay is now smaller, he no longer has any pension contributions to deduct from his pay before working out the tax.
b For simplicity, ignoring any other contributions the employer makes on Hank's behalf.

Keeping track

If your employer is not yet within the auto-enrolment rules and runs a pension scheme that you are eligible to join, you should be given information about the scheme within two months of starting work.

If auto-enrolment applies (see Chapter 4), your employer must establish whether you are eligible to join a workplace scheme and from what date. The date will usually be the day you start work, become eligible to join (for example, because of your age or earnings), or your employer's staging date (see page 68) arrives. However, your employer may be able to defer the date by up to three months. Once the date is reached, you must be given details about the workplace scheme within one month. If you have been automatically enrolled, this will include details of how to opt out if you want to. If you have not been automatically enrolled,

but have the right to join a workplace scheme, the information will include how to opt in or join.

Benefit statements

Benefit statements show an estimate of the pension you might get at normal pension age based on a variety of assumptions. The future could turn out to be different. So it is important to check your statements each year to see if you are still on track for the pension you want and adjust your planning if necessary. For information about your occupational pension scheme, contact the pension scheme administrator (usually located in the HR department at work). For information about a multi-employer scheme or a workplace personal pension, check paperwork you have been sent for contact details and the scheme website.

What a combined benefit statement might look like

Your Combined Benefit statement

When you reach State Pension age (65) the Department for Work and Pensions (DWP) expect your total state retirement pension to be £450 a month

If you stay in the Good2U plc Retirement Benefit Scheme until you reach 65 (the normal pension age for the scheme) your pension is forecast to be £1,600 a month

Your combined pension from Good2U plc Retirement Benefit Scheme and the State when you are 65 is forecast to be £2,050 a month

As a member of a workplace pension scheme, you should receive a yearly benefit statement estimating the amount of pension you are likely to get from normal pension age. The estimate will be in terms of today's money – in other words, after taking into account the effects of inflation. Some employers and pension providers issue combined benefit statements – see left – which also include an estimate of the amount of State Pension you might get at retirement based on your actual National Insurance record (see Chapter 2).

Summary

Unless you work for a very small employer, you will already be able to join a pension scheme through your workplace and, by February 2018, nearly all employees will be enrolled into a workplace pension scheme.

If, under current rules, your employer will pay into the scheme on your behalf, it is usually a good idea to join. Where you are automatically enrolled into a scheme or have the right to opt in (see Chapter 4), your employer must make contributions on your behalf. Not joining or opting out is like turning down part of your pay package.

The best work-based schemes are defined-benefit schemes, such as final salary or career-average schemes. These are still common if you work in the public sector but are generally being replaced in the private sector with less generous schemes. A defined-benefit scheme promises you a set level of pension at retirement and so lets you plan ahead with some certainty.

In many cases, especially if you work for a small employer, you will be offered a defined-contribution (money purchase) scheme. It is harder to plan for retirement because the value of your pension depends on stock-market movements and the life expectancy of the population as whole. The impact of these factors is explained in detail in Chapter 6. Nonetheless, where your employer pays into a defined-contribution scheme for you, this is still usually better than trying to save for retirement on your own.

You may be able to increase the pension you will get from a scheme at work, for example, by paying additional voluntary contributions or through a salary sacrifice scheme.

Personal pensions

Some of the pension schemes offered through the workplace are personal to you rather than linked to a particular job. And, if you are self-employed, a personal pension is generally a tax-efficient way to save for retirement. Personal pensions are defined-contribution schemes where you build up your own personal pot of savings. Other types of defined-contribution schemes (for example, some occupational schemes) work in the same way.

Personal pension and similar schemes

Auto-enrolment aims to ensure that, by 2018, nearly all employees have access to a work-based scheme to which their employer makes at least some contribution. But personal pension plans still have a place, especially for people who are not employees, such as the self-employed.

The nature of personal pension plans

Chapter 5 described how some of the workplace schemes that your employer might offer work on a defined-contribution basis. Virtually all the pensions that you arrange for yourself, or that are personal to you, are also defined-contribution schemes, including personal pensions, group personal pension schemes, stakeholder schemes and self-invested personal pensions (SIPPs).

With these pension schemes, you invest to accumulate a fund of savings. When you come to retire, you use the pension fund that has built up to provide your retirement income. The most common way to do this is to buy an 'annuity'. This is a type of investment where you exchange a lump sum for an income, usually payable for the rest of your life (see page 113).

When you might use a personal pension

The main reasons you might take out a personal pension or any of the other defined-contribution schemes covered in this chapter are:

- If you are self-employed and consequently have to arrange your own pension savings.
- If you are an employee but there is no occupational scheme or multi-employer scheme, you may be able to join a group personal pension scheme or stakeholder scheme through your workplace.
- If you belong to an occupational scheme or multi-employer scheme (see Chapter 5) and want to top up the amount you save for retirement.
- If you are an employee who decides not to join a pension scheme through your workplace, currently there is no workplace scheme, or you are not entitled to join it.
- If you are not working but want to save for retirement.
- If you are arranging a scheme for someone else, such as your partner or your child. There is no lower limit on the age at which a person can have a pension scheme.

If you already have your own personal pension or already belong to a work-based defined-contribution scheme and want to check out your choices at retirement, go to page 113.

Different types of defi...
contribution scheme

There are many types of defined-contribution pe... ...eme. Underneath they all work the same, but there are differences mainly in the choice of investments you can put into your pension wrapper and charges. In some cases, access is restricted to workers with a particular employer only.

Personal pensions and stakeholder schemes

The standard type of pension that you arrange for yourself is a personal plan. Typically this is offered by an insurance company.

You agree either to pay in regular amounts or make single lump sum contributions. Usually you are offered a choice of different investment funds (see Chapter 7). Charges vary greatly from one provider to another, and are often lower if you have a large pension fund (see Chapter 8).

When you want to start your pension, you do not have to stay with the same company, but can switch to another provider who may offer a wider range of choices and/or a better deal (see page 127).

Conditions that stakeholder pension schemes must meet	
Condition	**Details**
Capped charges	Charges must be no more than 1.5 per cent a year for the first ten years and 1 per cent a year thereafter. This must cover all the costs of running the scheme, managing your investments and providing information and basic advice. If there is a fee for detailed advice, this must be set out in a separate contract and charged separately. See Chapter 8 for more about charges.
Low and flexible contributions	The minimum contribution must be no higher than £20 whether as a one-off payment or a regular contribution. It's up to you when and how often you pay – you can't be tied in to regular contributions.
Portability	You must be able to transfer to another pension scheme without penalty.
Simplicity	There must be a default investment option if you don't want to make this choice yourself. The default must be a 'lifestyle fund' where the investments are automatically adjusted as you approach retirement to reduce the risks you take – see Chapter 7 for details.

Compare different personal pensions and stakeholder schemes using the Money Advice Service comparative tables at **http://pluto.moneyadviceservice.org.uk/ pensions** or call 0300 500 5000.

Your employer may offer a group personal pension scheme (GPPS) through your workplace. This is essentially the same as any other personal pension, but your employer may have negotiated some special terms, such as lower charges and might make contributions to the scheme on your behalf.

Stakeholder schemes are simply personal pensions that meet certain conditions – see the table opposite. You can arrange your own stakeholder scheme. If you are an employee, you may find that your employer offers a scheme through your workplace.

Self-invested personal pension (SIPP)

SIPPs are a type of personal pension offering extra choice and control. Instead of being a single product, typically SIPPs are segregated into their component parts and you can choose different firms to manage each bit:

- **The SIPP wrapper** You pay for a SIPP manager to handle the administration of your scheme. This may be an insurance company or a specialist SIPP provider.
- **The investments inside the wrapper** You choose which investments to use. Unlike ordinary personal pensions, you are not limited to a small range of funds selected by the scheme provider. You can select funds from different providers and invest direct in things like shares and commercial property. But not all SIPP managers will allow the full range of permitted investments – see Chapter 7.
- **Any other services** For example, you may wish to receive investment advice or hand over the detailed investment decisions to an investment manager (called a 'discretionary service').

In the beginning, SIPPs were very much aimed at wealthier investors, but these days there are two main types: low-cost SIPPs that cater for anyone who wants to control their own retirement savings and invest mainly through investment funds and mainstream shares and bonds; and comprehensive SIPPs that allow a much wider range of investments and typically levy higher charges.

Retirement annuity contract (RAC)

An old-style personal pension started before July 1988. Although you can no longer start new RACs, you can continue to pay into a scheme you already have.

Occupational defined-contribution scheme

See Chapter 5 for details of occupational defined-contribution schemes and in-house Additional Voluntary Contribution (AVC) schemes that work on a defined-contribution basis.

> **'When starting a personal pension, make sure you shop around for a wider choice or better deal.'**

Multi-employer defined-contribution scheme

See Chapter 5 for information about the National Employment Savings Trust (NEST) and its two main rivals, NOW and The People's Pension. These all work on a defined-contribution basis.

Small self-administered scheme (SSAS)

SSASs are occupational defined-contribution schemes for up to 11 members and used, typically, by family companies. The members of an SSAS are usually the people who control the company and often their close relatives. The company is the employer in relation to the scheme. This indirectly gives the members a high degree of control over: how much is paid into the scheme by the employer and/or members, how the scheme is invested (which may include owning the company's premises or lending to the employer – see Chapter 7) and the type and amount of benefits provided by the scheme.

Contributions paid into by an employer on behalf of a member do not count towards member's limit on contributions that qualify for tax relief. This gives a lot of scope for large contributions to be paid in via the employer. Employers get tax relief on whatever they pay into a scheme provided the contributions amount to a genuine business expense. This means the contributions for a particular member would have to be compatible with the person's value to the company and the salary they receive.

> 'With an SSAS pension scheme, employers get tax relief on whatever they pay into the scheme.'

How much pension?

Defined-contribution schemes come in many forms: plans that are personal to you, schemes offered through work or run by your employer, plans with limited investment choice, plans with lots of choice. But these are differences in detail only. They all work in the same basic way.

You can't know in advance how much pension a defined-contribution scheme will produce. This depends on:
- The contributions paid in.
- How well the invested contributions grow.
- The charges deducted.
- Annuity rates at the time you start the pension.

Contributions paid in
Who pays what?
With an occupational defined-contribution scheme, your employer pays in contributions on your behalf and so bears at least part of the cost of providing your pension.

Once your employer is covered by the auto-enrolment rules (see Chapter 4), employer contributions of at least a minimum amount become compulsory for eligible jobholders and non-eligible jobholders who opt in (see pages 72 and 73), and your employer may agree to pay more than this.

Although the requirement for employer contributions is a welcome aspect of auto-enrolment, the minimum employer contribution required is low compared with the amount that those employers who have so far voluntarily run

occupational schemes pay in on behalf of their employees – see the table, opposite. There is a fear that, just as employers are abandoning defined-benefit schemes for cheaper defined-contribution schemes, they might also over time 'level down' to the low employer contribution level required by auto-enrolment. As you can see, levelling down to this level would substantially reduce the employer contribution compared with a defined-benefit arrangement. It would also more than halve the employer contribution to a defined-contribution scheme, although in this case the total contribution would not be dissimilar with more of the total cost shifted to the employee.

If you are an employee who is not eligible to join the auto-enrolment scheme at work, you are self-employed or you are not working, there is no employer help, so you alone must normally bear the full cost of providing your pension.

There are no restrictions on other people paying into your pension scheme for you. For example, your partner could pay into your scheme.

Contributions must normally be in the form of money (for example, paid by cheque, direct debit or bank

Contributions as % of pay	Occupational defined-benefit scheme [1]	Occupational defined-contribution scheme [1]	Auto-enrolment scheme Minimum requirement [2]
Workplace pension schemes: average contributions compared			
Average employer contribution	15.8%	6.2%	3%
Average employee contribution	5.1%	2.7%	4%
Tax relief on employee contributions	[3]	[3]	1%
Total	20.9%	8.9%	8%

[1] ONS, 2012, *Pension Trends*, Chapter 8. Data for 2010 (latest available).
[2] Minimum contributions once auto-enrolment is fully operational. Lower contribution levels apply until September 2017.
[3] Tax relief on employee contributions is not normally paid into the scheme and instead reduces the employee's tax bill on their pay.

transfer) but you can transfer shares you have acquired through some types of employee share scheme at work (SAYE share option scheme and share incentive plan) direct to your pension scheme within 90 days of getting the shares.

Tax relief on contributions

Chapter 3 explained the tax advantages of saving through a pension scheme including tax relief on contributions (see page 64).

With most defined-contribution schemes, including those used for auto-enrolment, contributions paid in by you, or by someone else other than your employer, are treated as 'net' contributions from which tax relief at the basic rate has already been deducted. Everyone gets this relief, regardless of whether they are a taxpayer or the rate of tax they pay. So for non-taxpayers the tax relief is like a bonus added to the scheme – see the case study on Lyn and Wies on page 112.

You may get extra relief if you are a higher-rate taxpayer. Normally you

Case study Arif

Arif works for himself as a journalist. In 2013-14, he pays a lump sum of £5,000 into his personal pension. This is treated as a net contribution. The pension provider then claims tax relief at the basic rate from HM Revenue & Customs and adds it to Arif's scheme The basic rate is 20 per cent, so £1,250 tax relief is added bringing Arif's gross contribution to £6,250. (£1,250 is 20 per cent of £6,250.) Arif is a higher rate taxpayer. The higher tax rate is 40 per cent, so Arif can claim a further 20 per cent of £6,250 = £1,250 in tax relief through his tax return. In total £6,250 has gone into Arif's pension scheme at a cost to Arif of just £5,000 – £1,250 = £3,750.

do this by claiming through your tax return. If you don't get a tax return, contact your tax office.

If you pay into somebody else's scheme for them, the basic rate relief is added to their scheme as normal. But you would not be able to claim any further tax relief even if you were a higher-rate taxpayer.

Tax relief on some defined-contribution schemes is given differently. With occupational schemes, commonly you have paid in gross contributions with the amount deducted from your pay before tax is worked out and deducted through Pay-As-You-Earn (PAYE) – however, this way of giving relief may become less common as more employers become covered by auto-enrolment. With retirement annuity contracts (old-style personal pensions started before July 1988), you pay gross contributions and claim all the tax relief through your tax return or tax office.

Investment growth

It is important to realise that the investment decisions you make will have a big impact on how much pension you eventually receive.

Case study Lyn and Wies

Lyn and Wies have a family. At present Lyn stays home to look after the children and they rely on Wies's earnings. Although Lyn is not earning, they both feel it is important that she carries on saving for retirement, so Lyn has taken out a stakeholder pension scheme and Wies helps her to pay regular amounts into it. Lyn is a non-taxpayer. She pays £50 a month into her stakeholder pension scheme. This is treated as a contribution from which tax relief at the basic rate has been deducted. The pension provider claims the relief of £12.50 from HM Revenue & Customs and adds it to her scheme. So, at a cost to Lyn of £50, £62.50 has gone into her scheme.

Analysts reckon that the major influence on your return is not the individual funds you choose but the balance between broad types of investments, called asset classes. These include cash (deposits where your money earns interest), bonds (loans to governments or companies), property (investments in commercial properties, either directly or by owning shares in companies that run them) and equities (shares in companies). The return you might get from each of these generally varies according to the risk involved. Cash is the 'safest', but also earns the lowest return. Equities, on the other hand, offer the prospect of a higher return, but carry the risk of losses. The best strategy for most people is to keep a spread of different types of investment. You can achieve this by choosing a mix of different investment funds or a single fund that automatically holds a mix of different assets. For details about investing your pension scheme, see Chapter 7.

Charges

Charges have a big impact on the value of your pension fund, easily reducing the value of your pension fund at retirement by a quarter or more. However, charges are often complicated, so that it is hard to work out their full impact. Chapter 8 looks at the range of charges you may have to pay, compares the impact of charges across different pension arrangements and suggests how you can keep charges to a minimum.

For information about your investment options, see Chapter 7 starting on page 129.

Your choices at retirement

The decisions you make when you start your pension usually define the income you will have throughout retirement. It's important to understand your options and how you can choose between them. Many people use a financial adviser – perhaps for the first time in their life – to help them with these decisions.

How you draw your benefits

You may be able to take part of the fund that has built up as a tax-free lump sum (see page 58). The rest is normally used to provide a pension using:

■ An annuity (see below), and/or
■ Income drawdown (see page 119).

If you belong to an occupational defined-contribution scheme, the scheme might normally arrange a scheme pension by buying an annuity for you, but it must give you the option of shopping around for your own lifetime annuity if you want to.

Starting your pension

Under the tax rules, you can normally start your pension at any age from 55 onwards, but sooner if you have to retire early because of ill health.

In practice, your ability to start drawing your pension at an early age – whether through ill health or otherwise – is likely to be limited since, with defined-contribution schemes, the earlier you start your pension, the smaller it will be for the following reasons:

■ Generally, fewer contributions will have been paid in.
■ The pension fund has had less time to grow.

■ The annuity rate determining the pension you get will be lower, reflecting the fact that the pension has to be paid out for longer.

Conversely, the later you leave starting your pension, in general the larger the pension you may get. You do not actually have to retire in order to start drawing your pension.

Increases to your pension after it starts

There is no requirement for the pension from any defined-contribution scheme to increase automatically (for example, in line with inflation). It is up to you to decide whether you want this feature.

Using an annuity to provide your pension

Annuities are a special type of investment where you pay a lump sum (in this case, all or part of your

'You can start your pension at any age from 55 onwards – sooner if you have to retire early owing to ill-health.'

Jargon buster

Annuity An investment where you swap a lump sum (such as a pension fund) for an income either for life or a specified number of years. You can't get your money back as a lump sum.

Annuity rate The amount of pension you get in return for your lump sum.

---

pension fund) and in return get an income either for the rest of your life (a 'lifetime annuity') or for a specified period (a 'short-term annuity'). Lifetime annuities are more than just an investment, they are also a type of insurance (see box opposite).

How annuities work

The 'annuity rate' tells you the amount of regular income you will get in return for your lump sum, Generally, it is expressed as so many pounds a year for each £10,000 you invest. For example, an annuity rate of £650 would mean you get £650 a year for each £10,000 invested. Therefore, say, £30,000 would bring £30,000/10,000 × £650 = £1,950 a year.

The annuity rate at the time you buy the annuity determines the income you will get for the rest of your life with a lifetime annuity or for the whole annuity period in the case of a short-term annuity. This does not necessarily mean you will get the same income every year. Some types of annuity do provide the same income year-in, year-out. But others give you built-in increases or an income that fluctuates up and down.

The usual course is to use your pension fund to buy a lifetime annuity. This gives you the

reassurance that you will continue to receive a pension for the rest of your life, however long you live. In this way, lifetime annuities are a sort of insurance against living longer than expected – see the box opposite.

The table on page 116 sets out the main factors that determine the lifetime annuity rate you'll be offered. One of the most important is life expectancy – in other words, how many more years people like you can on average expect to live. This in turn depends on factors such as your current age, your state of health and lifestyle choices such as smoking.

One factor that no longer impacts on the annuity rate you will get from UK insurers – or indeed any insurance company in the European Union (EU) member states – is your gender. Statistically it is a fact that women tend to live longer than men. Until 20 December 2012, this was reflected in annuity rates, with a woman getting a lower income from a lifetime annuity than a man of the same age investing the same amount. This is because the pot of money used to fund the income would have to be spread more thinly over a longer period for the woman than the man. However, an EU court case found that any distinction between men and women when buying insurance amounted to unfair discrimination. Bear in mind that annuities are essentially a form of insurance and so they have been caught by the judgement in this court case. As a result, from 21 December 2012 onwards, it has been illegal for EU insurers to offer men and women different annuity rates (or other insurance rates).

Your choices at retirement

From that date onwards, men and women must be offered the same unisex rates. However, the court case does not affect the pensions offered by occupational pension schemes, which can continue to pay different amounts of scheme pensions to men and women whose circumstances are otherwise identical.

Average life expectancy in the UK has been steadily increasing and is expected to rise further. As a result, annuity rates have fallen dramatically over the last 20 years or so (see the chart below). For example, in 1990, a man aged 65 could invest his savings in an annuity to provide a pension of over £1,500 a year for each £10,000 invested. By end 2012, the amount had fallen by nearly two-thirds to under £550 a year. The decline has accelerated in recent years due to economic policies

Annuities as a type of insurance

With normal life insurance, you take out cover against dying prematurely. Your premiums are paid into a pool with those from lots of other people. The pool pays out to the survivors of those people who do die young; the people who survive get nothing but have had the peace of mind of knowing that the life insurance would have paid out if need be.

Lifetime annuities work in a very similar way. The money you invest is pooled with that from lots of other people. The average life expectancy of every one in the pool determines how much is paid out in yearly pensions. The people who live longer than expected get a bigger share of the pool over the years; the people who die younger than expected, get a smaller share, but have had the peace of mind of knowing that their pension would have carried on had they survived longer.

'An annuity gives you reassurance that you will continue to receive a pension for as long as you live.'

How annuity rates have fallen over 20 years

ANNUITY RATE (Yearly pension/£10,000)

Data for man aged 65, non-smoker, level annuity, no guarantee. Chart based on data from *Pension Management* and, for more recent figures, *Moneyfacts*.

Main factors determining your annuity rate		
Factor	How it affects the rate	Why it has an effect
Personal factors		
Your age	Older – higher rate Younger – lower rate	The younger you are, the longer your pension is likely to be paid out, so the more it is expected to cost in total (and so the less you get each year)
Your state of health [a]	Poor health – higher rate Good health – lower rate	Someone in poor health will probably live for a shorter period than someone in good health, so their pension will be cheaper in total
Your lifestyle [a]	Unhealthy (such as smoking, heavy manual job, and so on) – higher rate Healthy – lower rate	Someone who smokes, say, will probably live for a shorter period than someone with a healthy lifestyle so their pension will be cheaper in total
Economic factors		
Long-term interest rates	High interest rates – higher rate Low interest rates – lower rate	Pensions are funded partly by the money you invest and partly by the interest earned when that money is invested
Average life expectancy	Falling life expectancy – higher rate Increasing life expectancy – lower rate	The longer people live, the longer their pensions have to be paid out and so the more they cost in total

a Some annuity providers use postcode as a proxy for health and lifestyle factors that affect life expectancy. So you get a higher or lower annuity rate according to the average life expectancy of people living in your area.

How annuity rates vary with age	
Age	Yearly income per £10,000
55	£419
60	£470
65	£549
70	£643
75	£744

Source: Money Advice Service Comparison Tables
http://pluto.moneyadviceservice.org.uk/annuities. Accessed 29 December 2012.
Data for non-smoker, level annuity, no guarantee.

designed to tackle the aftermath of the global financial crisis and recession. These policies have entailed keeping interest rates very low, which has fed through to even lower annuity rates. The huge drop in annuity rates has caused many people to question whether annuities offer value for money any more and is one of the reasons for the great interest in alternatives to lifetime annuities, such as income drawdown (see page 119).

When to buy an annuity

Lifetime annuity rates reflect the cost of providing a pension year after year for as long as you live. So the older you are when you buy, the larger the yearly pension you get for any given sum invested – see the table bottom left. This contributes towards giving you a bigger pension if you retire later (see page 61).

Coping with inflation

The most basic type of lifetime annuity is a level annuity. It pays out the same income every year. The main drawback is that inflation eats into the buying power of your money over time (see page 21). For example, if you start with a level pension of £10,000 a year, after 10 years it will buy only the same as £7,800 today if inflation averages even a modest 2.5 per cent a year.

There are several ways you can plan to protect yourself against the effects of inflation. You could stick with a level annuity but save some of the income during the early years and use it to top up your pension later on. Maybe you could top up using other sources savings. Alternatively, you could choose an annuity with built-in increases. These are the main types:

- **Escalating annuity** This increases by a set percentage – for example, 3 per cent – each year. If inflation is lower, your income goes up by more than enough to retain the buying power of your money. If inflation is higher, you still lose some buying power
- **Index-linked annuity** This changes (up or down) each year in line with inflation so the buying power of your pension remains

> **Jargon buster**
>
> **Short-term annuity** An investment where you swap a lump sum for an income paid out for a specified period of time. At the end of the period, the income stops. You cannot normally get your original investment back as lump sum.

constant. Traditional inflation has been measured by changes in the Retail Prices Index (RPI). However, the Government is driving an economy-wide move towards using a different measure of inflation, the Consumer Price Index (CPI) and this is likely, over time, to affect annuities. A key difference between the two indices is that RPI includes housing costs, such as changes in the cost of repaying your mortgage. CPI tends to increase by less than RPI, so a CPI-linked annuity would normally have less generous annual increases than an RPI-linked annuity. At the time of writing, index-linked annuities were still normally RPI-linked and so these are the example rates shown in this chapter. You may also come across LPI annuities. 'LPI' stands for 'limited price indexation'. The income increases each year in line with an inflation index, but only up to a capped amount – say, 3 per cent or 5 per cent a year.

The cost of increasing annuities

The main drawback with increasing annuities is that the starting income is much lower than the amount you get from a level annuity (see table overleaf). Consider, for example, the

How starting income is affected by later increases

Type of income	Yearly income/£10,000
Level	£549
Escalating at 3% a year)	£382
RPI-linked	£343

Source: Money Advice Service Comparison Tables http://pluto.moneyadviceservice.org.uk/annuities. Accessed 29 December 2012.
Data for person aged 65, non-smoker, no guarantee.

position for a person aged 65. If they buy an annuity escalating at 3 per cent a year, the starting income is 30 per cent lower than the £549 a year they would get from a level annuity. It will take 13 years before the income from this escalating annuity catches up and 24 years before it has paid out as much in total as the level annuity. With the RPI-linked annuity, the starting income is nearly 40 per cent lower, but how long it takes to catch up depends on how inflation turns out in future. With a low rate of inflation, it would take many years. But if inflation returned to the high levels seen in the past (a peak of 27 per cent a year in 1975) the income would catch up very quickly.

Key tip

Some options involve leaving part or all of your pension fund invested or linking your annuity income to investment performance. You generally need to invest in relatively risky share-based investments that offer the chance of a higher return if you are to beat the deal you would have had from buying a conventional lifetime annuity. For more information, see Mortality drag, page 123.

Providing for a partner

If you have a spouse, civil partner or other partner who will be dependent wholly or partly on your pension, one way to ensure they could manage if you die first is to choose a joint-life-last-survivor annuity. This continues paying out an income until the second of you dies. See Chapter 10 for further details.

Getting value for money

If it worries you that dying soon after your pension starts would mean getting back less in pension than the amount you invested, consider a 'guarantee'. This is an assurance that the pension will be paid for a minimum period (up to ten years) even if you die within that period. You can nominate who would receive the continuing income. Your starting income is reduced by an amount that depends on your age, the age of your partner if it's a joint annuity and the length of the guarantee.

Another option that might appeal to you for the same reason is a 'capital protected annuity'. With this, a lump sum can be paid out to anyone you nominate if you die before age 75. The sum is equal to the purchase price of the annuity less the value of the pension paid out so far. Tax at 55 per cent in 2013–14 is deducted before the sum is paid out. Again your starting income is reduced. For more information about benefits payable on death, see Chapter 10.

If you have specific reasons to think that your life expectancy is shorter than average – for example, because you are in poor health or smoke – some annuity providers offer 'enhanced annuities' and 'impaired life annuities', which pay a higher-than-normal pension.

With investment-linked annuities, instead of buying a predictable pension, the lifetime annuity provides an income whose value is linked to an underlying fund of stock-market investments. Your hope is that the income will be higher than from a conventional annuity, but the income you get will change from year to year as the value of the investments in the fund rises and falls. The income may even fall. You need to have sufficient income either from the annuity or other sources to be able to cope with these fluctuations.

If you think that annuity rates might improve later on, you could consider a short-term annuity. You use part of your pension fund to buy an annuity lasting up to five years. The rest of your pension fund remains invested. At the end of that time, you can buy another short-term annuity if you want to, again lasting up to five years.

Using income drawdown

Income drawdown means leaving your pension fund invested and drawing a pension straight from the fund instead of buying an annuity. It is a very versatile way of providing a pension but involves extra costs and risks. There are two types of drawdown: capped and flexible.

At any time, you can stop using income drawdown and use your remaining pension fund to buy a lifetime annuity instead.

Key tips

- Shop around before you buy an annuity. There is usually a big difference between the best and worst rates. Whatever rate you get now, you are locked into for life.
- Check whether your health or lifestyle qualifies you for an enhanced annuity rate.
- Think about how you will deal with inflation. An index-linked annuity gives you automatic protection but the starting income is low and the market for index-linked annuities is not particularly competitive. If you opt for a level annuity – as most people do – make sure you set aside some savings in early retirement to cope with rising prices later on.

Jargon buster

Capped drawdown
Arrangement where you leave your pension fund invested and can draw off an income up to a maximum amount.

Flexible drawdown
Arrangement where you leave your pension fund invested and draw off an income of any amount you choose. To qualify for this type of drawdown you must have a secure income from other sources of at least a specified minimum amount.

Did you know?

In early 2013-14, a person aged 65, would need a pension fund of £167,000 to produce a weekly index-linked pension of £110.15. So that is roughly how much your basic State Pension (see page 30) is worth.

Case study Mike and Tamsyn

Mike, aged 68, has built up a pension fund of £84,000 and wants to turn it into pension. He's not going to have a huge retirement income and does not want to take risks, so he'd prefer to use the whole lot to buy a lifetime annuity rather than leaving any invested in the stock market.

As a first step, Mike checks the Money Advice Service comparison tables (http://pluto. moneyadviceservice.org.uk/annuities) to get an idea of how much pension he can get and who is offering the best deals. If Mike buys a single-life annuity, it will provide him with a pension for as long as he lives and stop when he dies. From the comparison tables, he finds out:

- Shopping around makes a big difference, even just based just on the selection of providers in the table. The lowest level annuity in the table would give him £409 a month while the highest would give him 10 per cent more at £450 a month.

- Although he would like to have automatic protection against inflation, it would mean a big drop in the starting income from £450 a month (the best level annuity) to £297 a month (the best RPI-linked annuity). He isn't prepared to accept that big a drop and would prefer to set aside some income as savings to deal with rising prices.

- He needs to think about the financial position of his wife, Tamsyn, who is two years younger than him, if he were to die before her. The income from a single-life annuity would stop. He could buy a joint-life-last-survivor annuity that would carry on paying the same level income until they had both died, but again the starting income would be a lot lower at £365 a month. A compromise would be a joint-life annuity where the income carries on at half the previous amount after the first death. In that case, he could get a level income of £405 a month.

- Some firms offer higher annuities to smokers and people in poor health, but Mike is pretty sure he would not qualify for any of these.

Armed with what he has learned from the comparison tables, Mike phones an independent financial adviser specialising in annuities to help him find and buy the best joint-life level annuity.

Capped income drawdown

With this type of income drawdown, the tax rules restrict the maximum pension you can take from your pension fund each year. For this purpose, a year runs between the anniversaries of the date you started income drawdown. The maximum is set as a percentage of the income that a single-life annuity for a person of your age would provide and the Government Actuary's Department (GAD) publishes the tables to be used in this calculation. (Since 21 December 2012, the same GAD table applies to both men and women reflecting the move to unisex annuity rates – see page 114.) In late 2012, the maximum drawdown was set at 100 per cent of the equivalent annuity income. However, the Government announced that, from 26 March 2013, this would be restored to 120 per cent – the level that applied before 6 April 2011.

Under age 75, the maximum income is set for three years at a time and recalculated at every third anniversary using your remaining pension fund and your age at the date of the review. From age 75 onwards, the review is held annually. The reviews are a safeguard to prevent you running down your pension fund too fast.

Case study Geoff

Geoff, 65, has a remaining pension fund of £100,000 after taking part as a tax-free lump sum. Using the GAD tables, his provider works out that the equivalent annuity income from this fund in December 2012 would be £5,500. At that time, the maximum capped drawdown income was 100 per cent of this amount, in other words 100% x £5,500 = £5,500 a year. Once the change in the rules allowing the maximum to be 120% of the equivalent annuity comes into effect, the maximum would rise to 120% x £5,500 = £6,600 a year.

Up to the maximum available amount, you choose how much income you want to withdraw each year. There is no minimum income that you must have. This means you could just take the tax-free lump sum and put off drawing any pension at all until later. If you take less than the maximum income in one year, this does not mean you can draw off more in another – the maximum applies separately to each year.

Flexible income drawdown

With this type of drawdown, there is no restriction on the amount of income you take from your pension fund. It can be as little or as much as you like.

However, the Government does not want you running out of retirement income and having to fall back on claiming state benefits, so flexible drawdown is only open to people who can show that they have a secure pension income of at least a minimum amount from other

sources. This is called the minimum income requirement (MIR).

Only specified types of pension income can count towards the MIR. They are:

- Your state pension
- A pension from an occupational pension scheme
- An annuity that provides a level or increasing income
- An annuity that provides a variable income, but only the guaranteed minimum income.

Income that cannot count towards the minimum includes income from any other drawdown arrangement, income from a short-term annuity, pensions from a Small Self-Administered Scheme with fewer than 20 members receiving such pensions, income from a purchased life annuity (see page 126) and investment income.

Since April 2011, the minimum amount of income from the permitted sources must be at least £20,000 a year. For this purpose, income means the before-tax amount. Note that 'a year' means the amount actually received in a tax year. Therefore, if a new source of income starts late in a tax year, you might have to wait until the following year to have actually received enough from the new source to take you up to or over the £20,000 threshold.

To qualify for flexible drawdown, you must also have finished building up your retirement savings and you will need to sign a declaration to say that is the case. This means you cannot still be building up pension rights in a defined-benefit scheme, be making contributions to a defined-contribution scheme or allowing

'You should be especially mindful of the impact of auto-enrolment. If your employer automatically enrolls you into a workplace pension, you will need to act quickly to avoid a tax charge.'

anyone else to pay into a scheme for you. (You can, however, still be building up a State Pension.)

If, having started flexible drawdown, you do start building up new pension rights or contributions, then these will be treated as if they exceed your Annual Allowance (see page 64) and you will have to pay tax on the value of the rights or contributions. This tax bill aims to claw back the tax relief that the pension rights or contributions will attract. You should be especially mindful of the impact of auto-enrolment (see Chapter 4). If your employer automatically enrols you into a workplace pension scheme, you will need to act quickly to avoid a tax charge. You have a window of just one month from the date your auto-enrolment started in which to opt out. Otherwise, you can stay in the scheme but must accept that you will have to pay the tax charge.

'Some people who opted for income drawdown in 2007 had seen their income halve by 2012. Most of us could not cope with that kind of fall in pension.'

Advantages of income drawdown

Income drawdown gives you a lot of flexibility. For example, you can:

- Vary the amount of income you draw each year (subject to the maximum if you are in capped drawdown). For example, you might draw a low pension in the early years while you are still doing some paid work and increase the pension as you retire more fully.
- Just take the tax-free lump sum (for example, so that you can pay off your mortgage) but put off drawing the pension until you need it later on.
- Provide for your partner or other dependants because, if you die first, they can use your remaining pension fund to provide pensions – see Chapter 10. Therefore, by drawing a lower pension yourself, you can increase the amount available for their pensions.
- Leave a lump sum to your heirs if you die because your remaining fund can be paid out to them, though this will be taxed. By drawing a lower pension, you can increase the amount you leave but, if you are thought to be deliberately using your pension scheme for inheritance rather than pension purposes, there could be extra tax to pay. See Chapter 10 for more details.
- Keep control of the way your pension fund is invested. This may be important if you like to select your own investments or have strong ethical beliefs. For more information about investments, see Chapter 7.

Income drawdown also offers an alternative for people who have religious objections to annuities. For example, the Plymouth Brethren view annuities as gambling on life, which is unacceptable in their faith.

Drawbacks of income drawdown

Do not underestimate how volatile your income can be if you opt for income drawdown. The maximum income permitted under capped drawdown depends on the value of your invested pension fund, the equivalent annuity income and any changes the Government makes to the drawdown rules. Since the global financial crisis started in 2007, stock-market investments have been volatile, annuity rates have fallen sharply with the general fall in interest rates in the economy, and a government cut in the maximum permitted income from 120 per cent to 100 per cent of the equivalent annuity is only being reversed in 2013. The combination of these factors means that some people who opted for income drawdown in 2007 had seen their income halve by 2012. Most of us could not cope with that kind of fall in pension.

In addition to volatility, you should also consider the impact of charges. Once you have bought a lifetime annuity, there are usually no more charges for providing your pension. With income drawdown, investment management charges continue for as long as your pension fund remains invested and there are administration charges for example for carrying out the regular reviews. These all add up and make income drawdown

Key tip

Because of the charges and the fact that your pension can fall as well as rise, income drawdown will generally be suitable only if you have a six-figure pension fund and/or substantial other retirement income.

uneconomic if you have only a small pension fund.

You might think you could reduce volatility by choosing 'safer' ways to invest, such as cash and bonds (see Chapter 7). But, in general, to make income drawdown worthwhile, you need to invest in share-based investments. This is for two reasons:

- As noted on page 114, the income from an annuity is funded partly from the money you use to buy

Mortality drag

Mortality drag refers to the loss of a cross-subsidy you would have had if you had bought a lifetime annuity. The income you get from a lifetime annuity is based on the average life expectancy for a pool of people of your age at the time you buy the annuity. Some of the people in the pool will die early. As they do, money that would otherwise have paid their pensions becomes available to help pay the pensions of everyone left in the pool. In this way, there is a cross-subsidy from the people who die young to the people who live longer.

If you put off buying an annuity until later, these early-death people have already dropped out of the annuity pool. Moreover, the survivors who are left are now expected to live to a higher average age – for example, average life expectancy for men aged 60 is 26 years to age 86, but average life expectancy for men aged 70 is 17 years to age 87.

These factors have a dampening effect on the annuity rate, so that the later you leave buying an annuity, the poorer the deal you get. If you never buy an annuity, you lose out on the cross-subsidy altogether and must rely purely on your own investments to fund your own pension without any insurance element at all.

the annuity and partly from the interest that money earns by being invested. The annuity provider puts the money into fairly safe investments that provide a low but predictable income. If, using income drawdown, you are to get a higher income than the annuity could provide, you need to choose investments that are likely to give a higher return.

■ As discussed on page 114, annuities are a type of insurance. By choosing income drawdown, you lose this insurance element and your investments need to produce extra return to compensate for the loss if you are to beat the income from an annuity (see Mortality drag on page 123).

Finally, unlike a lifetime annuity and despite the limit on the maximum income you can draw each year, there is no guarantee that your pension fund will last your whole retirement. If you live 'too long', you could see the income from your dwindling pension fund fall. Since 21 December 2012, this may be a problem, especially for women who draw the maximum income each year since this cap is based on unisex annuity rates that do not fully capture their statistical likelihood of living longer than men of the same age.

A third way?

Many people approaching retirement would like the security of an annuity but the chance of a higher income that income drawdown offers. To some extent, these aims are in conflict, since risk and reward always go hand in hand: if you want higher rewards you must be prepared to

take higher risks (or pay someone else to take on the risks for you). Nonetheless, providers have been experimenting with a range of products that attempt to combine the best features of annuities and income drawdown. They are often called 'third way' products.

A third way product offers you an integrated package, but examine how it works, and you'll usually find it involves splitting your pension fund in two and using part to provide some sort of guarantee and the remainder to provide investment growth. For example, part might buy an annuity to provide a guaranteed minimum income while the rest goes into an investment fund hopefully to provide extra income on top. Alternatively, part might pay you a flexible income now, while guaranteeing that your remaining pension fund after, say, five years will be no less than a minimum amount. There are some important points to bear in mind about these products: guarantees often involve using part of your money to buy complex investments, such as derivative, which involve extra costs; and there may be some risk that the organisation(s) offering the underlying guarantee might not deliver.

To date, third-way products have not been widely popular and the general verdict is that the cost of the guarantees is too high. But, if you are attracted to the third way, bear in mind that there is nothing to stop you creating your own third way. Provided you have a reasonably large pension fund, you can use part of it to buy an annuity to give you a secure income and leave the rest in income drawdown where it can carry on growing if investments perform well.

Phased retirement

Whether you opt for annuities, income drawdown or a combination of both, you do not have to start all your pension(s) on the same day. In fact, it is becoming increasingly popular to ease gradually into retirement, cutting back work and slowly flexing the amount of pension you draw so that your continuing earnings, plus pension, together provide the income you want. There are a variety of different methods you can use to phase your retirement:

- Use your whole fund to buy a lifetime annuity where the income starts relatively low but increases as your retirement progresses (for example, an escalating or RPI-linked annuity). At the time of purchase, you can take part of your fund as a tax-free lump sum.
- Use part of your pension fund to buy a lifetime annuity. Leave the rest invested and use a further tranche later on to buy another lifetime annuity. Each time you buy an annuity, you can take part of your fund as a tax-free lump sum. You might use the lump sum to provide part of the income you need.
- Use part of your pension fund to buy a short-term annuity. Leave the rest invested and, when the short-term annuity comes to an end, buy another short-term annuity or a lifetime annuity for a higher amount. You cannot take any tax-free lump sum when you buy a short-term annuity,

only when your lifetime annuity or pension starts or you go into income drawdown.

- Use income drawdown and vary the amount of income you draw as your needs change. When you first start income drawdown, you can take part of your fund as a tax-free lump sum.

Taking a tax-free lump sum

The tax rules allow you to take a tax-free lump sum from any type of defined-contribution scheme (though a scheme's own rules will not necessarily permit this).

Case study Fiona

Fiona, 70, has a pension fund of £50,000. In late 2012, the level lifetime annuity rate for a woman of her age was £658. Therefore, Fiona could convert her whole fund into a pension of £50,000 × £658 / £10,000 = £3,290 a year. Assuming her personal allowance is used up against other income and she is a basic-rate taxpayer, her after-tax income would be 0.8 × £3,290 = £2,632 a year.

Alternatively, Fiona could take a quarter of the fund as a tax-free lump sum. The remaining £37,500 would buy a pension of £1,974 after tax. With the tax-free lump sum, she could buy a purchased life annuity offering a rate of £628. This is lower than the pension annuity rate because people who buy purchased life annuities tend to have higher life expectancy that the more varied group of people who buy pension annuities. However, the tax treatment of purchased life annuities works in Fiona's favour.

The gross income from the purchased life annuity is £12,500 × £628 / £10,000 = £785. But around four-fifths of this counts as the return of Fiona's original capital and only the remainder is taxable. After tax, the income from the annuity is £753. Together with the net income from the pension annuity of £1,974, Fiona has a total after-tax income of £2,728. This is £96 a year more than she would have had using her whole pension fund to buy a pension annuity.

The maximum lump sum is the lower of:

■ A quarter of the fund that has built up, and

■ A quarter of the standard Lifetime Allowance (see page 66) less the value of any benefits you have already taken.

In general, it is worth taking the largest possible lump sum even if you need income, because the lump sum is tax-free whereas the pension is taxable. You could invest the lump sum in, say, a 'purchased life annuity'. This works in the same way as the annuities already described except it is taxed differently: part of each payment you receive is treated as return of your original investment and is tax-free; the rest is taxable.

Shopping around for the right scheme

To compare personal pensions, stakeholder schemes or pension annuities, check out the comparison tables on the Money Advice Service website at www.moneyadviceservice.org.uk/en/articles/retirement or call their helpline on 0300 500 5000. Personal finance websites (such as www.moneyfacts.co.uk), pages in newspapers and some specialist financial adviser websites (see, for example, www.annuity-bureau.co.uk and www.annuitydirect.co.uk) have tools or tables comparing current annuity rates.

Get information about particular schemes or annuities direct from providers – many have websites. Look out for the 'key facts document'. This is required by the UK's financial regulator, which in 2013 becomes the Financial Conduct Authority (FCA) although, at the time of writing, is the Financial Services Authority (FSA). The key facts document gives information about a product in a standard format designed to explain the main features clearly and make it easy to compare one scheme with another.

Shopping around when you start to save

Check out the following details before committing yourself to a particular pension scheme:

■ **What's on offer at work?** If you can join an occupational scheme, this will usually be the best way to

Your Lifetime Allowance is the value of benefits (pensions, tax-free lump sums and payments to your survivors if you die) that can be drawn from all of your pension schemes without a special tax charge being payable. For further details see Chapter 3.

save for retirement – see Chapter 5. By 2018, your employer will in most cases be obliged to pay at least part of the cost of saving for your pension – see Chapter 4.

- **The provider's credentials** Is the provider 'authorised' by the financial regulator? Find out by checking the FCA Register at www.fca.gov.uk or phoning the FCA on 0800 111 6768. If it is not authorised, report the firm to the FSA.
- **Contributions** Is there a minimum contribution – is it too high? Are you happy to pay regularly or do you want the flexibility to vary your contributions? Check how much flexibility a scheme offers and, if it requires regular contributions, whether there are penalties if you miss payments. Stakeholder schemes must be flexible and penalty free.
- **Investments** Do you want to choose your own investments? If so, you probably need to look at self-invested personal pensions (or if you run your own business, a small self-administered scheme). Bigger choice usually means higher charges, so don't choose a scheme with more options than you need. See Chapter 7 for information on investments and Chapter 8 for charges.
- **Charges** What charges are there – see Chapter 8.
- **When can you start your pension?** Do you have to specify a particular age in advance? If so,

---

Jargon buster

Authorised Means a firm that has been checked out by the regulator and is allowed to conduct financial business in the UK. Provided you deal with an authorised firm, you benefit from consumer protection - for example, complaints procedures and a compensation scheme if things go wrong.

Financial Conduct Authority (FCA) Body that took over part of the FSA's remit from 1 April 2013, including regulating financial advice and the selling of products such as pensions and annuities.

Financial Services Authority (FSA) Body that until 2013 regulated the provision of, and advice about, most financial products and services in the UK.

Money Advice Service Independent organisation, set up by the financial regulator, with a statutory duty to promote public understanding of the financial system. It operates a consumer information website (www.moneyadviceservice.org.uk), consumer helpline (0300 500 5000) and national financial advice service.

Open market option Your option to shop around and buy an annuity from any provider of your choice rather than sticking with the provider with whom you have built up your pension fund.

---

can you change that age without penalty? Can you draw just part of your pension? Many schemes are set up as clusters of lots of mini-schemes, giving you the flexibility to cash in just part at a time.

Shopping around when you want to buy an annuity

All defined-contribution schemes must give you the option of shopping around for a lifetime annuity when you want your pension to start – this is called an 'open market option'. In general, it makes sense to use the option because annuity rates can vary greatly from one provider to

---

For personalised guidance on deciding how much to save, which options to choose and the right products and providers for you, seek help from a financial adviser – see Chapter 13.

another and the firm with whom you built up your pension scheme will not necessarily be the best buy when it comes to annuities. There are two situations when this might not hold:

■ If you belong to an occupational defined-contribution scheme that arranges scheme pensions for its members. Because the occupational scheme can buy annuities in bulk, it may be able to get better annuity terms than you can arrange for yourself.

■ If the provider with whom you have built up your pension scheme offers a 'guaranteed annuity rate'. This is fairly common with schemes taken out before the 1990s. The scheme may have guaranteed that, at retirement, your pension would be based on an annuity rate no less than a specified amount. As annuity rates have more than halved over the last 20 years, some of these rates now look high and are impossible to beat by shopping around.

Not all providers offer a full range of choices at retirement. For example, if you want a short-term annuity or income withdrawal, you may have to switch to a specialist provider.

Keeping track

With all defined-contribution schemes, you should receive a statement once a year setting out in today's money, the pension you are expected to get by a specified age based on various assumptions. The statement will be very similar to that described at the end of Chapter 4 (see page 74) and, if it is a combined statement, will also include a forecast of the State Pension you may get from State Pension age.

Summary

You may want to save for retirement through a personal pension plan to top up your occupational pension or if you cannot join an occupational pension scheme – for example, you are self-employed. Alternatively, where you join a pension scheme through your workplace, this could be a personal pension.

With all defined-contribution schemes – whether personal plans or occupational schemes – you have important choices to make when you want your pension to start. Usually, it is worth taking the maximum possible lump sum, even if you need to maximise your income. You use your remaining fund to provide a pension either by buying an annuity or through income drawdown.

An annuity is the safer option. Income drawdown is generally suitable only if you have a six-figure pension fund or other sources of retirement income to fall back on. Lifetime annuity rates have fallen by nearly two-thirds over the last 20 years, in large part because average life expectancy has been increasing but also because of economic policies since 2007. You might think annuities offer a poor deal, but bear in mind that they are not just an investment: annuities are also insurance against living a long time.

You do not have to start your pensions all at the same time. It is becoming increasingly popular to phase retirement, gradually building up retirement income as you wind down the amount of work you do.

Investing your pension savings

Increasingly, it is up to you to decide how the money in your pension scheme should be invested while it builds up over the years to retirement. Most people opt for a mix of different investments that give a good chance of a growing pension fund, but without too much risk.

Investing your pension fund

Saving is about giving up some consumption today so that you can spend in the future. But, at the very least, you will want your savings to grow by enough to keep pace with inflation between now and the time you need to draw on them. Therefore they need to be invested.

The choice of investments

The sorts of thing you can invest in depends on the type of pension scheme concerned – see the table.

Any 'self-directed pension scheme' – in other words, one where the member controls the choice of specific investments – has the freedom to invest very widely, but is prohibited from investing either directly or indirectly in residential property (though see box on page 132) or possessions such as cars, fine wine, art and antiques. If your scheme were to invest in such assets you personally would be charged 40 per cent tax on the value of the assets and the scheme would face severe penalties. For more about self-directed pension schemes, see page 144 onwards.

Other types of pension scheme that are not 'self-directed' tend to limit your choice to selecting investment funds.

How you can invest your pension fund	
Type of scheme	**Your investment choice**
Occupational defined-contribution scheme	With many schemes, investments are chosen by the people running the scheme and you have no choice. With some, you can choose from a (usually limited) range of investment funds.
Multi-employer defined-contribution scheme	Usually a limited choice of investments and/or investment strategies (see page 140). These include a lifestyle fund or target-date fund (see page 139).
In-house AVC scheme	With some schemes there is no choice and your contributions are automatically paid into an account or fund selected by the people running the scheme. With others, you can choose from a (usually limited) range of investment funds.
Personal pensions (other than SIPPs) and retirement annuity contracts	You normally choose from a limited range of investment funds offered by the insurance company. If you make no choice, your contributions are usually automatically invested in a 'lifestyle fund' – see page 139.
SIPPs and SSAS	You choose the specific investments, which may be, for example, investment funds (which can be unit trusts and investment trusts, not just funds offered by insurance companies), shares, commercial property and so on. You may not invest in residential property or possessions such as cars, fine wine, art and antiques.

Basic investment strategy

The return on your investments will be the single biggest factor determining the size of your pension fund at retirement and the amount of pension you can buy. But unfortunately you can't know in advance what that return will be and there is no foolproof way of picking tomorrow's investment winners.

Asset classes

Many people spend a lot of time trying to spot the investment funds they think will perform best, but academic research shows that there is only a very weak correlation between current and future fund performance. Moreover, academics reckon that the major influence on your return is not the individual funds you pick, but the balance between broad types of investment, called 'asset classes':

■ **Cash** This refers to deposits similar to the accounts you would have with a bank or building society. Your money earns interest and, generally, you cannot lose any of your original investment (your 'capital').

■ **Bonds** These are loans to governments or companies. The borrower agrees to pay your money back at a set future date and in the meantime you may earn interest. You do not have to hold the bonds until repayment – instead you can sell them on the stock market. The price you can sell at depends on market conditions and could be more or less than the amount you invested. There is also some risk that the borrower might fail to pay the interest or repay the capital as agreed. This risk is very low in the case of loans to the UK government (called 'gilts').

■ **Property** This means investing in things like office blocks and shopping centres either directly or by owning shares in companies that hold and run such properties. Your return is generated by the rents that tenants pay and any increase in the value of the properties. But, if property prices fall or expenses exceed the rental income, you could make a loss.

■ **Equities** This means shares in companies. When you buy shares, you become part-owner of the company along with all the other shareholders. The return you get depends on how well the company performs. You may receive dividends (a slice of the company's profits paid out as income to shareholders) and/or a gain if the shares' price rises over the time you have held them. If the share price falls, you make a loss.

The asset classes above are listed in order of increasing 'capital risk' – in other words, the likelihood of losing your capital or previous growth. The

Jargon buster

Bond A loan to either a government or a company that can be bought and sold on a stock market.
Capital The amount of money you originally invest.
Capital risk The likelihood of losing part or all of your original investment and/or gains you have already built up.
Equities Another name for shares in companies.
Gilts The name for bonds issued by the UK government.
Shares An investment that makes you a part-owner of a company, along with all the other shareowners. The return you get depends on how well the company performs.

assets are also listed in increasing order of the return you are likely to get. This is no coincidence. A fundamental rule of investing is that risk and return go hand in hand.

The higher the likely return, the greater the risk. The lower the risk, the lower the return. It's easy to see why this is so. Ideally everyone would like to invest with no risk at

all. If investors are to be tempted away from very safe investments there must be a reward for doing so. That reward is the prospect of a higher return.

The chart below illustrates where the asset classes typically lie in relation to each other if you were to plot their returns against the risk involved.

Balancing risk and return

Most people do not like taking risks. So it could be tempting to save for retirement by putting all your money into cash assets. But reducing capital risk in this way increases the amount you need to save and could make it impossible for you to afford your pension target.

The chart opposite shows how much a person aged 30 might need to start saving each month to produce a pension of £10,000 a year in today's

The trade off between risk and return

Risk escalates with each asset class plotted on the chart below, although the return on your investment grows too.

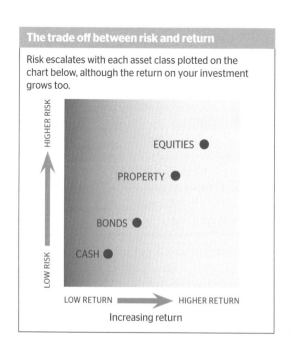

Increasing return

Property funds

Although a SIPP or other 'self-directed' pension scheme may not invest directly in residential property, it can invest in a fund that holds a spread of properties. Many property funds invest in commercial property, but some specialise in residential property, for example, investing in freeholds, holiday homes abroad or student accommodation. Property funds include Real Estate Investment Trusts (REITs) and Property Authorised Investment Funds (PAIFs) which can pay income direct to your pension scheme without any tax having been first deducted from the income (which would normally be the case with other types of property fund).

Return from equities compared with cash and gilts					
	Over the 111 years to 2011				
Holding period	Equities outperformed cash	Probability of equity outperformance	Equities outperformed gilts	Probability of equity outperformance	
2 years	74	67%	76	68%	
5 years	80	74%	80	74%	
10 years	93	90%	81	79%	
18 years	94	99%	84	88%	

Source: Barclays Capital (2012)

money by age 65 given different returns on his investment. If he chose investments paying on average 3 per cent a year, he would need to start saving £574 a month (nearly £7,000 a year). This is almost double the amount he would need to save if he opted for investments producing an average return of 7 per cent a year. But the higher-returning assets will almost certainly involve more capital risk than the lower-returning assets.

Managing the amount of risk

Saving for retirement is a long-term goal. The table above shows that, looking back over the last 111 years, over periods of ten years equities have produced higher returns than cash nine times out of ten. If you extend the investment term to 18 years, equities beat cash 99 times out of 100. The table also shows that, based on the past, equities are also highly likely to beat the return from gilts when investing for the long term. However, these long-run trends have been disrupted by recent experience. First the dot.com crash of 2000 and then the global financial crisis that started in 2007 have produced what is sometimes called a 'lost decade' for equities,

with the return from equities over the ten years to 2011 being a dismal 1.2 per cent over and above inflation, compared with 3.9 per cent from gilts but only 0.2 per cent from cash.

While evidence from the past suggests that equities are the more sensible way to invest for the long term, there are several important points to bear in mind given overleaf.

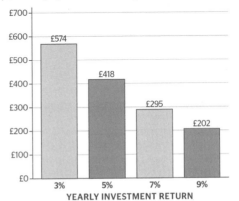

Saving rates

The chart shows how much a person might need to save each month from age 30 to produce £10,000 a year pension by age 65 with differing rates of return.

Assumes: charges average 1 per cent a year, price inflation averages 2.5 per cent a year, earnings inflation averages 4 per cent a year, monthly savings increase once a year in line with earnings inflation and pension increases in line with price inflation once it starts to be paid.

■ **The past is no guide to the future** Although past trends can help you to form a view about what might happen in future, they are not a reliable guide. The future could turn out to be different.

■ **Risks can, and do, materialise** Although there is a consistent trend of equities outperforming gilts and cash over most long-term periods, this does not mean that equities were the best performer in every year. In recent times, there have been major share price collapses in 1974, 1987, 2000 and 2007.

■ **Different assets usually behave differently** When equities do slump, usually cash and gilts perform well. The same is often true of other pairs of assets. But that does not mean that the unexpected cannot occur. For example, following the global financial crisis that started in 2007, cash, equities and property all performed badly.

■ **Spread your money** Despite occasional unusual outcomes, it makes sense to spread your money across assets that are expected to respond differently to economic events so that if one type slumps, others may be expected to do better. And, because risks do materialise from time to time, you either want to be in a position to sit tight and ride out a bad patch or, if you are close to retiring, to avoid the more risky investments.

How to manage investment risk

Don't be recklessly cautious If you avoid all capital risk, you increase the risk of being unable to meet your investment targets. You also increase the risk that your investments might not grow enough even to beat inflation.

Don't put all your eggs in one basket Have a spread of different types of investment – some equities, some property, some bonds and some cash. You can achieve this by, say, choosing a mix of different investment funds or a single fund that automatically holds a mix of different assets – see the table opposite.

Match the risks to your circumstances and temperament Normally you should take less risk, the lower the amount you have to invest. When you are young, you can usually afford to take more risks with your pension fund than when you are older. This is for two reasons. Firstly, you can ride out even a fairly lengthy slump in share prices, because you have a long time to go until you need to convert your pension fund into income. Secondly, if you do make losses, you still have many earning years left which gives you a chance to replace your losses. As you get older, you should generally reduce your exposure to risk. Whatever your age, you need to be comfortable with the degree of risk you take – there is no point being fully invested in shares if every movement of the stock market will keep you awake at night.

Lock in your gains as retirement approaches Protect yourself from a share slump just as you need to cash in your investments to buy a pension. Do this by shifting your fund away from equities and into bonds and cash over, say, the ten year run-up to starting your pension. 'Lifestyle funds' and target date funds (see page 139) make this shift for you automatically.

To get an idea of your own attitude towards risk, you could use an online profiling tool, such as Finametrica – see **www.riskprofiling.com**.

Examples of investments in funds

The table shows how the main investment funds differ in terms of risk.

Asset class	Type of fund	Description	Risk indication
Cash	Money market	Money in the fund is mainly on deposit earning interest. Normally little or no risk of losing your capital.	LOW RISK
Bonds	Gilt	Invested mainly in gilts. Value of fund can fall as well as rise, because gilts being bought and sold on stock market.	
	UK and fixed interest	Invested mainly in gilts and other bonds. Value of fund can fall as well as rise because bonds being bought and sold on stock market.	
Mix of asset classes	Targeted absolute fund return	Uses a mix of cash, short-term bonds and derivatives, with the aim of producing a specified return over a medium-term period. Aims to beat the return on cash funds.	
	Protected/ guaranteed	Fund aims to return either all or a set percentage of your capital, but also to give you some chance of stock market growth.	
	Mixed investment 20-60%	Maximum 60 per cent of the fund in equities (which can include overseas as well as UK shares). Rest in bonds and cash.	
	With profit	Your investment earns bonuses that are linked to an underlying fund invested in equities, property, bonds and cash.	
	Mixed investment 40-85%	Maximum 85 per cent of the fund in equities (with at least some in UK shares). Rest in bonds and cash.	
	Lifestyle	Fund starts by being invested mainly in equities but, in the ten years or so up to drawing your pension, automatically shifts to bonds and cash in order to lock in your past gains.	
	Target date	Designed to be wound up on a specified date. Fund starts by being invested largely in equities but, as the wind-up date approaches shifts to less risky assets to lock in past gains.	
Property	Property	Invested mainly in commercial property. Real estate investment trusts (REITs) can invest instead. or as well as, in residential property.	
Equities	UK all companies	Invested mainly in the shares of UK companies.	
	Tracker	Invested to mimic the performance of a selected stock market index.	
	Global equities	Invested mainly in shares of companies from around the world.	
	Europe	Invested mainly in the shares of companies based in continental Europe. Some funds include the UK.	
	UK smaller companies	Invested mainly in the shares of small UK companies.	
	Global emerging markets	Invested mainly in shares of companies in countries whose economies are developing or growing fast.	
	Asia Pacific	Invested in the shares of companies based in Asian countries around the Pacific. Some funds exclude Japan, which increases risk.	HIGHER RISK

Investment funds

Investing in different asset classes helps you spread risk. Equally, within each asset class, it is important to have a spread of different shares, bonds, and so on. Then, if one investment fails, it should have only a small impact on your overall fund.

Building up your own spread of investments is costly and requires knowledge and confidence. For most people, investment funds are the most cost-effective and convenient way to hold a spread of investments. These are ready-made portfolios that automatically give you a wide spread of investments. You invest by buying units in a fund and the return you get is in proportion to the number of units you hold. The table on page 135 gives an overview of the main funds available. This section contains more details. Funds come in different forms:

■ Insurance companies that offer pension schemes may operate their own insurance/pension funds. These are owned by the insurance company and the performance of your savings is linked to the performance of these funds.

■ You might instead invest in funds that are set up as unit trusts or open-ended investment companies (OEICs). These are run by a management company on behalf of the investors. Again the value of your investment is linked directly to the performance of the fund.

■ Investment trusts are also funds run by a management company, but you do not directly invest in the fund. Instead you buy shares on the stock market in the investment company. The value of your investment will tend to go up and down with the value of the fund but will also be affected by other factors that influence the share price.

■ Exchange-traded funds (ETFs) are also funds where you invest by buying shares on the stock market, but the value of your investment is more closely aligned with the value of the fund. Most ETFs are tracker funds (see page 142).

Money market funds

The money in the fund is used to make very short-term deposits and loans that earn interest, for example overnight or 90-day loans to banks,

Jargon buster

Derivatives Investments that derive their value from some underlying investment. For example, a traded option gives you the right to buy or sell some underlying shares by a set future date and the price of the option depends on how the price of the underlying shares is expected to move. Derivatives can be used in a variety of ways to expand the strategies an investment manager can take, for example, making profits when share prices fall as well as when they rise.

government and high-quality companies. Because the fund is large, it can normally get much better rates than you would at your bank or building society. Money market funds are particularly useful in the run up to retirement, when you want to avoid any risk of losing your capital or previous gains. However, be aware that you are not necessarily fully protected from capital losses. The global financial crisis and its aftermath have shown that seemingly invulnerable banks can go bust, leaving money market funds with worthless loans and very low interest rates, which can mean a fund makes losses after charges.

Gilt and fixed interest funds

The investments in these funds are gilts, corporate bonds (in other words, bonds issued by companies) and similar investments, all of which are known collectively as 'fixed interest'.

A single bond typically offers a fixed income and usually a set capital gain (or loss) payable at the set date when the bond is repaid. A fund investing in bonds does not offer the same guaranteed returns, because the fund manager will be constantly buying and selling different bonds. However, because of the nature of the bonds, the fund as a whole provides a reasonably stable return. Over the long-term, this is unlikely to be as exciting as the return on shares, so you generally do not want too much of your money in bonds if you are a long way from retirement. But as

retirement approaches it may be sensible gradually to switch your investments away from volatile equities to more stable bonds in order to lock in past growth.

Targeted absolute return funds

These use a variety of low-risk investments, such as cash and short-term bonds, plus derivatives, with the aim of producing a target return over a specified period. For example, the target might be 2 per cent more than the interest rate at which banks lend to each other. The strategies employed often have to stay in place for a set time in order to work and so an absolute return fund will not necessarily meet its target over short periods. Past performance data suggest these funds have a mixed record in meeting their goals at all.

Protected/guaranteed funds

These funds are examples of a group of investments more widely referred to as 'structured products'. They use a combination of two (or sometimes more) types of financial product to produce an investment that can deliver a particular aim. With protected and guaranteed funds, the aim is to guarantee the return of part

> ' As retirement approaches it may be an idea to switch your investments away from volatile equities.'

Useful websites for gathering information about, and comparing, different investment funds include **www.trustnet.com** and **www.morningstar.co.uk**.

or all of your capital, but also give you the chance to benefit from stock market growth.

These funds can be structured in different ways. Here is one example of a guaranteed fund. Say, you invest £1,000; £950 might be invested in a bond or put on deposit to provide a fixed return of £1,000 at a set future date. This provides the return of your capital. The remaining £50 is used to buy derivatives linked to a stock market index that will make a gain if the stock market rises by the set future date but return nothing if the stock market falls. Once the set date is reached, the cycle starts again. Even with this type of guarantee, your investment is not completely safe since there is always some risk that the provider of the bond or the derivative might default.

With a protected fund, only part of your capital is protected. For example, some of your money buys a bond that will provide a fixed return equal to 90 per cent of your capital. This leaves a larger sum to be invested in stock market linked products and so increases the gains if the stock market rises. But, if the stock market fails to rise, you lose some of your capital.

With-profits schemes and funds

Traditional with-profits pension schemes were conceived as an alternative to the sort where you bought units in an investment fund, and there are still some with-profits

schemes like this. They are offered by insurance companies and some friendly societies.

Your money is invested by the scheme provider in its with-profits fund, which holds a diverse range of shares, bonds, property, and so on. Your return depends largely on how well the fund grows, but also on other factors such as the expenses incurred by the provider, whether it has to pay out some of the profits to its shareholders, for example. The provider also uses a process of 'smoothing' to avoid sharp fluctuations in your return from one year to the next. Smoothing means holding back some of the return from good years to top up the pay-out in bad years. The scheme's actuary decides how much is available to be paid to the scheme members each year.

Your return is in the form of two types of bonus. Reversionary bonuses are added to your scheme regularly, usually once a year. A terminal bonus is added at the time you convert your investment into pension. The level of future bonuses is not guaranteed and can be varied from year to year or even missed altogether. Once a reversionary bonus has been added to your plan, in general it can't be taken away, so your plan should be on a constantly growing path. However, if you transfer your pension fund out of the scheme before your planned pension date, charges are likely to be deducted from the transfer value and may recoup some of the bonuses you had previously received.

For more information on asset performance see publications such as Money Mangement and Money Observer, available from larger newsagents.

These days, many with-profits schemes are organised, like most other investment funds, on a unit-linked basis. The with-profits fund is just one of the many different investment funds you can choose from and your money buys units in the fund. The value of the units increases in line with the bonuses as they are declared. But, instead of the provider's expenses being implicit in the level of bonuses, they are separated out and charged separately in the usual way that applies with any unit-linked fund (see Chapter 8). This makes unit-linked with-profits funds more transparent than the traditional with-profits schemes.

Lifestyle funds and target date funds

When you start your pension scheme, your money is invested in a fund that takes into account your attitude towards risk and the length of time until your pension is planned to start. A mix of shares, bonds, property and cash is chosen to reflect these factors and then automatically adjusted as time goes by.

For example, if you start a lifestyle fund in your 30s and plan to retire at age 65 and are comfortable with a reasonably high level of risk, your fund might be invested initially entirely in shares. When you are around age 50, the fund manager may start to switch some of your investments into bonds. By the time you are 60, say a quarter of your fund might be in bonds. During the last

five years, the manager may start shifting you into cash as well, so that by 65 your fund might be invested, say 25 per cent in cash and 75 per cent in bonds, with no shares at all.

A target date fund is very similar but instead of shifting assets in response to your age, at the outset you select a fund designed to be wound up at your chosen retirement age. The fund is designed so that it automatically and progressively shifts into lower risk investments, such as cash and bonds, to lock in future gains, as the wind-up date approaches. The funds have names that indicate when they will be wound up, so if you are planning to retire in, say, 2020, you should choose a 2020 target date fund. If you change your mind and decide to retire in 2025 instead, you could switch out of the 2020 fund and into a 2025 fund.

The advantage of lifestyle funds and target date funds is that you avoid any worry about making investment decisions but will automatically have been exposed to stock market growth while you were younger and have had your gains locked in as retirement approached.

Jargon buster

Default fund Investment fund that your pension scheme will be invested in if you do not actively choose the investments yourself. Typically, it will be a lifestyle fund or target date fund. Default funds are built into the design of stakeholder pensions and the multi-employer schemes being set up for auto-enrolment.

If you do not feel confident making your own investment choices, you could either allow yourself to be put into a default fund, if there is one, or get help from a financial adviser – see Chapter 13.

Key tip

If you like the idea of stock market growth but low or no capital risk, a protected or guaranteed fund could be the answer. However, these funds are varied and complex – make sure you understand how the fund works and the nature of the guarantee or protection before you invest. Be aware, too, that any gains you make will be less than if you had invested directly in equities because guaranteed and protected funds have extra charges and the return is linked only to stock market growth without the benefit of any dividend income.

They are used as default funds for stakeholder pensions and for the multi-employer schemes being set up in response to auto-enrolment (see below).

Auto-enrolment and investment choice

In response to auto-enrolment (see Chapter 4), three new multi-employer schemes have been established. Your employer, rather than you, will decide if you are enrolled into one of these schemes, but it is then up to you to decide how your savings will be invested, where the scheme offers a choice. The options available with each of the three schemes are as follows:

■ **National Employment Savings Trust (NEST)** This scheme operates target date funds (called Retirement Date Funds) and recommends this route as the suitable option for most people. Each target date fund has three phases:
  – The foundation phase is unusual and invests in low-risk assets with the aim of getting savers used to investments by avoiding a large short-term dip in value that might scare its members away from continuing to save.

  – The growth phase puts a higher proportion of your money into equities with the aim of building up your fund.
  – The consolidation phase shifts your savings to safer assets as retirement approaches.
  As an alternative to a target date fund, you can instead choose from five other funds and you are then recommended to have all your savings in one of these at any time. The funds are: ethical, Sharia, higher-risk, lower-growth and pre-retirement.

■ **NOW** This scheme (see page 95) does not offer any choice. Your savings follow a single lifestyling strategy. Initially they are invested in a growth fund and as retirement approaches part is shifted to a bond-based fund in preparation for buying an annuity and part to a cash fund to prepare for taking a tax-free cash lump sum.

■ **The People's Pension** (see page 95) You are asked to choose from three investment profiles: cautious, balanced or adventurous. If you make no choice, you are treated as balanced. All three use a lifestyling approach with a shift to safer assets as retirement approaches. If you prefer, you can instead put your savings into one or a mix of other funds, which are: ethical, Sharia, global growth (60% shares), global growth (85% shares), global growth (100% shares), pre-retirement and cash.

Property funds

Property funds often invest in the shares of property companies rather than holding property direct. In general, property is considered to be a lower-risk, more steady investment than equities. But property, if held direct, is fairly illiquid because it takes time to find a buyer and organise a sale. Therefore, the terms and conditions of the fund may allow for a delay, if necessary, of up to six or twelve months before your money can be released. This delay can be extended with the agreement of the financial services regulator. Following the global financial crisis that started in 2007 and the slump in economic activity that followed, a number of property funds ran into trouble. This has caused some investors to ask whether property as an investment is higher risk than they had been led to expect. However, bear in mind that any degree of risk, however small, means that bad outcomes will occur some of the time. The purpose of building a portfolio with a balance of different assets is to limit your exposure to the bad outcomes for any one asset class.

Equity funds

These are funds investing mainly or wholly in company shares. There is a huge range to choose from, for example:

- **UK shares** This lets you participate in the performance of companies whose prospects are likely to depend largely on the performance of the UK economy.
- **Overseas (global) shares** Here you are hooking into the performance of economies overseas. There is an extra layer of risk because the return will initially be in a foreign currency and has to be converted into sterling. Therefore,

movements in the exchange rate affect the return you get.

- **Small company shares** These funds offer the chance of high returns, because small companies may have the potential to grow very fast, but equally there is extra risk because small companies often find it harder to compete and may fail.
- **Specialist funds** These may invest in, say, companies that trade commodities or energy. Some funds seek out companies that are in poor shape now but look as if they have a good chance of recovery. Specialist funds are often high risk.
- **Ethical funds** Some funds either seek out companies that have good trade, employment or environmental practices or avoid companies that participate in, say, the arms trade, tobacco, alcohol or gambling. Check the ethical aims of individual funds to find the ones that match your own ethical stance or religious beliefs. For information, consult the Ethical Investment Research Information Service (EIRIS) at www.eiris.org.

Key tip

Some financial advisers suggest that the percentage of your pension fund invested in equities should be roughly 100 less your age. For example, if you are 30, you should have 100-30 = 70 per cent of your fund in share-based investments. (But not all financial advisers agree with this rule of thumb.)

■ **Sharia funds** These are similar to ethical funds, but the principles guiding the investments that are chosen and avoided are those laid down by Sharia law, making the funds particularly suitable if you are a Muslim.

Tracker funds

With most investment funds, the fund manager tries to select the underlying shares or other investments that he or she believes will give the best returns. This involves continuously monitoring the relevant markets and being prepared to switch investments as conditions change. This is called 'active' fund management. Of course, there is no guarantee that the fund manager will succeed in outguessing the markets – indeed there is some evidence that active fund management does not beat the market at all. And the downside of active fund management is the costs involved in paying for so much input from the fund manager and the charges for frequent sales and purchases of the investments (see Chapter 8). As a result, some funds have opted for 'passive' management.

Passive managers run tracker funds. With a tracker fund, the main input from the manager is when the fund is first set up. The underlying investments are selected to mimic a particular stock market index – for

example, the FTSE 100 Index. This could mean the fund invests in all the shares that make up that index or invests in a selection of investments that give a close approximation. The fund is then left to track the index, with no attempt made to identify and switch to the expected best performers. Because there is less manager involvement and less buying and selling of investments, tracker fund charges should be lower than charges levied by actively managed funds.

An increasingly popular way to invest in tracker funds is to choose exchange-traded funds (ETFs). Some of these are funds of the investments making up the particular index being tracked. But others are 'synthetic trackers' that use derivatives and other strategies to mimic the performance of the index. Synthetic trackers can be more risky than those holding the actual investments because the companies involved in providing the derivatives could default on their part of the bargain.

> **Jargon buster**
>
> **Active fund management**
> Trying to improve the returns from an investment fund by constantly monitoring and trading the underlying investments in an attempt to pick the best performers.
> **FTSE 100 Index** A measure of stock market performance based on the share prices of the 100 largest companies quoted on the London Stock Exchange.
> **Passive fund management** Setting up an investment fund to mimic the performance of a stock market index.

> ' Passive fund management aims to mimic a particular stock market index, such as the FTSE 100 Index.'

More information

Use the sources below to get information about investment funds and help you analyse and choose between the funds to create the right balance of risk and return. Here are suggestions, too, for finding out about self-directed pension schemes.

Investment funds

You can find further information about the various investment funds available for pension scheme investments from:

- Pension scheme literature and providers' websites. These should describe each fund and point out any significant risks involved.
- Independent websites, for example, TrustNet (www.trustnet.com) and Morningstar (www.morningstar.co.uk).
- Personal finance magazines, such as Money Management.

If you are not confident making your own choice of funds, you may want simply to go with the default fund or strategy for your scheme if there is one. Alternatively, get advice either from the salesperson or agent of the provider you are investing with, or a financial adviser. For more information about using an adviser, see Chapter 13.

SIPPs and SSASs

SIPPs are offered by a range of companies, for example, insurers, fund managers, actuaries and stockbrokers. SSASs are more specialist schemes offered by some insurers and actuaries. For a list of providers and their pension schemes, see the regular surveys published by Money Management magazine or get advice from a financial adviser.

Using a pension scheme to support your business is a complex matter with many aspects and trade-offs to take into account. Therefore, get specialist advice from an accountant or financial adviser.

'If you are not confident making your own choice of funds, go with the default fund or get advice from a financial adviser.'

Self-directed pension schemes

Despite the ban on pension schemes investing in residential property, cars, antiques and so on ('prohibited assets'), the tax rules still allow for a wide choice of investments.

To benefit from the widest choice you will need to take out either a:

- **Self-invested personal pension (SIPP)** This is a type of personal pension suitable for individuals who want a high degree of control over their pension scheme, or a

- **Small self-administered scheme (SSAS)** This is a type of occupational scheme particularly useful if you run your own small company and want to use the pension scheme to help your business. Your company is the 'sponsoring employer' of the scheme, which opens up various options not available with personal pensions.

The SIPP or SSAS itself is an empty pension wrapper. The firm offering it is selling you the framework and administration for your scheme. You then fill it up with the investments of your choice.

SSASs and some SIPPS involve substantial charges for setting up and running the schemes. Typically, you'll pay a set-up fee and annual management charge for the SIPP or SSAS framework and then transaction charges each time you buy and sell investments plus a variety of other incidental costs. Charges generally make these schemes uneconomic unless you have a minimum of around £100,000 to invest. However, low-cost SIPPs are now common – often set up and operated over the internet. They give you a wide choice of investment funds, but not other investments (such as commercial property). Charges are much lower, making these types of SIPP suitable for investments from a few thousand pounds upwards.

Jargon buster

Exchange traded funds Type of investment fund that usually tracks a specified stock market or other fund (so it is a tracker fund – see page 142). But you invest by buying shares in the fund on the stock market rather than going to a fund management company.
Sponsoring employer The employer who sets up, and contributes, to an occupational scheme.

For more information on pension scheme rules and regulations contact HM Revenue & Customs, website **www.hmrc.gov.uk/ pensionschemes/reliefs-charges.htm**.

Key tip

Even if you stick to investment funds, a SIPP gives you a much wider choice of funds than an ordinary personal pension.

Investments

SIPPs and SSASs are allowed to invest in any investments apart from prohibited assets. This can include, for example, direct investment in any types of shares (quoted on a stock exchange, unquoted, UK or overseas), gilts, bonds, commercial land and buildings, and so on. But, if a SSAS buys shares in the sponsoring employer's company, the value of the shares must be less than 5 per cent of the value of the pension scheme's assets. You can also invest some or all of the scheme in investment funds, choosing from the very wide range offered by unit trust and investment trust managers, as well as insurance companies.

The scheme might hold assets that you, your family or household use, in which case a value is put on the benefit you get and you personally are charged tax on that benefit. For example, a scheme might hold commercial premises that you decide to use for personal storage while they are standing vacant. You would be deemed to be getting a benefit in kind equal to the commercial rent you would otherwise be paying and have to pay tax at 40 per cent on that amount. You could reduce the tax bill by paying rent to the pension scheme.

There is no taxable benefit if the scheme receives a full commercial rent for the use of its assets. For example, the scheme could buy your business premises and rent them back to you on commercial terms. Your business could claim tax relief on the rent paid, the rent would be tax-free in the hands of the pension scheme and the scheme would pay no Capital Gains Tax (CGT) on the property when it was eventually sold.

The overriding aim of the scheme is to provide you with a pension for life and the investments must be compatible with that aim. Therefore, the scheme must have enough liquid assets to pay your pension when it falls due. This could mean, for example, selling property before that day arrives.

If the assets in the scheme are not compatible with providing the pensions due, HM Revenue & Customs could challenge the arrangement, clawing back previous tax reliefs and imposing penalty tax charges.

Buying from and selling to you

There are no restrictions on the scheme buying its investments from you or anyone connected with you or selling investments to you or your associates. But the purchase or sale must be on the same commercial terms that would apply if an unconnected person were involved.

'The scheme must have enough liquid assets to pay your pension when it falls due.'

Borrowing by the pension scheme

The pension scheme is allowed to borrow money in order to buy assets, but all such borrowings must not come to more than half the value of the assets in the pension fund just before the loan was taken out. For example, a scheme with assets worth £100,000 could, at most, borrow £50,000.

Loans from the scheme

Pension schemes may not lend to their members or people connected

Pension scheme investments

Pension schemes may not invest in residential property or assets, such as classic cars, wine and antiques. But this does not mean you have to stick just to investment funds. Here are some of the more unusual investments that you are allowed to invest in:

- Gold bullion (but not, for example, gold jewellery).
- Hotels, except where they provide accommodation on a timeshare basis.
- Children's homes.
- Student halls of residence (but not normal flats and houses let out to students).
- Residential care homes.
- Hospitals and hospices.
- Prisons.
- Job-related residential accommodation occupied by an employee, for example, a caretaker's flat. The employee must not be a member or the pension scheme or connected to a member of the scheme.
- Residential accommodation used in connection with business premises, such as a flat over a shop occupied by the trader. Once again it must not be occupied by a member of the pension scheme or anyone connected to a scheme member.

with their members. This means, for example, that you can't borrow money from your SIPP.

But occupational schemes, like SSASs, can lend to their sponsoring employer, provided all such loans come to no more than half the value of the pension fund and various other conditions are met.

Summary

As discussed in Chapter 1, pension schemes are really just a tax wrapper. Key to the success of your retirement planning is the investments that you put inside. In an ideal world you would invest without risk and end up with a handsome pension. In practice, risk and return go hand in hand: if you want the chance of a good pension by investing affordable amounts, you will normally need to take on some investment risk.

Spreading your money across different asset classes helps you to manage risk while pursuing reasonable returns. Investment funds let you pool your money with lots of other people to invest in a wide range of assets and investments. Increasingly, pension schemes offer a default fund or investment strategy that makes decisions for you about which assets and investments to choose and when to switch to a lower-risk approach.

If you prefer to control your own investments, a self-invested personal pension could be the answer. If you need help making your investment choices, talk to a financial adviser.

Where does your money go?

Charges can be complex and hidden. Even a completely transparent low annual rate of charges can take a surprisingly large chunk out of your pension savings. Therefore, it makes sense to opt for low-cost schemes.

Choosing a low-cost pension scheme

It has taken decades, but gradually pension scheme charges are becoming simpler, more transparent and lower. Take advantage of low-cost schemes when you can.

Recent trends in charges

All pension schemes involve a bevy of professionals and middlemen, each of whom has to be paid. They may include, for example, an external firm that administers the collection and passing on of contributions, an insurance company or other firm that provides the pension 'wrapper' and deals with the administration and governance involved, financial advisers who recommend suitable investment managers and funds, investment managers who run funds, selecting appropriate investments, custodians who keep safe the investments owned by the funds, brokers who act on instructions to buy and sell investments, and so on – see the table opposite.

Employers running large occupational schemes generally have the bargaining power to achieve a reasonable deal on charges, but for decades personal pensions levied a wide range of charges that were confusing and hard to add up. These complex charges could take away a big chunk of your pension savings. This was especially the case if the amount you were saving was relatively small, because charges are often tiered and come down substantially only once the value of your pension fund exceeds specified levels.

The first attempt to reduce the charges for personal pensions came with the introduction of stakeholder pensions in 2001. Employers with five or more employees were for the first time obliged to offer some kind of pension scheme through the workplace and the Government, wanting to ensure that good-value schemes would be available, introduced a set of rules for personal pensions that could be branded as 'stakeholder' schemes. These rules included a requirement for charges simply to be a percentage of the fund and, initially, not to exceed 1 per cent a year of the fund value.

> ' Complex charges could take away a big chunk of your pension.'

Typical pension scheme charges

Type of charge	Description
Investment fund charges	
Bid-offer spread	The difference between the higher 'offer price' at which you buy units and the lower 'bid price' at which you sell them. Typically the spread is around 5 to 6 per cent. 'Single priced' funds do not have this charge – they buy and sell units at the same price and levy charges in other ways.
Exit charge	A charge when you sell your units, often levied only if you sell during the first few years. Most commonly used by single-priced funds.
Annual management charge	A yearly charge deducted from the fund to cover the cost of managing the investments. Typically around 1 to 1.5 per cent a year of the value of the fund. Expect to pay less than 1 per cent for a tracker fund. The annual charge for exchange traded funds is typically 0.5 per cent or less. The annual management charge for the National Employment Savings Trust (NEST) is expected to be 0.3 per cent.
Performance fee	Some funds, particularly those using sophisticated investments like derivatives to boost returns, take a percentage (say 25 per cent) of any gains made. This might be instead of or on top of an annual management charge.
Fund expenses	The dealing costs of buying and selling investments in the fund and charges for their safekeeping are deducted direct from the fund and not normally counted with the other charges.
Other charges levied by pension providers	
Policy fee or administration charge	A one-off or regular charge to cover the costs of setting up and/or running the scheme.
Platform fee	Regular charge for providing administration of, and information about, your investments if details are collated by an online service.
Unit allocation	A given percentage of each payment is used to buy units. The percentage may be lower in the earlier years of the plan and/or if you pay, say, monthly rather than yearly. Don't be misled by an allocation of over 100 per cent – it generally means 100 per cent of your contributions after deducting a policy fee or other charges.
Capital units	Some insurance companies offer special units during the first year or two of the scheme – they usually have a much higher annual management charge (say 3 to 5 per cent a year) and this higher charge normally applies throughout the life of the scheme.
Surrender or transfer charges	You may be credited with only part of the value of your pension fund if you stop paying in regular contributions or transfer the scheme during the early years or switch your investments from one platform to another.
Market value adjustments (MVA)	If you transfer a with-profits scheme, your fund's transfer value may be reduced if the investment conditions are poor at the time of the transfer. The aim of the market value adjustment (MVA) is to claw back part of the bonuses already credited to your scheme to ensure a fair distribution of the with-profits fund between people who are transferring out and those who are left invested in the fund.

Stakeholder pensions were a mixed success. Providers were not keen to offer them, given the low charges cap, so this was increased to a maximum of 1.5 per cent a year during the first ten years – so not particularly low. However, alongside stakeholder pensions came a rule known as RU64, which required advisers recommending a personal pension with higher charges than a stakeholder scheme to explain to their customer why the personal pension was better and justified the higher cost. RU64 put downward pressure on personal pension charges generally.

The introduction of auto-enrolment from 2012 (see Chapter 4) has created another push towards lower pension charges. To ensure that all employers could offer a suitable

workplace pension scheme, this time the Government created the National Employment Savings Trust (NEST). The NEST rules require it to offer low-cost pensions. This has set the bar for NEST's rivals, so that all the multi-employer schemes are pitched at a low-cost level.

NEST is also open to the self-employed and people who have left the employer who originally auto-enrolled them into the scheme. To prevent NEST undercutting mainstream pension providers who might compete for this business, the NEST rules originally set fairly low limits on the amount that could be saved through the scheme (see page 96). However, at the time of writing, the Government was consulting on abolishing these constraints. If they go, the pressure will be on mainstream providers to cut their costs too.

Meanwhile, the rise of low-cost tracker funds (see page 142) has also put downward pressure on the cost of investing pension savings.

As a result, these days, you should be able to find relatively low-cost ways to save for retirement.

' Auto-enrolment has created another push towards lower pension charges.'

The impact of charges on your pension

The complexity and size of charges may be tending to improve, but do not underestimate the impact that even low-sounding charges will have on your eventual pension.

How much you could pay

The table below shows the proportion of your pension fund that would be eaten up in charges, given different levels and types of charge. For example, if you start to save regularly from age 20 and investment growth averaged 5 per cent a year, each £1,000 of your fund before charges would be reduced by over a fifth to £794 if charges averaged 1 per cent a year.

The impact of charges is greater the longer your money is invested because you lose not just the charges themselves but also the future

The effect charges can have on your pension fund				
	Value of each £1,000 of your pension fund in today's money [1] by age of 65 if you start to save regularly from age:			
Charges [2]	20	30	40	50
Before deducting charges	£1,000	£1,000	£1,000	£1,000
After charges of 0.5% a year	£889	£913	£934	£963
After charges of 1% a year	£794	£837	£881	£927
After charges of 1.5% a year	£712	£768	£829	£893
After charges of 2% a year	£642	£708	£781	£862
After stakeholder charges [3]	£790	£831	£872	£912
After NEST charges [4]	£915	£929	£945	£960
Afer NOW charges [5]	£920	£935	£950	£965
After The People's Pension charges [6]	£889	£913	£934	£963

[1] Assuming pension fund grows by 5% a year before charges, inflation averages 2.5% a year and you increase your contributions each year in line with average earnings (assumed to average 4 per cent a year).
[2] Percentages are percentage of the value of your fund.
[3] 1.5% a year for the first ten years and 1% a year thereafter.
[4] 1.8% of each contribution and 0.3% annual charge.
[5] £1.50 a month and 0.3% annual charge. (Lower admin charge applies until 2018 if you earn less than £18,000 a year.) Assumes minimum auto-enrolment contributions with employee paying £45 a month before tax relief is added.
[6] 0.5% a year.

growth that you would have had on that amount.

The last four rows of the table show the impact of charges on schemes that are designed to be low charging. You can see that the worst of the four schemes shown is the stakeholder scheme (assuming charges are set at the maximum allowed). Someone starting a stakeholder scheme at age 50 with a 15-year term until age 65 would lose around one-tenth of their pension fund to charges. The impact of the higher charges during the first ten years lessens as the term lengthens, so that a 20-year old starting a stakeholder scheme would lose around a fifth of their pension fund – little different from the impact had charges simply been set at 1 per cent a year throughout the whole term.

NEST, NOW and The People's Pension are schemes set up for auto-enrolment. They all charge in a slightly different way. NEST makes a low annual charge of 0.3 per cent a year of the fund value but also takes 1.8 per cent of the value of contributions paid in. This 1.8 per cent contribution charge funds the repayment of a loan from the Government used to set up the scheme and is due to stop when the loan is repaid, but this may take many years. The People's Pension does not have a contribution charge but has a slightly higher yearly charge of 0.5 per cent of the fund value. With both these schemes, the charges are percentages of the money involved and so proportionately have the same impact whether you are saving small sums or large.

By contrast, NOW, although having a low annual charge of 0.3 per cent, has a fixed contribution charge of £1.50 a month regardless of the size of the contribution. This would eat heavily into a small contribution but would be a small proportion of a large contribution. However, until 2018, NOW has temporarily reduced this contribution charge for people on relatively low earnings (less than £18,000 a year) to 30p per month until September 2017 and £1 a month from October 2017 to September 2018 before rising to the full £1.50 from October 2018. These staged increases are in line with the build up of the minimum contribution levels under the auto-enrolment rules (see page 71).

Information about charges

When you seek advice about or take out a personal pension, you should be given a key facts document (see page 126). Among other information, this includes an illustration of the pension you might get by your selected pension age based on various assumptions.

The illustration will include a table and statement showing the impact of charges on the value of your pension fund. Look for the statement that says something like: 'by age 65, charges would reduce the assumed growth of your pension fund from 7 per cent to 5.8 per cent'. In this example, the baseline assumed growth rate is 7 per cent a year. The financial regulator (the Financial Conduct Authority from 1 April 2013, but previously the Financial Services Authority) specifies the growth rates that providers must use in illustrations. There are three prescribed rates and the middle one must normally be used for the purpose of showing the impact of charges. In 2012, the middle rate was 7 per cent a year. From April 2014, this is being reduced to 5 per cent a year, though firms can start using this lower rate before then if they want to. The statement you see in an illustration

Jargon buster

Reduction in yield Figure in a key facts illustration that shows the effect of charges on the value of your pension savings.

would then start: 'by age 65, charges would reduce the assumed growth of your pension fund from 5 per cent to...'

The second figure in the statement is the yearly growth rate after charges have been deducted. The difference between the two rates – in the example above 7% – 5.8% = 1.2% a year – is called the 'reduction in yield' (RIY). However the charges are levied – contribution charges, admin fees, annual management charge, and so on – the RIY tells you in a single figure the overall yearly impact of the charges on your pension savings. By comparing the RIYs for different pensions, you can see which are cheaper and which are more expensive. For example, a scheme with a reduction in yield of 1.9 per cent would be more expensive than one with the reduction in yield of 1.2 per cent.

If you get advice from a financial adviser, on top of the charges for your pension scheme, you will pay fees for the advice – see Chapter 13.

Key tip

To keep control of the cost of saving for retirement:

- Check whether there is a low-cost pension scheme available through work. Talk to your HR department.
- If you need to arrange your own scheme, shop around. For example, use the comparison tables on the Money Advice Service website at http://pluto. moneyadviceservice.org.uk/pensions.
- Check and compare the reduction in yield (RIY) given in the key facts illustration for each scheme.
- If you are happy to choose your own investments, consider those investment funds that have lower charges, such as tracker funds (see page 142) rather than actively managed funds.
- If you need help, consult a financial adviser – see Chapter 13. Although you will have to pay fees for the advice, this could work out cheaper in the long run than making a poor choice on your own.

' By comparing the RIYs for different pensions, you can see which are cheaper and which are more expensive.'

Summary

Traditionally, charges for personal pensions have been complicated, hard to compare and hefty. Gradually this is changing.

Even seemingly low annual charges will over time eat away a hefty chunk of your pension savings, so it pays to shop around for a good value pension.

Generally, you will pay less if you can save through an occupational scheme run by your employer or one of the low-cost schemes set up for auto-enrolment. Bear in mind that the National Employment Savings Trusts (NEST) is open to self-employed people. You can also keep costs down by opting for low charging tracker funds rather than actively managed investment funds.

'You can keep costs down by opting for low charging tracker funds.'

Leaving a scheme early

9

If you leave a scheme before you retire, usually you must decide whether to leave your pension rights or fund in the old scheme or to transfer them to a new scheme. What's right for you depends on various factors and you may want advice to help you make the best choice.

Leaving a scheme before retirement

Your working life typically lasts around 50 years. It is unlikely that you will stay in the same job the whole time, so equally you are likely to build up pensions through a variety of different schemes. There are other situations, too, when you might leave a pension scheme even if you are not changing job.

Your options when you leave a scheme

There are various reasons why you might leave a pension scheme before retirement. You might decide to leave an occupational scheme on, for example, changing jobs or being made redundant. (You might have to leave if the scheme is being wound up – in which case, see Chapter 12.) You might leave a personal pension because an alternative scheme seems to offer a better deal or greater choice.

Whatever the reason, you face a range of options. They are complicated choices and you may want to get professional advice. You will have some or all of these options:

■ Cancel your pension rights and take a refund of contributions.

■ Leave your pension rights where they are in the old scheme.

■ Transfer your rights to a new scheme.

Refund of your contributions

Getting a refund is an option only if:

■ You are leaving an occupational pension scheme.

■ You have been in the pension scheme less than two years.

■ The scheme rules allow refunds.

You can have a refund only of your own contributions, not any made on your behalf by your employer. For refunds in 2013–14, tax will have been deducted at a rate of 20 per cent on the first £20,000 and 50 per cent on anything above that. You cannot reclaim any of this tax but neither is there further tax to pay.

The scheme might add interest to the refund. This is treated separately from the refund and paid with tax at the basic rate (20 per cent in 2013–14) already deducted. If you are a non-taxpayer or starting-rate taxpayer, you can reclaim all or part

To keep track of how much a 'preserved' occupational pension might pay out, the scheme will provide you with regular benefit statements – see page 103.

of the tax. If you are a higher-rate or additional-rate taxpayer, there is extra tax to pay.

If, through being a member of a defined-benefit scheme, you have been contracted out of the additional State Pension (see Chapter 2), there will also be a deduction from your refund to cover the cost of buying you back into the State Second Pension (The period of contracting out is then cancelled and your State Pension reinstated.)

Leaving pension rights in the old scheme

If you leave an occupational scheme before retirement, but after being a member for at least two years, you must be allowed to leave your pension rights behind so you still get

Case study Elspeth

Elspeth is changing jobs. She has been in her employer's occupational scheme for 18 months. The scheme tells her she can either have a refund of her contributions or, if she prefers, transfer her pension rights to a new scheme of her choice. The refund being offered is £1,350 (18 months' worth of contributions at 5 per cent of Elspeth's earnings of £18,000 a year without any interest) less tax at 20 per cent of £270, giving a net refund of £1,080.

Key tip

If you leave your pension rights in an old scheme, make sure to give the scheme your new address whenever you move so that it can send you regular statements and you know who to contact when you want to start your pension. If you lose touch with a pension scheme, you may be able to trace it through the Pension Tracing Service (www.gov.uk/find-lost-pension).

Case study Sayed

Sayed, 40, currently earns £40,000 and has been in a final-salary scheme for the last 15 years. It promises 1/60 of final salary for each year of membership. If he stays on until retirement at 65, with promotion, he expects his pay then to be about £60,000 in today's money. His 15 years' membership so far would be worth 15 × 1/60 × £60,000 = £15,000 a year in pension. But Sayed is changing job. If he leaves the scheme now, his pension will be just 15 × 1/60 × £40,000 = £10,000 and this will be increased in line with prices up to a maximum of 2.5 per cent a year (not earnings) up to age 65. Sayed needs to ensure the pay package in his new job adequately compensates for the reduction in pension from his old job.

a pension from the scheme later on. (Some occupational schemes also offer this option to members of less than two years.) Similarly, if you have a personal pension, you can stop paying in but leave your savings in the scheme to provide a pension later on. Whatever the type of scheme, this eventual 'preserved pension' will be lower than if you had not left.

Preserved pension: salary-related scheme

When you leave a salary-related scheme, your eventual pension is worked out in two steps:

■ First, calculate the pension according to the normal formula that we looked at in Chapter 5: **Years in scheme × Accrual rate × Salary = Pension**

■ Then, increase the formula pension, under current rules

usually, in line with price inflation up to a maximum of 2.5 per cent a year on average over the period from when you left the scheme up to the date when you start to draw your pension.

This will produce a lower pension than had you not left, firstly, because you have spent fewer years in the scheme. Secondly, 'salary' means your pay calculated at the time you leave the scheme not at retirement. So you lose the effect of any career progression – this could be particularly important if you belong to a final salary scheme. Thirdly, although preserved pensions are increased up to the time they start, the increase is in line only with price inflation and up to a maximum limit. Had you stayed, your pension – by being linked to your pay – would have tended to keep pace with general earnings inflation. So losing the earnings link reduces your pension.

Preserved pension: defined-contribution scheme

When you leave a defined-contribution scheme (whether an occupational scheme or personal pension), the pension fund you have built up so far is left invested to continue growing. The pension you eventually get will be lower than had you not left because:

- Future contributions cease. With an occupational scheme, this means losing the future contributions your employer would have paid in on your behalf.
- With a personal pension (other than a stakeholder scheme – see page 116), there might be extra charges if you stop paying in and had previously agreed to make regular contributions.

Preserved pension: contracted-out scheme

Contracted-out pension rights are treated the same as above, except where you are leaving a contracted-out salary-related scheme and had built up rights before April 1997. In that case, you are entitled to a guaranteed minimum pension (GMP) broadly equivalent to the additional State Pension given up. If you leave before normal pension age, this GMP must be increased between the time you leave and State Pension age by either:

- The increase in national average earnings. This method tends to produce the best increases, but in practice is used only by public sector schemes, or
- A fixed percentage, regardless of actual price or earnings inflation. For people leaving since 2007, the fixed rate is 4 per cent a year.

Under current rules, the State tops up the increased GMPs through your remaining additional State Pension

---

Jargon buster

Preserved pension The pension you are promised at normal pension age from a scheme you have left.

Key tip

In general, be wary of transferring from a salary-related pension scheme to a defined-contribution scheme. You are giving up a promised level of pension and getting, instead, benefits whose value will depend on investment returns and annuity rates - in other words, you will be taking on extra risks (see Chapter 5).

to ensure that you get no less pension overall than you would have done had you not contracted out. See Chapter 2 for how the State system may be changing.

Transferring your pension rights

Instead of leaving pension rights in an old scheme, you may be able to transfer them to a new one, but you need to check:

- The rules of the old scheme allow transfers – most do.
- Whether the new scheme is willing to accept the transfer. It doesn't have to and in some cases may not be able to – for example, if you are transferring contracted-out rights but the new scheme is not contracted out.

You don't have to transfer at the time you leave – you can do it at any

> **Jargon buster**
>
> **Section 32 scheme** A pension scheme offered by insurance companies. It is designed to accept preserved pension rights from an occupational scheme and can maintain them in their original form (say, salary-related).

time provided you haven't started to draw the benefits. Whether or not to transfer is one of the most difficult pension decisions you'll have to make. The benefits from the new scheme will be different from the benefits you give up in the old scheme, making comparison tricky. The decision is especially difficult where you are exchanging a salary-related for a defined-contribution pension or vice versa. The table below summarises when this will be the case.

Transferring your pension

Transferring your pension may involve moving from a salary-related scheme to a defined-contribution scheme. You should be aware of what this implies in terms of risk before deciding to move. See key tip opposite.

Scheme you are transferring out of	Scheme you are transferring into			
	Occupational salary-related	Occupational or multi-employer defined-contribution	Section 32	Personal pension (inc. stakeholder pension scheme)
Occupational salary-related	SR-SR	SR-DC	SR-SR	SR-DC
Occupational or multi-employer defined-contribution	DC-SR	DC-DC	DC-DC	DC-DC
Personal pension (inc. stakeholder pension scheme	DC-SR	DC-DC	not applicable	DC-DC

SR = salary-related; DC = defined-contribution

Pros and cons of pension transfers

It's not easy to decide whether or not you will benefit from transferring your pension. You need to weigh up a range of factors.

PROS

1 **Convenience** It is easier to keep track of just one scheme rather than several and easier to draw a pension from just one.

2 **Better deal** You might reckon the new scheme is likely to produce a higher pension than the old one.

3 **Future benefit improvements** A scheme might include transferred rights in any improvements to the scheme, but probably not preserved pension rights.

4 **Economies of scale** With personal pensions, charges may be lower for bigger funds.

5 **Greater choice** A new scheme might offer, say, a wider range of investments.

6 **Sever contact with a former employer** – for example, if you parted on bad terms.

7 **Fears about the employer's solvency** If your former employer's business fails, there is some risk that any salary-related pension scheme might be left short of enough funds to meet its pension promises (but see Chapter 12).

CONS

1 **Loss of guaranteed benefits** Some defined-contribution schemes offer guaranteed annuity rates when you start your pension. Because annuity rates have fallen sharply in recent years, these rates are now hard to beat.

2 **Reduced pension from salary-related schemes** Because each scheme uses different assumptions, the benefits you are promised in the new scheme may well be lower than the benefits you are giving up (but see page 163).

3 **Extra charges** The scheme you leave may deduct a surrender charge – most likely with personal pensions (other than stakeholder schemes) and some defined-contribution occupational schemes. If you switch from an occupational scheme to a personal pension, the charges you bear will almost certainly increase.

4 **Extra risk** Consolidating your pensions in one scheme means putting all your eggs in one basket. Transferring from a salary-related to a defined-contribution scheme means you taking on extra risk.ou need to weigh up a range of factors.

How transfers work

When a pension transfer takes place, the old scheme pays a cash sum to the new scheme. The big questions are: how much cash will the old scheme pay and what benefits will that sum buy in the new scheme? The answers depend on the types of scheme involved.

Transferring from a salary-related scheme

A salary-related scheme generally promises a given level of pension, tax-free lump sum, dependants' pensions if you die, and so on. A value – called the 'cash equivalent transfer value' (CETV) or just 'transfer value'– has to be put on these benefits to arrive at the cash sum the old scheme is willing to pay if you give them up.

Calculating the transfer value is complex and carried out by the scheme's actuary. However, the broad steps are:

- Work out your preserved pension at the time you leave the scheme.
- Increase the pension between now and the normal pension age for the scheme as described on page 87.
- Work out the lump sum that would be required at retirement to buy that pension, based on assumptions about annuity rates, dependant's pension and pension increases in retirement.
- Work out the amount of cash you would need to invest today to produce the required lump sum at retirement based on assumptions about investment returns and the sort of investments the pension scheme would be invested in.
- Similarly, work out the value of other benefits, based on appropriate assumptions (for example, the probability of dying at any given age). However, the actuary does not necessarily take into account benefits that are 'discretionary', in other words, not promised but paid only if the trustees decide to.
- The resulting transfer value can be reduced – but not below a minimum level worked out on a statutory basis – if the pension fund does not have enough in it to meet all the members' promised benefits in full.

Jargon buster

Actuary Financial and statistical expert who uses mathematical techniques to estimate how the future may turn out. With pension schemes, actuaries design schemes and advise on issues, such as, the expected size of future benefits and level of contributions needed to ensure those benefits can be paid.

Transfer value The lump sum which, if invested now, is deemed to be enough to provide a given level of pension at retirement plus other benefits. This cash sum can be transferred from one scheme to another.

> **'The transfer value from a defined-contribution scheme is the value of the fund earmarked for you.'**

As you can see, the actuary has to make a number of assumptions. Even quite small changes in the assumptions can have a big impact on the resulting transfer value. Although there are standard professional guidelines and the statutory minimum basis for the calculation, the actuary has a lot of discretion to choose assumptions that are relevant to the particular scheme.

The assumptions depend also on economic conditions at the time, so any transfer value quoted is valid for

a maximum of three months. If you don't make your decision within that time, you need to ask the scheme for a new quote. If conditions have changed the new quote may give a higher or lower transfer value.

Transferring from a defined-contribution scheme

The transfer value from a defined-contribution scheme (whether an occupational scheme or a personal pension) is simply the value of the pension fund earmarked for you, less any surrender charges.

The value of the pension fund of course depends on the value of the past contributions paid in by your employer and, if it is a contributory scheme, by you as well, together with past investment income and growth. The value of the fund rises and falls with stock market conditions, so the transfer value only becomes a fixed precise amount at the date of transfer.

Transferring to a salary-related scheme

When you approach a salary-related scheme with a transfer value to pay in, you may be able to use it in one or a choice of the following ways:

- Buy a fixed amount of pension payable at the normal pension age for the scheme. This is basically a preserved pension but it is unlikely to be the same as the amount of preserved pension you have given up in the old scheme – see below.
- Buy 'added years' in the new scheme. This means that when your pension and other benefits are worked out, a higher number of years are included in the

Case study Sayed

Sayed is leaving a final salary scheme at age 40 and is entitled to a preserved pension of £10,000 a year payable from age 65. For simplicity, assume there are no other benefits and that the pension, once it starts, will be increased in line with price inflation. Instead of the preserved pension, Sayed wants to transfer to a new scheme. The old scheme's actuary works out the transfer value as follows:

- The preserved pension is £10,000 a year payable in 25 years' time.
- Assuming inflation averages 2.5 per cent a year, the revalued preserved pension would be £18,500 by age 65.
- Using an RPI-linked annuity rate for a single man aged 65, the actuary works out that a lump sum of £540,500 would be needed at age 65 to provide a pension of £18,500.
- Assuming investment returns average 5 per cent a year and scheme costs 0.5 per cent a year, £179,800 would need to be invested today to generate the required lump sum by age 65.

Therefore, Sayed's transfer value is £179,800.

formula than your actual years of membership. This results in a higher pension and other benefits. The number of years in the new scheme that you can buy may be fewer than the number of years you had in the old scheme – see below.

■ Invest on a defined-contribution basis and eventually use the resulting fund to buy extra pension or other benefits. This is generally the least desirable option if you are transferring from a salary-related scheme, because you will be taking on extra risk compared with the salary-related preserved pension you have given up in the old scheme.

To convert your transfer value into a fixed pension or added years, the actuary of the new scheme has basically to reverse the steps of the old scheme's actuary described on page 161. This means working out how much the transfer value, if invested now, could be worth by the normal pension age for the scheme, then calculating how much pension that fund could provide, based once again on various assumptions.

The calculations by the actuaries in the old and new schemes are similar but the assumptions they use are likely to differ. The benefits that make up the package from each scheme will also differ. The upshot is that what you can buy in the new scheme is very unlikely to be identical to the benefits you give up in the old scheme. It can seem very confusing

> **'What you can buy in a new scheme may not be identical to what you are giving up.'**

but, just because the pension or number of added years in the new scheme is lower than that from the old scheme, it does not necessarily mean you are being offered an inferior deal.

Transferring to a defined-contribution scheme

Transfers into defined-contribution schemes are very straightforward. Your transfer value is a cash sum, which is invested in the pension fund and earmarked to buy your pension and other benefits in the normal way. As with all defined-contribution schemes, your eventual pension will depend on:

■ The amount paid in.
■ How well the invested transfer value grows.
■ Charges deducted.
■ Annuity rates at the time you want to start the pension.

Transfer clubs

A transfer club is an arrangement between different salary-related pension schemes to pay transfers out and accept transfers in using the same or similar assumptions. This means that you should be treated more or less as if you had been a continuous member of one scheme

Deciding to transfer is a complex decision, especially if a salary-related scheme is involved. You may want to get advice from a financial adviser – see Chapter 13.

Transfer checklist

These are the main factors to consider before deciding whether or not to transfer

1 Guaranteed benefits

If the old scheme offers guaranteed benefits – for example, a retirement annuity contract with a guaranteed annuity rate – be wary of any transfer that means giving up the guarantee.

2 Transfer club

If both schemes are in a transfer club (see page 163), transferring is likely to be worthwhile.

3 Expected pension

Compare the benefits from the old scheme with what you might get from the new scheme. Get help making the comparison (see page 153).

4 Risk

Before choosing a defined-contribution scheme over a salary-related one, make sure you understand, and are comfortable with, the extra risks (see Chapter 5).

5 When you can start your pension

Check the normal pension age and early/late retirement options for both schemes. Are you happy with the options?

6 Death benefits

If you have dependants, check out the life cover and dependants' pensions. If you are not married or registered to your partner, check they are eligible for a dependant's pension under the scheme rules – see Chapter 10.

7 Retiring early through ill health

Check the pension that would be payable from each scheme in this event.

8 Other benefits

Does the old scheme offer any extras to members with preserved pensions and/or to its pensioners? For example, medical insurance, discounts on the employer's products, membership of a pensioners' club, use of company sports facilities? Does the new scheme offer anything similar?

for the whole time you spent in the various schemes in the club.

The biggest of these clubs is the Public Sector Transfer Club which links around 120 public sector schemes (covering, for example, the armed forces, teachers, universities, police, the NHS, and so on) and some other schemes mainly for charitable and similar bodies. Each of the schemes you are leaving and joining can tell you whether or not they are members of a transfer club.

Transferring contracted-out pension rights

Since April 2012, contracting out of the additional State Pension scheme on a defined-contribution basis has been abolished (see page 39) and pension rights built up are now treated just the same as any other defined-contribution pension savings.

If you have been contracted-out on a defined-benefit basis, there are some special points to consider:

- The defined-benefit scheme you are leaving promises you a given level of pension – your GMP. The only way to preserve this promise if you transfer these rights is to switch them to a new employer's contracted-out salary-related occupational scheme, if there is one available, or to a section 32 scheme. However, the insurance companies that offer section 32

> **Key tip**
>
> Each time you leave a salary-related scheme early, you suffer the drawbacks described on page 160. So anyone who changes jobs often should generally be wary of transferring their pension from one salary-related scheme to another, unless they can take advantage of a transfer club – see page 163.

schemes are reluctant to accept GMP transfers because the benefits are costly to replicate.

- You can transfer your GMP to a defined-contribution scheme (for example, a workplace scheme or personal pension you arrange yourself), but you then lose the pension promise. The amount you are given to transfer must be at least the cash equivalent transfer value (CETV – see page 161) and you must consent in writing to the transfer.

> **Key tip**
>
> If you are in a public sector pension scheme, ask your HR department or pension scheme administrator for details of the Public Sector Transfer Club or look for information about it on your scheme's website.

Getting information and advice

If you are leaving or joining an occupational scheme, the pension scheme administrator can give you information about the scheme, your scheme benefits and the options you face, but they are unlikely to be able to give you advice.

Your employer might recommend a financial adviser (IFA) and might be willing to pay towards the advice. (Pensions advice costing no more than £150 a year paid for by your employer normally counts as a tax-free benefit from your job.) Otherwise, you might decide to get financial advice for yourself – see Chapter 13.

Key tip

Over a million people received redress amounting to over £10 billion after being wrongly advised in the late-1980s/ early-1990s to transfer from occupational schemes to personal pensions, losing valuable benefits in the process. Make sure you understand what you are giving up if you transfer out of an occupational scheme.

Summary

If you leave a pension scheme before retirement, you can either leave your pension rights with that scheme or transfer them to another pension arrangement.

If you leave a salary-related pension scheme, be wary of transferring your rights to a defined-contribution scheme. You will be giving up the security of a promised level of pension and, instead, taking on the risks of stock-market volatility and increasing life expectancy. Consider getting financial advice – see Chapter 13.

Pensions and your family

10

Pension schemes are designed mainly to provide income in retirement, but have other features too. Usually, they pay out a lump sum and/or income for survivors in the event of death. Since pensions are valuable assets, they are also taken into account when a marriage or civil partnership breaks down.

Pensions and dependants

The main purpose of pension schemes is to provide retirement income, but they also provide a range of other benefits that can help you plan for your family's financial security. The pensions and other benefits are also valuable assets to take into account when couples split up.

State Pensions and benefits on death

The State currently provides specific help for widows, widowers and bereaved civil partners but not for unmarried or unregistered partners. The rules are complicated and an outline is given here – see the table on page 170 for sources of further information.

Death before retirement

If you die before your spouse or civil partner has reached State Pension age, they may be able to claim the following state bereavement benefits if you had built up the appropriate National Insurance record over your working life up to the time of your death:

- **Bereavement payment** This is a tax-free lump sum of £2,000.
- **Widowed Parent's Allowance** A regular taxable income (£108.30 a week in 2013–14) plus half of any additional State Pension (S2P) you had built up. The payment continues until the youngest child ceases to be dependent or until your widow, widower or civil partner, enters a new marriage or civil partnership or starts to live with someone as if they were married or registered. Your spouse or civil partner might also be able to claim Child Tax Credit (CTC, a means-tested state benefit available to households with children) or from October 2013, Universal Credit (a new means-tested state benefit being phased in to replace a range of other benefits for working age people, including CTC).
- **Bereavement Allowance** A regular taxable income payable to spouses and civil partners over age 45 without any dependent children. The amount increases with their age. This income is payable for a maximum of 52 weeks and stops

Survivor pensions and the additional State Pension

There is a cap on the maximum additional State Pension that a person can receive from all sources. In 2012-13, the cap was just under £162 a week. The pensions that count towards or affect this cap are any additional pension you have built up in your own right, any additional pension inherited from your spouse or civil partner and any Guaranteed Minimum Pensions (GMPs) or their equivalent paid from contracted-out schemes either as retirement pension or as survivor's pension. In some cases, this could mean that receiving a survivor pension from your late spouse's or partner's occupational pension scheme reduces the additional pension you get from the State.

earlier if your spouse or partner enters a new marriage or civil relationship or starts to live with someone as if they were married or registered.

Death after retirement

If you die after you and your spouse or civil partner have both reached State Pension age, help is given through the State Pension system under the current rules. Your spouse or partner, if they do not receive a full basic pension in their own right, may be able to make up the pension to the full rate a single person can have (£110.13 a week in 2013-14) by using your contribution record. In addition, they can inherit up to half of any additional State Pension you had built up.

Other state benefits

Although there are no specific state benefits for bereaved unmarried or unregistered partners, they may be able to claim other state benefits. The most important of these are Working Tax Credit (WTC) if they are in work but on a low income, Child Tax Credit (CTC) if they have children (due to be replaced by Universal Credit starting in October 2013), Pension Credit if they are already retired and on a low income, and other means-tested help such as Housing Benefit (also due to be replaced by Universal Credit) and Council Tax Benefit. See the Government website, www.gov.uk for information. If you don't have

> **Key tip**
>
> If you have gaps in your National Insurance record, it could be worth paying voluntary Class 3 National Insurance contributions (see page 50) to ensure that your spouse or civil partner would qualify for maximum bereavement benefits in the event of your death – see chart on page 157. But consider whether to put the amount you would pay in Class 3 contributions towards buying life insurance instead.

access to the internet, see the Address section at the back of this book for alternative contact details.

You can check whether or not you may be able to claim state benefits and the amount you might get using the Government's online tool, Benefits Adviser, at www.gov.uk/benefits-adviser.

Death benefits from occupational and personal schemes

Occupational and personal schemes may offer pensions and lump sum pay-outs for your survivors when you die.

> **Your National Insurance record**
>
> Under current rules, a bereaved or divorced spouse or civil partner can claim state help based on their late or ex-partner's National Insurance record. (For this purpose, the partner must have at least 10 years of contributions and credits and, for maximum state help, they must have National Insurance contributions and credits for approximately nine-tenths of their working life.) From April 2016, the government is proposing to end this ability to use your spouse's or partner's record. State help (if any) should you become bereaved or divorced will then be based purely on your own circumstances.

 To find out more about bereavement benefits contact your local Jobcentre Plus (see your phonebook) if you are of working age or visit their website at **www.gov.uk**.

Dependants' pensions – the tax rules

Schemes can pay pensions to your dependants (but not anyone who was not dependent or co-dependent on you) whether you die before or after starting your pension. 'Dependant' means:

■ Your husband, wife or civil partner.

■ Your child(ren) under the age of 23 or, if older, dependent on you because of physical or mental impairment.

■ Anyone else financially dependent on you.

■ Anyone financially interdependent with you – for example, an unmarried or unregistered partner with whom you share a home and the associated expenses.

■ Anyone dependent on you because of physical or mental impairment.

Under the tax rules, all the dependants' pensions added together must not come to more than the retirement pension you would have been entitled to, but otherwise there is no limit on the amount of any one pension. (However, individual scheme rules may set some limit.)

The pension choices for your dependants are virtually the same as those for a person starting a retirement pension (see Chapters 5 and 6). The only difference is that, where a dependant's pension is to be provided by an annuity, no 'guarantee period' (as described on page 118) is allowed.

Dependants' pensions are taxable income, so the recipient will have to pay tax on it if their income from all sources is high enough. Tax is normally deducted through PAYE before the pension is paid out.

Dependants' pensions from occupational salary-related schemes

Subject to the tax rules already described, a scheme can set its own rules about how much pension it will provide for dependants. If the scheme is contracted out (see Chapter 2), there are additional rules.

Typically, a scheme will provide a pension for a widow, widower, civil partner or unmarried partner on:

■ Death before you have started your pension. Pension of, say, half or two thirds of the pension you would have been entitled to based on your pay now and either your years of membership to date or the number of years you would have completed had you reached the normal pension age for the scheme.

■ Death after you have started your pension. Pension of, say, half or two thirds of the pension you were

Free leaflets about state benefits		
Ref	**Title**	**From**
NP45	A guide to Bereavement Benefits	Department for Work and Pensions
PC10S	A detailed guide to Pension Credit for advisers and others	Department for Work and Pensions
RR2	A guide to Housing Benefit and Council Tax Benefit	Department for Work and Pensions
WTC2	A guide to Child Tax Credit and Working Tax Credit	HM Revenue & Customs

getting at the time of death. A higher pension might be payable for, say, the first three or six months following death.

The pension must be increased each year at least in line with inflation up to a maximum of 2.5 per cent a year on average. The rules of the scheme may state that the pension stops if your widow, widower or civil partner remarries or forms a new civil partnership.

If you have been contracted out through a salary-related pension scheme before April 1997, the scheme must pay a guaranteed minimum pension (GMP) to your widow, widower or civil partner equal to half the GMPs you had built up (see page 38). Note that these GMPs may affect the amount of additional State Pension you can receive (see page 168). The scheme and state together provide increases that ensure the pension is fully increased each year in line with inflation. If you have been contracted out through a salary-related scheme since April 1997, the scheme must provide a pension for

Case study Joan

Joan's husband, Len, had a pension of £14,000 a year from his occupational scheme. When Len died, under the scheme rules, Joan was entitled to a pension of half Len's entitlement but only in respect of the pension he had built up in the last 13 years of his 22 years with the employer (because the scheme had not offered family benefits at all during the earlier years). Instead of getting a widow's pension of around £7,000 a year from the scheme, Joan was told she would get only £4,800 a year.

your spouse or civil partner of at least half the pension you would have had.

Most salary-related schemes also provide separate pensions for dependent children.

Jargon buster

Joint-life-last-survivor annuity An investment where you exchange a lump sum (say, your pension fund) for an income payable until both you and your partner have died. You can choose whether or not the income reduces following the first death.

Single-life annuity An investment where you exchange a lump sum (say, your pension fund) for an income payable for as long as you live.

Key tip

■ If schemes have, at some stage, improved the death benefits, the improvement will not necessarily have been backdated so the survivor pension may be smaller than you expected. For example, most public sector schemes started to pay survivor pensions to unmarried partners only from around 2007 onwards. Only years of scheme membership from that date on count towards the survivor pension. Check your latest benefit statement to see how much the pension would be and contact your pension scheme administrator to see if you can pay extra contributions to increase the amount.

Dependants' pensions from all types of defined-contribution scheme

If you die before starting your pension, the pension fund you have built up can be used to provide a dependant's pension. The amount of pension depends on the size of the fund and annuity rates at the time (which determine either the annuity your dependant can buy or the amount of pension they can take through income withdrawal). The same applies if you had already started your pension but still had some pension fund left invested (because you were using income withdrawal or short-term annuities).

Where you die after starting your pension and you had opted for a lifetime annuity, what happens depends on whether you had chosen a single-life annuity or a joint-life-last-survivor annuity. A single-life annuity dies with you and your survivor gets no pension at all. A joint-life-last-survivor annuity carries on paying out after the first of you and your partner dies and continues for as long as the survivor lives. The starting income will be less to reflect the fact that the pension may have to be paid out for longer – see table opposite. You can choose for the income to continue after the first death either at the same or a reduced rate (say, two thirds or a half of the full pension).

In general, annuities can be purchased for any couple regardless of married or registered status, so there is no discrimination against unmarried and unregistered partners.

Lump sum death benefits – the tax rules

If you die and have an occupational scheme or personal pension, the

Case study Sonia

Richard retired at age 65 with a pension fund of £80,000. He opted to buy a single-life annuity which provided an income of £80,000 × £549/£10,000 = £4,392 a year. Unfortunately, he died before his partner Sonia and his pension died with him. This left Sonia struggling to make ends meet.

Income from a joint-life-last-survivor annuity

	Level annuity	Annuity escalating by 3% a year	RPI-linked annuity
Single-life annuity			
For person aged 65.	£549	£382	£343
Joint-life-last-survivor annuity			
For person aged 65, partner aged 60, income reducing by half if older person dies first.	£454	£303	£251
For person aged 65, partner aged 60, income reducing by one third if older person dies first.	£433	£287	£233
For person aged 65, partner aged 60, no reduction in income if older person dies first.	£390	£255	£202

Source: annuity rates from http://pluto.moneyadviceservice.org.uk/annuities, accessed 1 January 2013.

scheme may pay out a lump sum. This might be a multiple of salary in a defined-benefit scheme or typically the value of the pension fund in a defined-contribution scheme. Under the tax rules, this can be paid to anyone – they do not have to be your dependant. However, the scheme might have its own restrictions on who can receive the lump sum. Usually the scheme will ask you to nominate the person or people you would like to receive it. The scheme does not have to follow your wishes, but generally will do so.

If you die before starting your pension, whether or not the amount paid out is taxable depends on your age at the time you died. If you were under 75, the lump sum is tax-free unless it exceeds your remaining Lifetime Allowance (see page 66). Any part that does exceed your Lifetime Allowance is taxed at 55 per cent. For most people, the pay out will be comfortably within the allowance and so tax-free. If you were 75 or over, the whole lump sum is taxed at a rate of 55 per cent.

If you die after you have started your pension or an income withdrawal arrangement, any lump sum paid out is taxed at a rate of 55 per cent. The possible lump sums are:

- **Pension or annuity with a guarantee period** (see page 118). The balance of pension due for the remainder of the period can be rolled up and paid as a lump sum.
- **Capital protection** (see page 118) If the pension to date comes to

less than you paid, the remainder can be paid out on death as a lump sum.
- **Income drawdown** (see page 119) The remainder of the pension fund that has not been paid out in pension can be paid out on death as a lump sum.

In general, pensions and lump sums payable on your death from your pension scheme are outside the scope of Inheritance Tax. Rules that applied before 6 April 2011 that could give rise to an Inheritance Tax Bill have been abolished.

Key tip

Your pension scheme or provider will send you a nomination form (sometimes called an 'expression of wish' form) so you can say who you want to receive any lump sum payable on death. Make sure you complete this form and send it back. Review your nomination whenever your circumstances change, for example you start a new relationship, get divorced, your children become independent, and so on.

Case study Kristin

Kristin is a teacher and belongs to the Teachers' Pension Scheme which, if she dies before retiring, would pay out a lump sum of twice her final salary. Based on her current salary of £28,000 this would be £56,000. The lump sum would be tax-free and paid in addition to any survivors' pensions to her dependants.

For more information on annuities see Chapter 6 and, in particular, pages 123–5 for an explanation of how annuities work.

Pensions and divorce

Pension rights are a valuable asset, and one that will be taken into consideration in any divorce settlement. There are various orders the court can make in the event of divorce, and similar arrangements you can adopt voluntarily.

Divorce is stressful financially as well as emotionally. Assets and income that have supported one household have to be split to support two. You might think the family home is your biggest possession, but do not overlook pensions. Pension rights can be the family's largest single asset. On the basis the Government uses to compare pensions against your Lifetime Allowance, an occupational pension of, say £20,000 a year would be worth a capital sum of 20 × £20,000 = £400,000.

As discussed in Chapter 1, women often end up with lower pensions than men. Today, it is still more likely that a woman, rather than a man, will take on the care of children and elderly relatives resulting in breaks from work, and a greater likelihood of taking on part-time and low-paid

jobs. As a result, a husband typically has much greater pension rights than his wife. On divorce, the wife then stands to lose:

- The opportunity to share her husband's pension in retirement or the living standard that his pension would allow.
- A widow's pension if her husband dies before her.
- A lump sum payment if her husband dies before her.

The same applies to a husband if his wife has the lion's share of the pensions. But, as that is less typical, this section is written as if the wife is the main loser. This section also applies to civil partners who break up, since the process of dissolving a civil partnership is directly equivalent to a divorce. On divorce, the pension rights of each person may be counted alongside the other family assets to be shared out appropriately.

How pensions are taken into account

Courts must take pension rights into account when determining how a family's assets should be shared on divorce. In England, Wales and Northern Ireland, all pension rights whether built up before or during the

Unmarried and unregistered couples

If an unmarried or unregistered couple breaks up, there is no formal process of sharing out the family assets. You should try to take account of pensions, but an ex-partner with the larger pension rights may be unwilling to do this. Therefore, it is especially important that anyone in an unmarried or unregistered partnership has their own pension scheme and builds up pension rights in their own name rather than relying on their partner.

marriage are considered. In Scotland, only rights built up during the marriage are included.

There are three ways in which the pension rights can be treated:

- **Offsetting** The person with less in pensions may be granted a bigger share of other assets to compensate for the lost pension rights. For example, the wife might be given a large lump sum or the family home and the husband retains his pension rights in full. The main drawback with this approach is that there might not be sufficient other assets to provide the compensation. However, offsetting is likely to be the only option if the pension scheme involved is not UK-based.
- **Earmarking** (more formally called 'attachment orders'). The

> **Key tip**
> Pension sharing is an arrangement that both provides a clean break and ensures each of you will have some pension in retirement.

court can order that part of the husband's pension, once it starts to be paid, is handed over to the ex-wife. This could be a pension that has already started or a deferred order relating to a pension that will become payable in future. In addition, or instead, the court could order that part or all of the tax-free lump sum payable at the start of retirement and/or any lump sum paid on death in service be handed over to the ex-wife. In Scotland, only lump sums not pensions can be earmarked in this way. There are several problems

Options for pensions on divorce

For convenience, the table is written assuming the husband has the bulk of the pension rights but applies equally if the wife or a civil partner has the main pension assets.

	Offsetting	Earmarking	Pension-sharing
Does arrangement achieve a clean break?	Yes	No	Yes
Is ex-wife unaffected by subsequent pension decisions of husband?	Yes	No	Yes
Can arrangement be used even if the family has few other non-pension assets?	No	Yes	Yes
Does it ensure the ex-wife will get a retirement pension?	No*	Maybe**	Yes
Does it ensure the ex-husband still has a retirement pension?	Yes, full pension rights retained	Yes, part of pension retained	Yes, part of pension rights retained

* If she receives a lump sum, she may be able to pay part or all into a pension scheme. But if she receives illiquid assets (such as the family home) this is unlikely to be an option.

** But if husband dies, the pension stops or never becomes payable.

Pension sharing

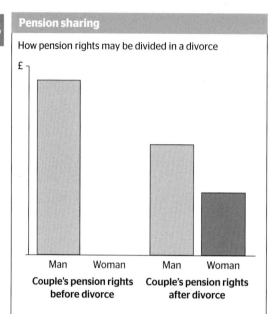

How pension rights may be divided in a divorce

£

| Man | Woman | Man | Woman |

Couple's pension rights before divorce   **Couple's pension rights after divorce**

husband's life. Pension sharing orders first became possible for divorces started on or after 1 December 2000 and their use has been steadily increasing.

Only one of these approaches can be taken in the case of any one pension scheme. But, if the husband has more than one scheme, a different approach could be taken with each – for example, the death-in-service lump sum from one scheme could be earmarked for the wife to tide her over if need be until a pension secured through a pension sharing order starts.

How pension sharing works

In essence, pension sharing is very simple. One person's pension rights are reduced – the reduction is called a 'pension debit'. The other person is given a corresponding 'pension credit' with which to secure their own pension. Most pension rights can be shared, including those from occupational schemes, multi-employer schemes, personal pensions (including stakeholder schemes), retirement annuity contracts and the additional State Pension scheme. The main pension rights that can't be shared are the basic State Pension (but see page 42) and any schemes that are not based in the UK.

Early in the divorce, each of you will be required to list for the court all your financial interests. This includes any pension schemes you belong to. You will have to contact

with this approach – for example, the ex-wife's share of any pension would stop if the husband died, or the husband might delay retiring in order to put off handing over part of the pension and/or the tax-free lump sum. Earmarking tends to be most useful as a way of providing the ex-wife with a lump sum on the death of the husband – for example, to replace maintenance payments that would then cease.

■ **Pension sharing** The court can order that part of the husband's pension rights be transferred to the ex-wife. These rights then become the wife's own and are unaffected by anything that subsequently happens in the

---

For advice on the legal aspects of divorce and separation contact Resolution. Their website is at **www.resolution.org.uk** or telephone 01689 820272 for further details.

each pension scheme and ask them to give a valuation. This will be essentially the same as the transfer value you would be given if you wanted to transfer your pension to another scheme (see Chapter 9).

This section assumes that the husband has most or all of the pension rights and the court decides that part should be transferred to the wife. Taking into account the circumstances of the couple, the length of their marriage, ages, earnings potential, other assets available, and so on, the court determines a fair share of the pension to be transferred and this is expressed as a percentage of the transfer value.

The husband has lost some of his pension rights and so stands to get a lower pension at retirement. Only the reduced rights count towards the Lifetime Allowance and Annual Allowance, so provided the husband can afford to, there is plenty of scope to rebuild the lost pension rights by making extra contributions.

The ex-wife has received pension rights. This increase – the Pension Credit – counts towards her Lifetime Allowance but this will only be an issue for a minority of people with very substantial pension savings. Pension Credits do not count towards the Annual Allowance or the yearly limit on contributions that qualify for tax relief. The ex-wife can generally do one of two things with the Pension Credit.

Case study Mel and Chris

Mel and Chris divorce. The court awards Mel a 30 per cent share of Chris' pension rights in his occupational scheme. Chris belongs to a final-salary scheme and, based on his pay and years' of membership so far, has built up a pension of £12,500 a year. The scheme works out the transfer value of this pension as £77,000. Taking 30 per cent of this gives a pension debit for Chris and Pension Credit for Mel of £23,000. Chris' pension to date is reduced to £8,750 a year. Mel can either keep her Pension Credit in the scheme Chris belongs to and is told that this is expected to produce a pension of £3,200 a year at the normal pension age for the scheme. Alternatively she looks at transferring the credit to a personal pension and receives an illustration showing that it might produce a pension of £2,235 a year by her chosen pension age. Mel decides to retain the credit in Chris' scheme.

- **Internal transfer** She can become a member in her own right of her ex-husband's pension scheme. Assuming her husband had not started to draw a pension, she is treated in the same way as an early leaver who has left their rights in the old scheme (see Chapter 9) and will start to get a pension once she reaches the normal pension age for the scheme. If her husband had already started his pension, she gets a pension straight away.
- **External transfer** If her husband had not yet started his pension, she can transfer the credit to another scheme of her choosing. This could, for example, be her own employer's scheme if applicable or a personal pension.

For more details on how pension transfer values (from one scheme to another) are calculated, see Chapter 9. The valuation for pension sharing is very similar.

The basic State Pension and divorce

Currently, the State scheme has special rules to help people who get divorced. Broadly, you can substitute your ex-spouse's or ex-civil partner's National Insurance record for part or all of your own if this would result in a higher basic pension than you can get based on your own record. You lose this right if you subsequently remarry or enter a new civil partnership. The Government has proposed that, from 2016, the ability to use an ex-spouse's or ex-civil partner's National insurance record in this way will end.

If the pension has already started, an external transfer is unlikely to be allowed. External transfer is also not possible from a public sector scheme, which is unfunded (see page 83).

Getting advice

You can agree a financial settlement on divorce without the involvement of the courts. In that case, do make sure you still take account of the value of any pension rights. This is complicated and you are strongly advised to get help from a solicitor who will know what steps to take to obtain the necessary pension

Key tip

If your ex-spouse belongs to an unfunded public sector scheme (such as the schemes for teachers or NHS workers), a pension sharing order would give you a Pension Credit with that scheme. You cannot transfer the credit to another scheme but that's normally no hardship because public sector schemes are very secure (see Chapter 11) and offer good benefits including index-linked pensions.

valuations and be able to call in other experts if necessary. To find a solicitor, get in touch with Resolution at www.resolution.org.uk.

Summary

Pension schemes provide more than just a retirement income. They can also provide an income and/or lump sum for your dependants or heirs if you die before retirement.

They may also provide an income or lump sum if you die after retirement, but this will depend either on the scheme rules or, in the case of a defined-contribution arrangement, the choices you made at the time you started your pension.

It is important to let pension schemes and providers know who you would like to receive any pay-outs in the event of your death.

Pension rights are treated as family assets to be taken into account in the divorce settlement when a married couple or civil partners split up. Unmarried couples have no legal claim on each other's pension savings.

Is your pension safe?

11

A number of high-profile scandals over the last 30 years or so, company schemes closing down and persistent talk of a pensions crisis have understandably made people nervous about saving through pension schemes. It is important to understand the risks and keep them in perspective.

Pensions and risk

State Pension cutbacks, and a series of pension scandals in the 1980s and 1990s, followed by closing final-salary schemes, some unable to pay the pensions they had promised, has sorely tested the faith of the UK population.

Keeping a clear perspective

Although private pension scandals (see opposite) have undermined public confidence in pension schemes, even the State Pension scheme is not without risk. The State system has been changed on numerous occasions and, all too often, change means cutbacks – see the table on page 182. In general, changes have been phased in so that people close to retirement are affected less or not at all. But if you are relatively young now, you should be aware that what the State promises today could be very different by the time you become a pensioner. This, together with the low amount the State pays, makes it essential that you do not turn your back on making your own savings through occupational and personal schemes. Recall that Chapter 1 showed that a key difference between the poorest and richest pensioners was access to an occupational pension scheme.

You have seen in Chapters 3 to 6 how tax reliefs and, where applicable, employer contributions make pension schemes an efficient way to save. While problems have arisen in the past and, human nature being what it is, probably will again in future, keep these in perspective. The majority of pension schemes are soundly run and should deliver pensions that will help you to achieve a more financially secure retirement.

> **'What the State offers now could be very different by the time you reach retirement.'**

To keep abreast of general information about the State Pension scheme, visit **www.gov.uk**.

Major pension scandals

A number of pension scandals have shaken public confidence over the years.

Maxwell

In 1991, it was discovered that Robert Maxwell, head of the Mirror Group Newspapers business empire, had stolen £450 million from his employees' pension funds. Some money was recovered but many employees were left with reduced pensions. The scandal led to changes in pension legislation and the setting up of a scheme to compensate future pension scheme members who lose rights owing to fraud.

Equitable Life

During the 1950s Equitable Life began selling pension plans that guaranteed customers a minimum level of income from their annuities when they started to draw their pension. Equitable did not foresee or make provision for the growing cost of honouring these guarantees. By the 1990s the guarantees had become too expensive and Equitable sought to cut back the pay-out to the customers holding guaranteed annuities. The House of Lords ruled the cutbacks illegal and Equitable, faced with a gaping hole in its finances, closed its doors to new business. Many customers were trapped and getting poor returns on their pension schemes and other policies. Others cut their losses and transferred. Only in 2012 did a compensation scheme finally start to make pay-outs to the Equitable victims.

Pensions mis-selling

In the late 1980s up to the mid-1990s, many people who belonged to occupational pension schemes were wrongly persuaded by financial advisers to switch to personal pensions even though they offered inferior pensions and other benefits. The regulator for the industry ordered a review, which took several years but eventually over 1.1 million customers received over £10 billion in compensation.

Schemes winding up where the employer is insolvent

In the early 2000s, there was a spate of schemes winding up with too little in the pension fund to pay all the promised pensions. Normally the employer should have stepped in to make good the shortfall, but where the employer was insolvent, there was no one to bale out the scheme. It is estimated that, as a result, some 85,000 scheme members lost substantial amounts of their promised pension, with at least 35,000 of these losing a half or more. The Government set up an assistance scheme to help these members. The scandal also led to the setting up of a compensation scheme to help pension scheme members should they in future find themselves in a similar situation.

State Pension cutbacks

State Pension provision has changed significantly over recent decades.

Date	Change	Effect
1980	Link to earnings inflation cut.	Pensions being paid had been increased each year in line with the higher of earnings or price inflation. Now they are increased only in line with prices. Pensioners are becoming progressively poorer relative to people in work.
1988	State earnings related pension scheme (SERPS) pensions cut.	Lower additional State Pension for people retiring and their widows (and subsequently widowers and bereaved civil partners).
1988	Introduction of contracting out on a defined-contribution basis.	Contracting out this new way might leave you better or worse off.
1997	Changes to contracting out through a salary-related scheme.	Before the change, you could not lose by contracting out this way. After the change, you could be either better or worse off.
1997	Reduced protection against inflation for contracted-out pensions.	Contracted-out pensions being paid no longer fully protected against inflation – only inflation up to a maximum of 5 per cent a year.
2002	SERPS replaced by the State Second Pension.	No one worse off and carers, some low earners and some people with long-term illness or disabilities better off.
2005	Reduced protection against inflation for contracted-out pensions.	Contracted-out salary-related only have to be protected against inflation up to a maximum of 2.5 per cent a year. Contracted-out defined-contribution pensions no longer have to be protected against inflation at all.
2009-2030	State Second Pension becoming flat-rate.	Higher earners will get less pension than originally intended.
2010	Improvements to State Second Pension.	Better access for people with caring roles and with disabilities.
2010	Access to basic State Pension improved.	Number of qualifying years needed for a full pension reduced substantially. Especially helps women get a better pension.
2010-2018	Women's State Pension age being raised from 60 to 65.	Women have to wait longer to receive their State Pension.
2011-12	Basic State Pension to be increased to the higher of price inflation, earnings inflation or 2.5 per cent a year.	More generous basic pension. Other parts of the pension, such as additional pension, will increase only with price inflation.
2011-12	Where State Pensions and benefits are increased with price inflation, this becomes the Consumer Price Index (CPI) instead of the Retail Prices Index (RPI).	Lower increases each year, because CPI tends to rise more slowly than RPI. There is also a knock-on effect, as public sector and some private sector occupational pensions also switch to CPI-linking.
2012	Defined-contribution contracting out abolished.	Employees can no longer take a gamble on contracting out in this higher risk way, but must either stay in the additional scheme or be contracted out through less risky salary-related schemes.
2016	New flat-rate State Pension to be introduced.	Replaces the current basic and additional pensions payable at a rate of £144 a week in today's money. This should reduce reliance on means-tested benefits. Spouses and civil partners will no longer be able to use their partner's National Insurance record to get or top up their own pension. Defined-benefit contracting out will end.
2018-2020	State pension age increases to 66.	This affects men and women born on or after 6 December 1953.
2024 onwards	State Pension age being raised.	People born after March 1960 will have to wait longer for their pensions. Five-yearly reviews will link increases to longevity.

Occupational pension schemes

There are two main risks with occupational schemes: first that money intended to pay for pensions is embezzled; and secondly that the scheme cannot pay the pensions it has promised. The first risk can affect any scheme; the second is peculiar to defined-benefit schemes.

A further risk is that your expectations might not be met because of a change in the rules or the scheme. This is particularly relevant now, with many final-salary schemes closing and being replaced with less generous schemes and could be an issue if auto-enrolment (see Chapter 4) and the abolition of defined-benefit contracting out (see page 39) prompt more employers to close the remaining final salary schemes.

Keeping pensions safe

Occupational pension schemes must normally either be statutory schemes or set up under trust. A statutory scheme is set up under an Act of Parliament and is the normal arrangement for most public sector schemes – covering, for example, NHS workers, teachers, the police, and so on. Often these schemes are unfunded and the pensions derive their security from the fact that future taxpayers can be called upon to pay for them – but see also the

section entitled Renegotiating the pension promise on page 186.

A private sector scheme is nearly always set up as a trust, a device that ensures the scheme is at arm's length from the employer and his or her business. With any trust, there are three key players:

- **The sponsor who sets up the trust** – in this case the employer. The employer usually decides on the initial benefits and rules of the scheme (which may later be altered if the rules allow for this).
- **The beneficiaries** who are the scheme members. These are the people for whom the trust has been set up. The aim of the trust is to provide them with pensions and other benefits. The beneficiaries include not just the 'active' members, who are working for the employer now, but also people with preserved pensions and people who might benefit if, say, a scheme member dies. The employer is usually also a beneficiary who can, in certain

---

 For details of how personal pension schemes are regulated, see page 188. See also Chapter 7 for advice on managing investment risk.

Key tip

You can get actively involved in ensuring your pension scheme is run well by standing for election as a trustee. Most occupational schemes must have at least some trustees nominated by the scheme members. To find out more, talk to the pension scheme administrator at work.

circumstances, receive money back from the scheme.

■ **The trustees who have the task of looking after the trust property** – in this case, the pension fund – and making sure that it is used in accordance with the scheme rules for the good of the beneficiaries.

The trustees are responsible for the running of the scheme but can employ help and have a duty to seek specialist help as required. They normally appoint a scheme administrator to handle day-to-day matters, investment managers to advise on investment strategy and the selection of investments, an actuary to evaluate the assets and liabilities and advise on the level of contributions required, a lawyer to advise on any legal aspects and an auditor to check the accounts.

The trustees and the advisers are all responsible for seeing that the employer meets its obligations to the scheme, the scheme is properly run and blowing the whistle if they suspect there is something wrong. They are supported and overseen by the Pensions Regulator – see the box bottom left.

The aim is that the trustees, advisers and Pensions Regulator together create a tough regulatory framework that will ensure no one can steal from, or defraud, the pension scheme. But, in those cases where it does happen, there is a compensation scheme.

The Fraud Compensation Fund can pay out where an occupational pension scheme's assets have been reduced as the result of dishonesty. The scheme is expected first to do all it can to recover the lost assets. Where a shortfall is left, the compensation scheme can step in. The fund is financed by a levy on all occupational pension schemes.

The pensions regulator

If you suspect your pension scheme is breaking the law or your employer is not acting properly in relation to the scheme (for example, failing to pay in contributions on time), tell the Pensions Regulator – see www.thepensionsregulator.gov.uk for more information.

This is the official body that regulates all work-based pension schemes (occupational schemes and also those personal pensions and stakeholder schemes organised through your workplace). It promotes good practice, monitors risks, investigates schemes if something seems to be wrong, has powers to put things right and can fine and prosecute individual wrong-doers.

Failing to meet the pension promise

In a salary-related scheme (or other defined-benefit scheme), you are promised a given amount of pension, worked out according to the pension formula for your scheme (see Chapter 5). Enough has to be paid into the scheme to ensure that each member's pension can be paid as it falls due. You are usually required to pay some contributions but the employer pays the balance of the cost.

The employer's contributions rise and fall in line as the cost of providing the promised pensions increases or reduces. The scheme actuary works out the level of contributions required based on assumptions about, for example, how well the invested contributions might grow and how long the pensions will have to be paid out (in other words, the life expectancy of the members). In a pension scheme where most of the members are a long way from retirement, the actuary usually assumes that the pension scheme will be invested largely in shares which, as discussed in Chapter 7, tend to be more suitable for the long-term than lower-risk but lower-returning investments.

In theory, the scheme is simultaneously required to have enough in the fund to meet all its obligations if the scheme came to an end today (in other words, if the scheme were to 'wind up'). In that case you would be entitled to a preserved pension or transfer value as described in Chapter 9. To be sure of doing this, the pension fund would have to be invested in assets that offered a known and stable return (in other words, gilts).

In practice, there is a lot of leeway in the way this funding requirement is applied and schemes are allowed to hold a high proportion of shares. But, at any point in time, share prices could be in a short-term fall. Therefore, a scheme can be

> **' The aim is that the trustees, advisers and Pensions Regulator together create a tough regulatory framework.'**

broadly on track to pay its long-term promises but have too little in the fund to meet all its obligations if the scheme were wound up today.

Normally, if there is a shortfall when a pension scheme is wound up, this is a debt on the employer who must pump extra money into the scheme. But this is not possible if the employer is insolvent. Between 1997 and April 2005, it is estimated that some 85,000 members of occupational salary-related schemes lost some of their promised pension because their employer went out of business leaving a big hole in the pension fund. As a result two compensation schemes were established:

■ **Financial Assistance Scheme (FAS)** This scheme was set up and funded by the Government to provide help for those pension scheme members in greatest need where their pension scheme started to wind up during the period 1 January 1997 to 5 April 2005, the scheme was under-funded and their employer is insolvent. The trustees of the scheme make the application to the fund and help is directed generally at members who

---

 To find out more about the Pension Protection Fund (PPF) and the scope of its provisions, see the website **www.pensionprotectionfund.org.uk**.

Occupational pension schemes

The role of employers, trustees and members in a typical scheme.

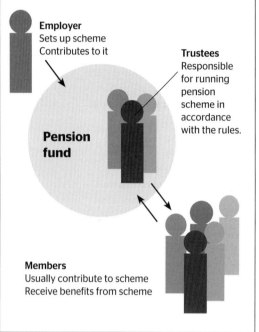

Employer
Sets up scheme
Contributes to it

Trustees
Responsible for running pension scheme in accordance with the rules.

Pension fund

Members
Usually contribute to scheme
Receive benefits from scheme

are within three years of their scheme's normal pension age or older.

■ **Pension Protection Fund (PPF)**
This scheme takes over to provide compensation where a scheme winds up on or after 6 April 2005 with too little in the fund and an insolvent employer. In general, compensation ensures that

existing pensioners carry on getting the full amount of their pension and that other scheme members get 90 per cent of their promised pension up to a maximum limit (the cap is £34,049.84 at age 65 in 2012-13 of which 90 per cent is £30,644.85). The PPF is financed by a levy on occupational salary-related schemes.

Public sector pension schemes are not covered by the above compensation schemes because they are instead ultimately backed by tax revenues.

Renegotiating the pension promise

Many final-salary schemes are realising they cannot afford to provide the pensions they had promised, because the cost of the pension scheme is increasing dramatically. There are various reasons for this, in particular the fact that, on average, employees are now expected to live much longer than originally thought. The abolition of defined-benefit contracting out (see page 39), which will increase the cost to the employer of providing any scheme affected (because the employer's National Insurance contributions will rise), is also a factor that may trigger pension promise renegotiations. Employers are looking at ways to cut the cost, for example, closing schemes to new members, stopping existing members from building up further benefits, switching to career-average or defined-contribution schemes capping the amount of pay that is pensionable and/or trying to

'**Many final-salary schemes are realising they cannot afford to provide the pensions they have promised.**'

persuade workers to retire later.

Looking at the bigger picture, it is probably inevitable that these sorts of changes will happen at some time, given that we are all tending to live longer. But, at your personal level, a reduction in the pension you had been led to expect as part of the overall remuneration package for your job is effectively the same as a pay cut.

If your employer is trying to change your pension scheme, there might not be a lot a lot you can do stop it. But you should try taking the following steps:

- **Check your contract of employment** Does it give you the right to a particular type or amount of pension? (Most contracts don't.)
- **Contact the trustees** They may have the power to force the scheme to wind up rather than simply be altered. If the scheme is wound up, the employer must pay in extra contributions if there is a shortfall in the pension fund. Since this could be very costly, your employer might be forced to think again about changing the scheme.
- **Contact your union or staff association** They may be able to negotiate a better deal regarding the pension scheme.
- **Talk to your employer** Even if you can't stop the changes, you might be able to negotiate a compensating pay rise or extra pension contributions in your case.

Although renegotiating the pension promise is primarily an issue for members of defined-benefit schemes (see box), members of defined-contribution schemes may find their expectations dashed if their employer proposes to reduce the amount the employer contributes to the scheme. This has not been a particular issue so far, but could become one if, following the introduction of auto-enrolment (see Chapter 4), employers decide to level down to the auto-enrolment contribution rate.

Be aware that cuts in contributions could be achieved by narrowing the definition of pensionable pay rather than simply cutting the percentage contribution rate.

'The abolition of defined-benefit contracting out may trigger pension promise renegotiations.'

Members of defined-contribution schemes

If you belong to a defined-contribution scheme, there is no pension promise, so you are generally not affected by employers cutting back on and changing their pension schemes. But that's because you already bear the risks that employers are now trying to offload. As life expectancy increases, annuity rates tend to fall, so you either have to pay more into your pension scheme or end up with a lower pension when you retire.

Personal pensions

Personal pensions are by their nature risky in the sense that you cannot know how much pension you will eventually get and you are exposed to the ups and downs of the investment markets. In general, there is no protection against these risks, but you can lessen and manage them as described in Chapter 7.

There are other types of risk that you can expect to be protected against, for example, being mis-sold a scheme that is unsuitable for you or losing your money through fraud.

How you are protected

Nearly all personal pensions come within the scope of the financial regulator, which at the time of writing was the Financial Services Authority (FSA). During 2013, the FSA is to be replaced with its functions split between several new regulatory bodies. The new body most relevant to personal pension consumers will be the Financial Conduct Authority (FCA), but with some functions passing to a new Prudential Regulatory Authority

Key tip

Before doing business, check that the pensions firm or adviser you are dealing with is authorised by the FSA. Do this by consulting the FSA Register (www.fsa.gov.uk/fsaregister).

(PRA). The protections described here with reference to the FCA will be taken over by the FCA and PRA, probably from 1 April 2013.

In general, it is illegal for a firm to offer personal pensions to UK customers without being 'authorised' by the FSA. Provided you deal only with authorised firms, you can be confident that:

- The firm is solvent and run by people who appear to be honest.
- The personnel have at least a minimum level of training or are supervised.
- The business is run in accordance with rules set by the FSA. These include being open with you about the services it offers and their cost, providing you with key information about the firm's products and keeping proper records.

Jargon buster

Authorised Means that a firm has been checked out by the financial regulator and is allowed to conduct financial business in the UK. Provided you deal with an authorised firm, you benefit from consumer protection - for example, complaints procedures and a compensation scheme if things go wrong.

- If the firm is offering advice, it must be based on knowledge of you and your circumstances and be suitable advice.
- The firm must have a proper complaints procedure for you to use if things go wrong and belong to an independent complaints body (see page 191).
- The firm is covered by the Financial Services Compensation Scheme (FSCS).

The Financial Services Compensation Scheme (FSCS)

If you lose money because of the negligence or dishonesty of a financial firm, you would normally claim redress from the firm using the complaints procedures described on page 191. But if the firm has become insolvent, this will not be possible. In that case, the FSCS may step in and provide compensation instead. Compensation is capped at a maximum amount – see the table below – which varies according to the way your money has been invested. Most personal pensions offered by insurance companies technically count as insurance policies and so qualify for a higher level of compensation if your fund exceeds around £55,000. The scheme is funded by a levy paid by authorised firms.

> ' With a personal pension you are always exposed to the ups and downs of the investment markets.'

Maximum compensation available from the FSCS

Type of investment	Compensation limit	Maximum pay-out
Deposits	100% of first £50,000	£50,000
Investments (for example, unit trusts and investment trusts)	100% of first £50,000	£50,000
Long-term insurance (most personal pensions, life insurance and annuities)	90% of the claim without any upper limit	Unlimited

What to do if you have a complaint

Problems often stem from misunderstanding, so be prepared to work through an issue patiently, starting with the person or firm you originally dealt with. If that doesn't resolve the matter, there are independent complaints bodies that can help.

State Pensions

During the years you are building up your State Pension, you will be dealing with HM Revenue & Customs (regarding payment of National Insurance) and The Pension Service (concerning your State Pension forecasts).

If you have problems with the Revenue, first contact the office you normally deal with. If you need to take the matter further, ask to be put in touch with that office's complaints handler. If that still does not resolve the matter, you can ask for a different complaints handler to review your case – you can find details and addresses in the Revenue factsheet C/FS *Complaints* available from HM Revenue & Customs (www.hmrc.gov.uk/factsheets/complaints-factsheet.pdf).

If you are not happy with the HMRC's response, you can take your complaint to the Adjudicator's Office (www.adjudicatorsoffice.gov.uk). This is an independent body that can deal with complaints about

mistakes, delays, misleading advice, staff behaviour and the Revenue's use of its discretionary powers.

Similarly, first contact The Pension Service department dealing with pension forecasts if you have a problem in this area or your local Pension Service office – to find this, call 0845 606 0265 or use the search tool at www.gov.uk/find-pension-centre. If you want to take your complaint further, you can ask for it to be considered by an Independent Case Examiner.

If, having exhausted these complaints procedures, you are still unhappy with the way the Revenue or The Pension Service have dealt with you, try contacting your Member of Parliament who can refer your case to the Parliamentary and Health Service Ombudsman (www.ombudsman.org.uk). The Ombudsman investigates maladministration by government departments. You cannot complain direct to the Ombudsman and must go through your MP.

 If the firm that sold you the pension cannot resolve the problem, contact the Financial Ombudsman Service, **www.financial-ombudsman.org.uk**, tel: 080 00 234 567 or 0300 123 9 123.

If your complaint is a dispute about the amount of National Insurance you must pay or the amount of State Pension you have been awarded, you may want to take your case to the Tribunals Service (www.justice.gov.uk/ tribunals/tax for National Insurance and www.justice.gov.uk/tribunals/ sscs for State Pensions).

Occupational schemes

Initially contact the pensions administrator for your scheme. If the problem is not resolved, say that you want to use the formal complaints procedure, which all occupational schemes must have and must give you details about. If this does not produce a satisfactory outcome, then take your complaint to The Pensions Advisory Service (TPAS) – (website www. pensionsadvisoryservice.org.uk).

TPAS is an independent mediation service. It can investigate your case and help you and your scheme to reach agreement. If that doesn't work, you can take your complaint to the Pensions Ombudsman. The services of TPAS and the ombudsman are both free to complainants.

You must have gone through TPAS before the ombudsman will consider your case. The Ombudsman can make judgments that are binding on both you and the pension scheme and can order the scheme to pay redress if appropriate. (There is no limit on the amount.)

Instead of going to the Ombudsman, you could go to court, but this will be a lengthy and expensive process.

Personal pensions

Complain first to the firm with whom you have a problem. All firms authorised by the FSA must have a formal complaints procedure. If you are uncertain of your rights or need support making your case to the firm, TPAS may be able to help.

Provided you have exhausted the firm's complaints procedure, if you are still unhappy, you can take your case to the Financial Ombudsman Service (FOS) (www.financial-ombudsman.org.uk). The FOS is free to complainants. It will investigate your case and can make orders which are binding on the firm (but not you) to put the matter right. Where appropriate, FOS can order the firm to pay redress up to £150,000.

Commonly, complaints to the ombudsman concern advice – for example, failing to explain the risks of income withdrawal.

If you are unhappy with the FOS decision, you have the option to take your case to court, but this could be a lengthy and expensive process.

Key tips

- Always keep a record of phone calls and correspondence regarding your pensions, noting the date, who you dealt with and the key points covered. These records will be important if later you have a dispute.
- Preferably complain, in writing as this provides a clear, unambiguous record of what you have said. Head your letter, fax or email 'Complaint'. Quote any relevant reference numbers so that your case can be easily traced. Be clear, concise and polite. State all relevant events, giving dates and if relevant the people involved. Spell out clearly the response you are seeking to resolve the matter.

Free leaflets if you have a complaint		
Reference	Title	From
C/FS	Complaints	HM Revenue and Customs
AOI	The role of the adjudicator	Adjudicator's Office
	Bringing a complaint to the Parliamentary Ombudsman	Parliamentary and Health Service Ombudsman
	The Pensions Advisory Service and the Pensions Ombudsman	Pension Advisory Service
	Your complaint and the Ombudsman	Financial Ombudsman Service

> **'There is no certainty that the pension schemes you save with will stay the same year in year out.'**

The FOS is able to make decisions that go beyond the strict legal position and take into account other aspects, such as good industry practice. So, if FOS has not found in your favour, try to be realistic about your chances of winning before deciding to go to court.

Summary

Planning for retirement is a long-term process and there is no certainty that the pension schemes you save with will stay the same year in year out. There is little you can do to stop changes to the State system (beyond casting your vote for the party with the proposals you favour). Your contract of employment may state that you have access to a pension scheme but usually it does not embed any promise that this will be a particular type of scheme and so does not preclude future changes. All you can do is review your retirement planning regularly and adapt to changes as they arise, for example, by saving extra or resigning yourself to working a bit longer.

What you can expect is protection from dishonesty or negligence and this is provided by complaints mechanisms and compensation schemes that mean you should be able to seek redress without the delays and expense of going to court. In defined-benefit schemes, you may also be compensated if your employer fails to meet the pension promise owing to insolvency.

Other ways to finance retirement

12

Pension schemes are not the only way to save for retirement and, if you do not manage to save enough, there may be other ways to salvage your retirement income.

Non-pension saving and investments

You can use any type of savings and investments as a way of saving for retirement. Unless you are already very close to retiring, you will be saving over a long period.

Historically, share-based investments have tended to produce much higher returns over long periods (say, ten years or more) than lower-risk investments, such as building society accounts (see Chapter 7 for more details). For this reason, most professional advisers will normally suggest that you choose mainly share-based investments if your investment term is more than ten years, shifting to less risky investments as your chosen retirement date approaches. However, as you saw in Chapter 1, you do not have to put investments into a pension-scheme tax wrapper.

In most cases, if you save for retirement without using pension schemes, there are no particular tax incentives. An exception is if you invest through individual savings accounts (ISAs).

Individual savings accounts

An ISA is not an investment as such. Once again, think of it as a tax-free wrapper you can put around a whole range of different investments, including shares, unit trusts and savings accounts. There is no tax relief on money you pay in, but the investments in the ISA grow either completely or largely tax-free (depending on the type of investment) and there is no tax on money you draw out. There are no restrictions on when you can have your money back or in what form.

Each tax year, you have an ISA allowance, as shown in the table left. You can either invest the full amount in a stocks-and-shares ISA or you can put up to half in a cash ISA and the remainder in a stocks-and-shares ISA. You do not have to use your full allowance each year, but any unused amount cannot be carried forward and is lost for good.

As a way to save for retirement, ISAs are more flexible than pension schemes, since you can get your money back at any time and in any form you like.

Your yearly ISA allowance		
Tax year	Total allowance	Cash ISA allowance
2013-14	£11,520	£5,760
Subsequent years	As above but increased by price inflation and rounded to the nearest multiple of £120	As above but increased by price inflation and rounded to the nearest multiple of £120

Compared with using a pension scheme, ISAs are not quite as tax-efficient. Pension schemes give you tax relief as you pay your money in, but tax it as you draw it out. ISAs are a mirror image: there's no tax relief on the way in, but the proceeds are tax-free. What gives pensions the edge is that you can usually take part of the proceeds as a tax-free lump sum – which means you get tax relief on both the way in and the way out.

Property

During most of the 1970s to the 1990s, UK house prices were – apart from an occasional blip – generally on an upward trend. Despite house prices flatlining or even falling in most parts of the UK outside London since the global financial crisis that started in 2007, there remains an expectation that residential property tends to hold its value and prices are certainly less volatile than the stock market. This has prompted a lot of interest in the potential for using residential property as a substitute for pension savings, either by buying a large home that can be traded down at retirement to release money for a pension or by investing in buy-to-let property.

Trading down to a smaller home at retirement is a tax-efficient strategy, since the gain made on selling your home is normally tax-free. Investing in buy-to-let property does not have this advantage, so any gain made when you sell would, apart from various tax reliefs and allowances, be taxable.

To work out tax on a capital gain, after deducting reliefs and allowances, the gain is added to your income for the same tax year and tax is charged at two rates. In 2012–13, these rates were 18 per cent on any part of the gain falling within your basic-rate tax band and 28 per cent on anything more.

Relying mainly, or completely, on selling property as a way of financing retirement is a risky strategy. Who knows what the property market will be like in 30 or 40 years time? New house building could take away the pressure on house prices. Even if house prices generally rise, the particular properties that you own might not fare so well. A less risky alternative could be to invest in a fund that holds lots of different residential properties – see Chapter 7.

Equity release

An alternative to trading down as a way of releasing capital tied up in your home could be to use an equity release scheme. This provides a way of realising capital locked up in your home without having to move. The main drawback is that you will not get the full value of the part of your home that you sell or mortgage.

To understand why, consider this: if you invested, say £10,000 to be repaid on a distant but uncertain date – say, five, ten or 20 years' time – would you expect to get £10,000 back or a larger sum? Almost certainly your answer is: a larger sum because, if you invest, you expect to get a return as compensation

Property funds offer a way of investing in a portfolio of many different properties and/or shares in property companies. This spreads your risk across a wider range. See page 141 for further information.

for giving up the immediate use of your money and for any risks involved. That is a fundamental principle embedded in the pricing of equity release schemes. These schemes offer you a lump sum or income now but you – or more likely your estate – have to pay back a larger sum later to compensate the investors (the equity release companies) who supplied the money. Provided you are comfortable with that, equity release schemes could be worth looking at in retirement if you find yourself short of money,

Different ways to save for retirement

You can save for your retirement in many ways but, outside a pension scheme, there are no particular tax incentives, except in the case of ISAs. Flexibility is another issue you may want to consider.

Feature	Method of saving for retirement			
	Pension scheme	Individual savings account	Other non-pension investments	Direct investment in property
Your employer generally contributes	Yes, if occupational scheme. Sometimes in case of other schemes.	No	No	No
Tax relief on money you pay in	Yes	No	No	No
Your investment builds up tax-free	Partly	Partly	Usually no	Yes, if the property is your home. Otherwise, no.
Tax-free when you take your money out	No – you can usually take part as a tax-free lump sum, but the rest must be drawn as taxable pension.	Yes	Usually no	Yes, if the property is your home. Otherwise, no.
You can get your money back at any time	No, minimum age is 55.	Yes	Often – depends on the type of investment.	Yes, but may be slow to sell.
You have flexibility over how much you cash in and when	Maybe – see Chapter 6.	Yes	Often – depends on the type of investment.	When – yes, but must usually cash in whole property in one go.

but do not want to move home. But the low sums you can release relative to the amount of capital given up, especially at ages below 65, mean equity release is a poor way to plan to provide your pension.

Equity release schemes come in two basic forms: lifetime mortgages and home reversion schemes.

Lifetime mortgage

With a lifetime mortgage, you borrow against the value of your home but the capital and usually the interest too are repaid only when the home is sold on your death or when you move out permanently (for example, because you move into a care home). Different providers set different age limits, but you must be at least 55 or 60 with most schemes, and 70 with some, to be eligible. The older you are, the greater the sum you can borrow, but the absolute maximum for a roll-up loan is unlikely to be more than half the value of your home.

You can use a lifetime mortgage to raise a single, large cash lump sum. If you want an income, you can either draw out a series of smaller lump sums (called a drawdown mortgage) or use a single lump sum to buy an

> ### Jargon buster
>
> **Equity** In the context of a home you own, the difference between its value and any mortgages or other debts secured against it.
>
> **No-negative-equity guarantee** A guarantee that the amount to be repaid when a lifetime mortgage ends will not exceed the proceeds from selling the home.

investment, such as a purchased life annuity (see page 126). The former is usually more tax-efficient, because part or all of the return from investing a lump sum will normally be taxable, whereas the money raised through a series of small lump sum loans will be tax-free.

The interest rate on lifetime mortgages, which is often fixed but may be variable, is typically 3 or 4 percentage points higher than the rate for an ordinary mortgage. With the most common form of lifetime loan – a 'roll-up loan' – interest is added each month to the amount you owe. You are charged interest not just on the amount you originally borrowed, but also the interest that has already been added to the outstanding balance. This means the total that you owe can grow rapidly – see the table below. When your home

How a roll-up mortgage may grow

The table shows, for each £10,000 borrowed, how the amount you owe could grow once interest is added to the outstanding balance.

After this many years:	The balance would be this much if you were charged interest fixed at a yearly rate of:				
	5%	6%	7%	8%	9%
5	£12,834	£13,489	£14,176	£14,898	£15,657
10	£16,470	£18,194	£20,097	£22,196	£24,514
15	£21,137	£24,541	£28,489	£33,069	£38,380
20	£27,126	£33,102	£40,387	£49,268	£60,092

Case study Hannah

Hannah is 70 and owns her own home, worth £240,000. She is considering a lifetime mortgage and has been offered a maximum loan of 40 per cent of the value of her home, which would be 40% x £240,000 = £96,000. Interest, at a fixed rate of 7 per cent, will be rolled up and repaid when the mortgage comes to an end. If Hannah experiences the average life expectancy for a woman aged 70, which is 18 years, the outstanding loan will reach £337,200. This will be repaid from the proceeds of selling the home. How much, if anything, remains for her heirs depends on how house prices change over the 18 years. Hannah has been careful to choose a lifetime mortgage with a no-negative-equity guarantee. This means that if the sale proceeds are lower than the outstanding loan, her heirs will inherit nothing from the house but equally the lender will have no further claim against Hannah's estate or anyone else.

is eventually sold, the proceeds are used to repay the outstanding loan and what is left over – if anything – goes to you or your estate. Loans that come with a no-negative equity guarantee promise that the maximum you or your estate must repay will not exceed the proceeds from the eventual sale of your home.

Reversion scheme

With a reversion scheme you sell part or all of your home, but retain the right to carry on living there either rent-free or for a token rent. When the home is eventually sold, the reversion company takes a percentage of the sale proceeds (or the whole amount if you sold 100 per cent of your home). This means

that the reversion company, not you or your estate, gets the benefit of any appreciation in value of the part of the home you sold. But, equally, the reversion company has to accept any reduction in value of that part if house prices have fallen.

To qualify for a home reversion scheme, you must usually be aged at least 65 or 70 years. As with lifetime mortgages, reversion schemes can pay you a single lump sum or a series of smaller lump sums. If you need income, opting for a series of lump sums will usually be a more tax-efficient option than taking one large lump sum and investing it.

The money you get when you take out the scheme will be smaller than the value of the part of the home you sell. For example, a person aged 70 might get, say, £4,500 for every £10,000 they sell (see the case study, above). The difference (between £10,000 and £4,500 in this example) is the return to the reversion company, reflecting the delay until it can expect to get its money back and the fact that it earns no rent from the property (or only a tiny amount) in the meantime. A key factor that the reversion company uses in deciding how much to offer is how long it expects to wait to get its money back, which, in turn, depends on the average life expectancy for someone of your age. Therefore, the older you are when you take out the scheme, the larger the sum you should get for each £10,000 you sell.

Equity release providers that are members of the trade body, the Equity Release Council (formerly called SHIP), all offer no-negative-equity guarantees on their lifetime mortgages and have agreed to abide by a code of good business practice – see **www.equityreleasecouncil.com**.

Working in retirement

Deferring retirement or continuing to work after you have started to draw a pension can be part of your plan for funding retirement. But be aware that health or economic conditions could thwart your plan.

Since October 2006, age discrimination in the workplace has been illegal. As a result, normally you cannot be forced to retire at a specific age. This opens the way in theory to carry on working for as long as you like. Retiring later can help to fund retirement in two ways:

■ You continue to receive income from work. As you saw in Chapter 1, earnings are an important contribution to the incomes of wealthier pensioners.
■ You may be able to start your pension later, which could mean your eventual pension is higher (see pages 61, 87 and 92).

There is nothing to stop you drawing a pension while continuing to work for your current or another employer, or starting your own business. This may allow you to phase your retirement (see page 125), so that you gradually ease out of work, replacing earnings with a growing pension as you do so.

However, these plans assume that you retain the ability to work and that work will be available. It is easy when you are younger to underestimate the impact that ageing might have on your physical stamina, even if you do not encounter outright health problems that prevent you from working as much as you would like.

It is impossible to forecast the state of the economy many years ahead. If economic activity is low, there simply might not be jobs available for everyone who wants them. Moreover, while, the age discrimination rules do apply to recruitment and so place a general ban on turning down an applicant on the grounds of age, there are some exceptions. You can legally be turned down because of age if:

■ **There are objective grounds for turning you down.** For example, it is unlikely you could work for a reasonably long enough period following training.
■ **There is a genuine occupational reason,** such as, needing a younger person to act in a particular role in a play.

On top of that, it can be very hard to pin down why you have been rejected for a job. Although

> **'Normally you cannot be forced to retire at a specific age.'**

application forms frequently no longer ask for your date of birth or age (and there's no reason to include these details on your CV), it is easy for an employer to estimate your age from your qualifications and employment history. If employers have an (illegal) preference for younger workers – say, because they will accept lower pay and potentially stay with the firm for longer – it might be very hard to prove that was the case.

You avoid the potential problem of age discrimination if you work for yourself. However, whether or not you can make enough income from

running your own business will again depend on the state of the economy among other factors.

So planning to fund your retirement entirely by carrying on working would be a risky strategy.

Summary

Non-pension investments can provide a more flexible way of saving for retirement than pension schemes. Individual savings accounts (ISAs) provide a tax-free wrapper, albeit not quite as tax-efficient as a pension scheme.

Using your home as a source of retirement income may be a necessity if you find yourself short of money in retirement. However, it does not provide an efficient or robust plan for funding retirement.

Deferring or phasing your retirement can help you to build up a better pension, but you need to be realistic about your ability and the opportunities to carry on working into older age. Planning never to retire is no plan at all and extremely high risk.

Did you know?

A survey for Barings Asset management found that one in ten people in Britain who have not yet retired say property will be their sole source of retirement income. The survey also suggested that 4.3 million Britons do not plan to retire at all.

Getting advice

13

There are different types of advice available to help you make decisions about saving for retirement. Advice is not cheap, so make the most of your adviser's time by doing your homework first.

Using a financial adviser

There have been big changes to financial advice from 1 January 2013 onwards. They should mean you can be more confident of getting professional and impartial recommendations.

How advice has changed

In the past, many people have used financial advisers somewhat reluctantly, fearing they may be recommended unsuitable products but lacking the knowledge to make a choice without help. Many turned to their bank for help, because at least this was a familiar organisation with presumably a brand reputation to protect. However, Which? research over the years has consistently shown that independent financial advisers (IFAs) tended to give better advice than advisers based in banks or working for other large firms, such as insurance companies.

Yet, in the past, the way in which most advisers were paid – be they IFAs or bank/insurer-based – had the potential to bias the advice they gave. This is because advisers typically received commission from the providers whose products they sold. This created incentives to recommend types of product, such as insurance-based investments rather than exchange-traded funds, that paid commission over other products that might have been more suitable. They might also have recommended those companies offering the highest commissions, and have pushed at least some product when better advice would have been none.

Moreover, consumers have been confused by this system into wrongly thinking that financial advice has been free, when really they have been paying heavily through inflated charges for the financial products they were sold. Which? has campaigned against this system for decades, arguing the case for more transparent charges and unbiased advice.

There have been some attempts to improve the system and, as a result, prior to January 2013 some IFAs had already started to charge separate fees for the advice they gave, freeing them from the need to make any product sale. But, from 1 January 2013, a new system of regulation applies to nearly all investment advisers, which includes those giving advice about

> '**Consumers have been confused by this system into wrongly thinking that financial advice has been free.**'

pensions. The way they are paid is not the only aspect being changed and, under the new regulations, investment advisers must:

- Demonstrate their professionalism by being qualified to at least Level 4 (first-year university level) and keep up their knowledge and skills through continuous professional development. Advisers must belong to one of several professional organisations that issue certificates as evidence of the advisers' on-going competence.
- Be paid through a system of 'adviser charging', which means fees agreed between the adviser and you, the customer. See page 205 for more information.
- Declare what type of advice they can offer you at the outset and the nature of any restrictions that apply.

Types of advice

The new regulations were intended to make it easier for consumers to understand the type of advice they are being offered, but unfortunately have had the opposite effect. Whereas, in the past, Which? would recommend that you always go to an independent financial adviser (IFA) over any other type, the picture is now not so clear-cut.

The table overleaf summarises the types of investment advice available from 1 January 2013 onwards. A key difference from the pre-2013 world is a change to the rules an adviser must comply with to qualify to use the name 'independent'. To count as being independent, under both old and new regulations, an adviser

must make recommendations based on the 'whole of the market'. Under the old rules, this might mean, say, recommending the best unit trusts for you selected from all the providers' offerings. Under the new rules, an adviser must base their advice on a review of all relevant investments from all providers. Relevant investments is widely drawn, so that the adviser from the previous example will now have to consider not just unit trusts, but also investment trusts, exchange-traded funds, insurance-based funds, and so on (see Chapter 7). In some respects, this is good news for consumers because an IFA can no longer specialise in a narrow range of investments but must truly seek out the best strategy for you. But, if you know broadly the type of product you want, going to an IFA may now mean paying unnecessarily for a wider service than you need.

Any adviser not meeting the new standards for 'independent' advice must, by definition, be giving restricted advice. Furthermore, depending on your requirements, from January 2013 onwards, you may find that some type of 'restricted advice' is all that you need. However, the term 'restricted' covers all manner of restrictions from advisers selecting from the products of just one or a handful of providers to those covering the whole market in terms of providers, but limited to a particular type of product, such as personal pensions. So you will have to check the nature of the restriction carefully to make sure you get the type of advice you want.

All the types of advice listed in the table below may end with a recommendation that you buy a particular product.

Independent and restricted advisers must be regulated by the financial regulator. The same does not apply to generic advice. This falls short of giving personalised recommendations. Instead it aims to help you to decide what types of action might be suitable for you, but leaves you to take this further and choose particular products from particular providers suitable to your specific circumstances and needs. Providers of generic advice do not have to be authorised by the financial regulator. Generic advice comes in many forms – this book and

Types of adviser from January 2013 onwards		
Type of adviser	**Description**	**How the adviser may be paid**
Independent	Can recommend any type of product that is relevant from any provider	Adviser charging only
Restricted	Advice falls short of meeting the conditions for being 'independent'. The restriction could be of any type, for example, specialising only in certain types of product to representing just one or a few providers	Adviser charging only
Simplified	A type of restricted advice that typically addresses a particular consumer need without undertaking a full review of your finances. Typically it might be delivered by an internet tool or by phone.	Adviser charging only
Basic advice	Scripted advice, typically delivered by an internet tool or call centre to check your suitability for a particular product, such as a stakeholder pension.	Commission still allowed
Non-advised sale	Carrying out your instructions without any advice given	Commission still allowed

Examples of sites offering online tools and generic advice include: Fund Expert (**www.fundexpert.co.uk**), Money Advice Service (**www.moneyadviceservice.org.uk**), Money on Toast (**www.moneyontoast.com**), MoneyVista (**www.moneyvista.com**), RPlan (**www.rplan.co.uk**) and Wake up your Wealth (**www.wakeupyourwealth.com**).

the Which? website are examples. The Money Advice Service is a generic advice service set up by the Government.

The regulatory changes from January 2013 will make the cost of advice more transparent and it is expected this may make some consumers question whether they want to pay this much. At the same time, advisers are expected to shift to wealthier customers if they see little profit in clients with only small sums to invest. As a result, many pundits see an advice gap opening up that may be filled, in particular, by websites offering generic advice, in the form of DIY financial planning tools, in some cases mixed with authorised advice if users want to take the process further to be guided towards particular products. Typically, these sites are free or low cost.

How you pay for advice

From 1 January 2013 onwards, you will pay for most investment advice (including advice about pensions) through a system called adviser charging.

Under adviser charging, typically the adviser will tell you what fee it will charge for giving you advice. This might be a fixed fee or an hourly rate. According to a survey by accountancy firm, BDO, the average charge is likely to be around £160 an hour. There may be a choice of ways to pay. The most straightforward would be to pay a lump sum fee direct to the adviser – in much the same way as you would pay a solicitor or accountant for their services. However, the advice firm might offer some kind of instalment deal.

It is also permitted, if you do take out a product, for the provider of that product to collect instalment payments for the advice along with the charges for the product and pass those payments across to the adviser. While, on the face of it, this looks like commission, the key difference is that you and the adviser agreed what the charge would be, without any involvement from the product provider. This means there is no incentive for the adviser to recommend this provider over any other. However, to the extent that not all providers will necessarily agree to collect the adviser's fee in this way, your own choice might be swayed if you prefer to pay this way.

If you buy investments having received only basic advice or no advice at all, the firm you deal with is still permitted to receive commission from the product provider as payment rather than charging you a fee direct.

How to find an adviser

If you can join a workplace pension scheme, you may find that your employer has arranged access to a financial adviser. If you need to find your own adviser, the easiest way to find one is to use an online search tool – see the information at the foot of page 206. Typically, these let you state the type of advice you are looking for and return a selection of advisers close to the postcode or area you have specified.

It's a good idea to check the details of any adviser against the regulator's registry (the FCA Register – see Useful addresses). In particular, make sure the adviser is permitted to give

Key tips

When buying any financial product:

1. Do your homework. Work out roughly what you need and find out broadly what's available.

2. Gather together information you will need – for example, proof of your earnings, State Pension forecast, benefit statements.

3. Deal only with firms or advisers who are authorised. Check the FCA Register (www.fca.gov.uk/caregister).

4. Read the literature you get, especially key facts documents.

5. Ask questions about anything you do not understand.

6. Check the sort of advice an adviser offers and how much they will charge.

7. Check whether there is a choice of ways to pay.

8. Avoid advisers who do not ask enough questions to understand your needs and circumstances.

9. If a deal sounds too good to be true, avoid it.

10. Keep a file of all the information – product literature, notes of phone conversations and meetings, letters, and so on – that formed the basis of your decision. You'll need these details if you later have a complaint (see Chapter 11).

accept some degree of restricted advice, check that you are happy with the restrictions.

Bearing in mind that advice is not free, make sure you have assembled all the information you need before you have an advice session. For example, you will need details of your income, spending, existing pensions and life insurance, including a State Pension forecast, and any existing savings and investments, debts and so on. The adviser will take you through a 'fact find' to gather the information he or she needs as a basis for giving you suitable advice. Some advisers give you this fact find in advance so that you can fill it in and gather the necessary information on your own time rather than taking up adviser time. See the Key tips left for other ways to make most effective use of your adviser.

Summary

Since the start of 2013, there have been important changes to the types of advice you can get and the way you pay for it. Independent financial advisers are likely to continue to offer the 'Rolls Royce' service, but this might be more holistic than you need, so you could end up paying extra unnecessarily. If you are sure of the type of product you want – say, an annuity but not income drawdown – you might be happy going to an adviser who is restricted in the sense of specialising in annuities, provided they consider all the providers in the market.

the type of advice you need – for example, advisers require additional qualifications before they are allowed to advise on transfers of pensions from defined-benefit to defined-contribution schemes.

Contact two or three advisers for details of their service and charges and to see how comfortable you feel with the firm, before deciding to do business. In particular, if you want independent advice, check that the firm offers this. If you are happy to

---

 The following sites have tools that let you search for a financial adviser: **www.unbiased.co.uk**, **www.findanadviser.org**, **www.financialplanning.org.uk** and **www.mylocaladviser.co.uk**.

Useful addresses

The Adjudicator's Office
Tel: 0300 057 1111
www.adjudicatorsoffice.gov.uk

Age UK
Pension calculator
www.ageuk.org.uk/money-matters/
pensions/pension-calculator/

Court – going to
England & Wales
www.justice.gov.uk/about/hmcts/

Scotland
www.scotcourts.gov.uk

Northern Ireland
www.courtsni.gov.uk

Department for Work and Pensions (DWP)
DWP benefits for people of working age are administered through Jobcentre Plus. State Pensions are administered by The Pension Service.
http://dwp.gov.uk/gov/

Equality Advisory Support Service (EASS)
FREEPOST
Equality Advisory Support Service
FPN4431
Tel: 0808 800 0082

Equality and Human Rights Commission
For advice and enquiries, contact Equality Advisory Support Service

Equity Release Council (formerly SHIP)
www.equityreleasecouncil.com

Ethical Investment Research Information Service (EIRIS)
Tel: 020 7840 5700
www.eiris.org

Finametrica
Risk profiling tool
www.riskprofiling.com

Financial Assistance Scheme (FAS)
The trustees of your pension scheme contact the FAS

Financial Conduct Authority (FCA)
Tel: 0800 111 6768
www.fca.gov.uk

FCA Register:
www.fca.gov.uk/fcaregister

Financial Ombudsman Service (FOS)
Tel: 0800 0 234 567 or 0300 123 9 123
www.financial-ombudsman.org.uk

Financial Services Compensation Scheme (FSCS)
Tel: 0800 678 1100 or 020 7741 4100
www.fscs.org.uk

Fraud Compensation Fund
Tel: 0845 600 2541
www.pensionprotectionfund.org.uk

Generic advice
For sources of advice and online tools, go to:

Fund Expert
www.fundexpert.co.uk

Money Advice Service
see separate entry

Money on Toast
www.moneyontoast.com

MoneyVista
www.moneyvista.com

RPlan
www.rplan.co.uk

Wake up your Wealth
www.wakeupyourwealth.com

Gov.uk
www.gov.uk

Benefits Adviser interactive tool
www.gov.uk/benefits-adviser

Defer state pension guide
www.gov.uk/deferring-state-pension

Pension Credit calculator
www.gov.uk/pension-credit-calculator

HM Revenue & Customs
For local tax enquiry centres
Look in the phonebook.

For your local tax office
Check your tax return, other tax correspondence or check with your employer or scheme paying you a pension.

National Insurance (NI) Helpline
Tel: 0845 302 1479
www.hmrc.gov.uk

Complaints
www.hmrc.gov.uk/factsheets/complaints-factsheet.pdf

Married women's reduced NI rate
www.hmrc.gov.uk/ni/reducedrate/marriedwomen.html

Pension scheme rules
www.hmrc.gov.uk/pensionschemes/reliefs-charges.htm

Salary sacrifice
www.hmrc.gov.uk/specialist/salary_sacrifice.htm

Independent financial adviser (IFA)
For a list of IFAs in your area, contact these organisations:

The Institute of Financial Planning
Tel: 0117 945 2470
www.financialplanning.org.uk

MyLocalAdviser
www.mylocaladviser.co.uk

The Personal Finance Society
www.findanadviser.org/find-an-adviser.asp

Unbiased
www.unbiased.co.uk

Independent financial advisers specialising in annuities
The Annuity Bureau
Tel: 0845 850 8550
www.annuity-bureau.co.uk

Annuity Direct
Tel: 0500 50 65 75
www.annuitydirect.co.uk

Hargreaves Lansdown Annuity Supermarket
Tel: 0117 980 9940
www.hl.co.uk/pensions/annuities

WBA Ltd
Tel: 020 7636 7278
www.williamburrows.com

Investment fund comparison websites (examples)
www.morningstar.co.uk
www.trustnet.com

Jobcentre Plus
See phonebook for local office
http://dwp.gov.uk/gov/

Member of Parliament
To find your local MP
www.writetothem.com/

Money Advice Service
Tel: 0300 500 5000
www.moneyadviceservice.org.uk

Comparison tables
www.moneyadviceservice.org.uk/en/
categories/comparison-tables

Interactive tools
www.moneyadviceservice.org.uk/
en/categories/calculators (including
Budgeting Tool and Pension
Calculator)

Money Management Magazine
Available in larger newsagents.
Subscriptions and back issues:
Tel: 0845 456 1516

Money Observer
Magazine, available in newsagents
www.moneyobserver.com

MyCompanyPension
www.mycompanypension.co.uk

National Employment Savings Trust (NEST)
Tel: 0300 020 0090
www.nestpensions.org.uk

NOW
Tel: 0333 33 222 22
www.nowpensions.com

Pension Protection Fund
Tel: 0845 600 2541
www.pensionprotectionfund.org.uk

Pension scheme administrator
See scheme handbook, recent
benefit statement, annual
report or noticeboard at work
for contact details of pension
scheme administrator or trustees.
Alternatively, contact your HR
department.

The Pension Service
Tel: 0845 60 60 265

To find your local pension centre
www.gov.uk/find-pension-centre
http://dwp.gov.uk/gov/

Pension Credit application line
Tel: 0800 99 1234
www.gov.uk/pension-credit/
how-to-claim

To get a State Pension forecast
State Pension Forecasting Team
Tel: 0845 3000 168
www.gov.uk/state-pension-statement

State pension age calculator
www.gov.uk/calculate-state-pension

The People's Pension
www.thepeoplespension.co.uk

Pension Tracing Service
Tel: 0845 6002 537
www.gov.uk/find-lost-pension

The Pensions Advisory Service (TPAS)
Tel: 0845 601 2923
www.pensionsadvisoryservice.org.uk

Pensions Ombudsman
Tel: 020 7630 2200
www.pensions-ombudsman.org.uk

Pensions Regulator
(Note: does not deal with queries about individual pensions benefits)
Reporting a concern
Tel: 0845 600 7060
www.thepensionsregulator.gov.uk

Personal finance websites (examples)
www.moneyfacts.co.uk
www.moneysupermarket.com

Personal inflation calculator
www.neighbourhood.statistics.gov.uk/HTMLDocs/dvc14/index.html

Resolution
Tel: 01689 820272
www.resolution.org.uk

Tax office
See entry above for HM Revenue & Customs

Tribunals Service
National Insurance (NI)
www.justice.gov.uk/tribunals/tax

State Pensions
www.justice.gov.uk/tribunals/sscs

Glossary

Accrual rate In a salary-related pension scheme, the proportion of your pay that you get as pension for each year you have been in the scheme.

Active fund management Trying to improve the returns from an investment fund by attempting to pick the best performers.

Actuarial reduction A cut in your pension if you retire early to reflect the extra cost of paying your pension for longer.

Actuary Financial and statistical expert who uses mathematical techniques to estimate how the future may turn out.

Annual limit for relief The maximum contributions you can make to pension schemes each year that qualify for tax relief. The limit is £3,600 or, if higher, your total UK earnings for the year.

Annuity An investment where you swap a lump sum (such as a pension fund) for an income either for life or a specified number of years. You cannot get your money back as a lump sum.

Annuity rate The amount of pension you get in return for your lump sum.

Authorised Means that a firm has been checked out by the financial regulator and is allowed to conduct financial business in the UK. Provided you deal with an authorised firm, you benefit from consumer protection – for example, complaints procedures and a compensation scheme if things go wrong.

Basic State Pension Part of the State Pension (see Chapter 2), which nearly everyone gets.

Bond A loan to either a government or a company that can be bought and sold on a stock market.

Capital The amount of money you originally invest.

Capital risk The likelihood of losing part or all of your original investment and/or gains you have already built up.

Capped drawdown Arrangement where you leave your pension fund invested and can draw off an income up to a maximum amount.

Cash-balance scheme Type of pension scheme that promises you a set amount of pension fund at retirement for each year you have been in the scheme. The pension you get then depends on how much pension you can buy with fund.

Civil partner Since 5 December 2005, same-sex couples have been able to register their relationship as a civil partnership and, for most purposes, are then treated in the same way as husbands and wives.

If new laws being discussed by Parliament in early 2013 are passed, same-sex couples in England and Wales will also be able to marry (and convert a civil partnership into marriage) and be treated the same as husbands and wives.

Commutation The process of swapping part of your retirement pension for a tax-free lump sum.

Commutation factor The amount of tax-free lump sum you get for each £1 a year of pension you give up.

Contracted out Describes the situation where, instead of building up additional State Pension, a person is saving for retirement through a private pension scheme. Since 6 April 2012, contracting out has been restricted to defined-benefit schemes only. See pages 38–9.

Contracting out Giving up some additional State Pension and building up a pension, instead, through a private pension scheme.

Contribution Money paid into a pension scheme by you or someone else, for example, your employer.

Default fund Investment fund that your pension scheme will be invested in if you do not actively choose the investments yourself. Typically, it will be a lifestyle fund or target date fund. Default funds are built into the design of stakeholder pensions and the multi-employer schemes being set up for auto-enrolment.

Defined-benefit scheme Type of pension scheme that promises you a set level of pension typically based on your pay and length of time in the scheme.

Defined-contribution scheme Type of pension scheme where the pension you get depends on the amount paid in, how well the invested contributions grow and the amount of pension you can buy at retirement with the resulting fund.

Derivatives Investments that derive their value from some underlying investment. For example, a traded option gives you the right to buy or sell some underlying shares. Derivatives can be used in a variety of ways to expand the strategies an investment manager can take, for example, making profits when share prices fall as well as when they rise.

Equities Another name for shares in companies.

Equity In the context of a home you own, the difference between its value and any mortgages or other debts secured against it.

Equity release Schemes that enable you to draw off some of the capital tied up in your home without moving house.

Exchange traded funds Type of investment fund that usually tracks a specified stock market or other fund (so it is a tracker fund – see page 142). But you invest by buying shares in the fund on the stock market rather than going to a fund management company.

Financial Conduct Authority (FCA) One of the new bodies that took over regulating financial services from 1 April 2013, in particular regulating financial advice and the selling of products such as pensions and annuities.

Financial Services Authority (FSA)
Body that regulated most financial services in the UK up to end March 2013.

Flexible drawdown Arrangement where you leave your pension fund invested and draw off an income of any amount you choose. To qualify for this type of drawdown you must have a secure income from other sources of at least a specified minimum amount.

FTSE 100 Index A measure of stock market performance based on the share prices of the 100 largest companies quoted on the London Stock Exchange.

Gilts The name for bonds issued by the UK government.

Inflation A sustained rise in the price level. In the UK, inflation is often measured as the change in the Consumer Price Index (CPI) or Retail Prices Index (RPI).

Investment fund A wide range of different shares and/or other investments chosen by a fund manager. The investments are purchased by pooling your money with funds from lots of other investors.

Joint-life-last-survivor annuity An investment where you exchange a lump sum (say, your pension fund) for an income payable until both you and your partner have died. You can choose whether or not the income reduces following the first death.

Lower earnings limit (LEL) The lowest level of earnings that count towards the record on which certain state benefits, such as your State Pension, are based.

Means-tested Describes state benefits that you receive only if your income and, in some cases, your savings are below a specified level.

Money Advice Service Independent organisation, set up by the financial regulator, with a statutory duty to promote public understanding of the financial system.

National Insurance contributions
A tax paid by most people who work. There are different types of contribution, called 'classes'. Paying some classes of contribution entitles you to claim state benefits, such as the State Pension.

NICO Stands for National Insurance Contributions Office, the part of HM Revenue & Customs that deals with the collection and recording of National Insurance contributions.

No-negative-equity guarantee A guarantee that the amount to be repaid when a lifetime mortgage ends will not exceed the proceeds from selling the home.

Open market option Your option to shop around and buy an annuity from any provider of your choice rather than sticking with the provider with whom you have built up your pension fund.

Passive fund management Setting up an investment fund to mimic the performance of a stock market index.

Paye-As-You-Earn (PAYE) A system for collecting Income Tax you owe direct from your earnings or pension before the remainder is paid to you.

Pension fund A pool of investments into which contributions are paid and that is used to provide pensions and other pension scheme benefits as they fall due for payment.

Pensionable earnings The definition of pay used by a salary-related scheme when working out the pension it will pay and for setting contributions.

Preserved pension The pension you are promised at normal pension age from a scheme you have left.

Primary threshold The level of earnings at which employees start to pay National Insurance contributions.

Private sector The part of the economy that is independent of the State.

Public sector The part of the economy to do with the State. For example, public sector workers are people employed by central or local government or state services. They include, for example, NHS staff, teachers, firemen, police.

Purchased life annuity An annuity you choose to buy with money other than a pension fund. Part of each payment you receive counts as return of your original investment and is tax-free. The rest is taxable.

Qualifying year A tax year that counts towards your basic State Pension, because you have paid or been credited with enough National Insurance contributions

Reduction in yield Figure in a key facts illustration that shows the effect of charges on the value of your pension savings.

Registered pension scheme A scheme designed to provide a pension and often other benefits too (such as life cover and pensions for survivors if you die), which qualifies for advantageous tax treatment.

Retirement Used in this book to mean the period of life when you draw a pension. You might not have stopped work altogether.

Section 32 scheme A pension scheme offered by insurance companies. It is designed to accept preserved pension rights from an occupational scheme and can maintain them in their original form (say, salary-related).

Self-directed pension scheme A scheme where you choose the specific investments the fund invests in. The main examples are self-invested personal pensions (SIPPs) and small self-administered schemes (SSASs).

Shares An investment that makes you a part-owner of a company, along with all the other shareowners. The return you get depends on how well the company performs.

Short-term annuity An investment where you swap a lump sum for an income paid out for a specified period of time. At the end of the period, the income stops. You cannot normally get your original investment back as lump sum.

Single-life annuity An investment where you exchange a lump sum (say, your pension fund) for an income payable for as long as you live.

Sponsoring employer The employer who sets up, and contributes, to an occupational scheme.

State Pension age Age at which you become eligible to claim the State Pension. This is being gradually raised (see page 40).

Taxable Describes income or gains on which you may have to pay tax depending on your personal circumstances.

Tax deferral Putting off a tax bill until a later time. This could save tax if your tax rate in future is lower than now.

Tax year A period of a year running from 6 April to the following 5 April. Generally, both taxes and state benefits are set in relation to tax years.

Today's money The amount of money today that would be worth the same in terms of what it might buy as a sum of money that you will get at some time in the future. For example £100 in ten years' time would be worth £50 in today's money if prices doubled over the ten-year period.

Transfer value The lump sum which, if invested now, is deemed to be enough to provide a given level of pension at retirement plus other benefits. It can be transferred from one scheme to another.

Upper accruals point (UAP) The highest level of earnings that count towards the record on which your State Pension is based.

Upper earnings limit (UEL) National Insurance threshold at which the contribution rate changes.

Working life The tax years from the one in which you reach age 16 to the last complete tax year before you reach State Pension age.

Working Tax Credit (WTC) A state benefit for people who are in work, but on a low income.

Index

About Which?

Which? is the largest independent consumer organisation in the UK. A not-for-profit organisation, we exist to make individuals as powerful as the organisations they deal with in everyday life. Our campaigns make people's lives fairer, simpler and safer. The next few pages give you a taster of our many products and services. For more information, log onto www.which.co.uk or call 01992 822800.

Which? Online and Which? Local

www.which.co.uk is updated regularly, so you can read hundreds of product reports and Best Buy recommendations, keep up to date with Which? campaigns, compare products, use our financial planning tools and search for the best cars on the market. As a Which? member you can sign up to Which? Local, a website of 110,000 local business reviews created for Which? members, by Which? members. Covering everything from plumbers to plasterers and butchers to bakers, our independent member reviews will help you find the best service that won't charge you over the odds. To subscribe, go to www.which.co.uk.

Which? Legal Service

Which? Legal Service offers convenient access to first-class legal advice at unrivalled value. One low-cost annual subscription enables members to receive tailor-made legal advice by telephone or email on a wide variety of legal topics, including consumer law – problems with goods and services, employment law (for employees), holiday problems, neighbour disputes, parking tickets and Wills and Probate Administration in England and Wales. To subscribe, call the Members' helpline: 01992 822828 or go to www.whichlegalservice.co.uk.

Which? Money

Whether you want to boost your pension, make your savings work harder or simply need to find the best credit card, *Which? Money* has the information you need. *Which? Money* offers you honest, unbiased reviews of the best (and worst) personal finance deals, from bank accounts to loans, credit cards to savings accounts. It's also packed with investigations, revealing the truth behind the small print. As a Which? member you also have access to the Which? Money helpline offering free one-to-one guidance on any financial matter. To subscribe, go to www.which.co.uk/money-subscription.

Other Which? books

Which? Books provide impartial, expert advice on everyday matters from finance and law to gardening, property and major life events. We also publish the country's most trusted restaurant guide, *The Good Food Guide*. To find out more about Which? Books, log on to www.which.co.uk/books or call 01992 822800.

Tax Handbook 2013–14

Tony Levene
ISBN 978 1 84490 154 8
Price £10.99

Fully updated in line with the 2013 Budget, *Tax Handbook 2013-14* is essential reading for all tax payers. Jargon-busting advice explains how to complete a tax return and online assessment, check a tax code and National Insurance, and reduce Inheritance Tax or minimise Capital Gains Tax. This essential guide also demystifies Tax Credits and tax-free perks at work.

Wills and Probate

David Bunn
ISBN 978 1 84490 133 3
Price £10.99

Easy-to-follow guidance on writing or revising a will, valuing and distributing assets and all the legal concerns of an executor. Learn how to deal with official forms and timings, be informed on the charges to anticipate with tips for keeping costs down, learn the key mistakes to avoid, and get information on reducing your Inheritance Tax bill and setting up a trust. The second part of the book provides step-by-step guidance on probate and acting as an executor, making the process as straightforward and trouble-free as possible.

Other Which? books

Giving and Inheriting
Jonquil Lowe
ISBN 978 1 84490 118 0
Price £10.99

This indispensable book will help you reduce the tax bill faced by your heirs, ensuring your gifts go to those you choose and not to HMRC. Find out what you need to know about tax-free gifts and ways of reducing tax when you die, as well as the taxes on lifetime gifts and what you can do about them. *Giving & Inheriting* also looks at how trusts let you control how your gifts are used, explains gifts to children and charities, and highlights the tax pitfalls to consider if you are giving your home. There is also advice for those receiving an inheritance.

Buy, Sell & Move House
Kate Faulkner
ISBN 978 1 84490 142 5
Price £10.99

Buy, Sell and Move House covers the complete buying and selling process, from understanding the market and choosing a mortgage through to completing the sale. Includes guidance on everything from arranging a mortgage and dealing with estate agents, to managing a chain and getting a survey. Written by Kate Faulkner, a property expert, this edition is fully updated to cover the government's new housing strategy. Case studies and tips throughout highlight solutions to common problems and the pitfalls to avoid, so you can navigate the property maze with ease.

Renting & Letting
Kate Faulkner
ISBN 978 1 84490 146 3
Price £10.99

Now fully updated, *Renting & Letting* is essential reading for both landlords and tenants. Packed with expert guidance and jargon-free tips, this practical guide covers the legal rights and obligations of both landlords and tenants, advice on tenancy agreements and law, how to manage a let and rental income, Capital Gains Tax, energy performance certificates and deposit protection schemes. This edition includes fully up-to-date figures and changes to regulations, including the introduction of Universal Credit.